The Criminal Investigation Process

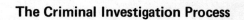

The Criminal Investigation Process

Peter W. Greenwood

Jan M. Chaiken

Joan Petersilia

with contributions from
Linda Prusoff
Robert Castro
Konrad Kellen
Sorrel Wildhorn

D.C. Heath and Company
Lexington, Massachusetts
Toronto

Clothbound Edition by Lexington Books

Library of Congress Cataloging in Publication Data

Greenwood, Peter W
    The criminal investigation process.

    Bibliography: p.
    Includes index.
    1. Criminal investigation. I. Chaiken, Jan M., joint author.
II. Petersilia, Joan, joint author. III. Title
HV8073.G827   364.12   76-27032   ISBN 0-669-00972-5

Published simultaneously in Canada

Printed in the United States of America

Paperbound International Standard Book Number: 0-669-01067-7

Clothbound International Standard Book Number: 0-669-00972-5

Library of Congress Catalog Card Number: 76-27032

Contents

List of Figures

List of Tables

Foreword

Before criminal justice ascended to a national political priority in the middle 1960s, the contemporary literature of police administration was sparse and somewhat conservative.

It is not denigration of the contribution of such leaders as O.W. Wilson and V.A. Leonard to say that their major police administration publications tended to be descriptions of the best practices of their times rather than advocacies for new directions.

This situation has drastically changed, however, in the wake of the politicization of the crime problem by the 1964 presidential campaign and the social disorders of the late 1960s. Literally billions of dollars have been spent on study and experimentation of possible changes in criminal justice.

Perhaps the most remarkable development of the past decade has been the ready willingness with which police administrations have sought, developed, and implemented changes within their organizations. I will confess that perhaps it is a bias, but my own observation has been that the police, often in the past stereotyped as the least flexible of the actors within the criminal justice system, have proved to be the most amenable to change and the most innovative under the pressures of the last generation.

In addition to the succession of commissioners, committees, and task forces which have addressed problems of criminal justice in general and of police administration in particular, we have been a proliferation of special studies on a wide variety of subjects, ranging from the broad to the specific.

In this climate of inquiry, it is not surprising that the processes of criminal investigations have come under scrutiny. A substantial proportion of local and state police personnel of America are assigned to the investigatory functions. Yet, by and large, there has been no careful thinking through of what realistic goals the majority of criminal investigations are expected to achieve.

Our tendency, as police administrators, has been to require that all but the most minor criminal cases be assigned for investigation, even though we realized that the likelihood of solution in many cases was so remote as to render investigative effort a poor investment of resources. Our tendency has been to measure the success of criminal investigations by clearance rates, realizing all the time that clearance data are unreliable indicators of success for most classes of crimes. Our tendency has been to disregard the outcome of cases in court as a measure of investigative success, leaving the presentation and proof of cases largely to the prosecutor. Our tendency, until recent years and to this day in many departments, has been to assign police officers to investigative duties with no training in investigative techniques and goals except that obtained through experience.

Now, this is not intended as, nor to suggest, self-flagellation of police administrators for not recognizing that we were operating a less than optimum criminal investigations process. Most police administrators with whom I am acquainted have been aware, intuitively, of the need for more rational organization of criminal investigations and for improved measures of success. The problem has not been lack of recognition that deficiencies existed nor an unwillingness to change. The problem has been that deficiencies have been hard to define effectively, and appropriate changes have been elusive. The problem has been lack of any blueprint for action.

There is not yet a blueprint for action! The book's authors make this clear. A department should not materially reduce its level of investigative efforts on the strength of their findings alone, they say. Rather, closely monitored experiments or demonstrations in different types of jurisdictions are suggested.

Thus, this Rand study disavows any intention of being the final word in this fertile field for improvement. Nonetheless, as the first extensive study of criminal investigative processes across multiple jurisdictions, it does offer a useful fund of knowledge, of impressions, and of suggestions for possible future directions.

Jerry V. Wilson

Preface

This book results from a two-year study at The Rand Corporation supported by a grant from the National Institute of Law Enforcement and Criminal Justice. We attempted to achieve findings of national interest by conducting a survey of all major U.S. police agencies, which included interviews and observations in twenty-nine departments. However, collection of detailed operational data was possible in only a small number of departments, so that many of our findings must be confirmed in other cities before they can be considered definitive.

In addition to describing the range of current investigative activities, the book attempts to evaluate the contribution which these activities make to overall law enforcement objectives. We also suggest a number of policy reforms which we believe are worthy of test to determine whether they can enhance police performance.

Our findings attracted considerable attention in the press, after which we received both praise and criticism from numerous police officials. But the reader who believes, from brief descriptions of our work, that we have taken an advocacy position on behalf of one side in some controversy will be surprised to discover that the book attempts only a balanced appraisal of the investigative process. It is a preliminary step toward better understanding of one part of police work that has historically been immune to outside inspection, even by some police chiefs. Our hope is that the results of our work will provide an objective basis for police administrators to explore more productive uses of their manpower and for the public to reach a more realistic appreciation of the accomplishments and limitations of law enforcement agencies.

Acknowledgments

The authors are indebted to the following persons and organizations for materials and assistance not acknowledged elsewhere in the study.

Foremost, a most sincere note of appreciation is expressed to the members of our Criminal Investigation Advisory Panel, who endured our early briefings, reviewed documents, suggested additional areas for research, and always made helpful comments at critical stages of the study: Chief Cornelius (Neil) J. Behan (New York City Police Department); James Fisk (member of the Los Angeles Police Commission); Chief Thomas Hastings (Rochester, New York, Police Department); Jerry Wilson (Former Chief, Washington, D.C. Police Department); and Eugene Zoglio (Professor, Prince George's Community College).

This study would not have been possible without the cooperation of the police personnel across the country who enriched our knowledge of police investigation through their own working experiences and allowed us access to various pieces of departmental information. We are particularly indebted to the following (organization affiliations date to the time of the study): Chief Edward Davis and the Los Angeles Police Commission, Commander Kenneth McCauley, Sergeant Joseph Horvath, Captain Carl Calkins, Mr. Robert Balderama, Lieutenant Robert Bovensiep, and Sergeant Henry Skeggs (Los Angeles Police Department); Deputy Chief Robert V. Hill and Sergeant John J. Rapecko (Long Beach Police Department); Captain Charles Plummer, Chief Wesley Pomeroy, and Officer Maurice Holman (Berkeley Police Department); Captain Roy E. Estes and Officer Robert Keller (Richmond Police Department); Chief George Tielsch, Captain Clarence Hansen, and Captain Eugene McCarthy (Santa Monica Police Department); Major Robert Knight, Chief Bernard Garmire, Mr. Joseph Musial, Sergeant Keith Hardin, Lieutenant Vic Kennedy, Captain Philip Doherty, Mr. Harry Peterson, Sergeant Chris Nassberg (Miami Police Department); Deputy Chief Burtell Jefferson, Sergeant Robert Reynolds, Mr. Norman Smith (Washington Metropolitan Police Department); Captain J. Lothrop (Oakland Police Department); Chief Joseph McNamara, Mr. Melvin Bockelman, and Officer Lee Gregory (Kansas City Police Department); Assistant Chief Donald F. Steele, Mr. Edwin D. Heath, Jr., Mr. Richard Seibert, Chief R. O. Dixon (Dallas Police Department); Captain Frank Herron, Lieutenant Edward Clark, Captain Daniel O'Brien, Chief Neil Behan, Lieutenant James Ghericich (New York City Police Department); Captain Eugene Gallagher and Sergeant Charles Davis (Indianapolis Police Department).

We also wish to thank the employees of the 153 police departments around the country who cooperated with us and responded to our national survey questionnaire. In addition, we are grateful to FBI Director Clarence Kelley, who authorized release of Uniform Crime Reporting data for purposes of the survey, and to Andrew McKean, who supplied us with the data tapes.

At the National Institute of Law Enforcement and Criminal Justice, Law Enforcement Assistance Administration, U.S. Department of Justice, considerable encouragement and advice were given by Gerald Caplan, current director of NILECJ; Martin Danziger, former director of NILECJ; and Richard Laymon, David Farmer, William Saulsbury, and Joseph Peterson, who all provided valuable guidance as grant monitors during the project.

During the course of the research, we brought together several investigators from different police departments to discuss our preliminary findings and determine how the findings conformed to their views based on experience. We are grateful to the following investigators for participation in these discussions and sharing their unique insights: Sergeant Gary Arnold, Sergeant Ted Bach, and sergeant Frank Gravante (Los Angeles Police Department); Inspector Frank Sabatini and Officer Patrick Phelps (Berkeley Police Department); and Sergeant Jack Greenleaf (Long Beach Police Department).

Several Rand colleagues and consultants offered valuable assistance during the conduct of the study. Eugene Poggio conducted a review of computer systems used in support of the investigative process. The extensive computer processing required for our analysis was ably completed by Robert Young. In addition, detailed coding and conversion of text responses to our national survey was performed by Robert Castro and Kathleen O'Hare. Assistance in designing the format of the survey instrument and associated materials was provided by the Rand Survey Research Group under Deborah Hensler. Management of the system for tracking the status of questionnaires and preparation of follow-up correspondence was handled by Bernice Jacobs.

Michael Lawless contributed to the research by collecting and analyzing statistical data as well as conducting several extensive interviews. Paul Berman, Irv Cohen, David deFerranti, Bernard Greenberg, Elwyn Harris, and Marvin Lavin made valuable and cogent comments on early drafts of our reports and their comments significantly improved its comprehensibility. Albert Seedman, Carmine Motto, Seymour Silver, Raymond J. Sinetar, and Sydney Cooper were involved in the initial research planning and Mr. Sinetar and Mr. Cooper subsequently assisted in collecting and analyzing portions of the data.

Mary Sauters, as well as other secretaries, provided excellent secretarial assistance during the conduct of the study and the preparation of the manuscript.

The research described in this book was conducted under a grant from the National Institute of Law Enforcement and Criminal Justice, Law Enforcement Assistance Administration, Department of Justice. Points of view or opinions expressed herein are those of the authors and do not necessarily represent the official position or policies of the funding agency or any of the law enforcement agencies that cooperated with the study.

The Criminal Investigation Process

1

Introduction

This book provides an in-depth look at the criminal investigation process, an aspect of police work that is of increasing public concern given the rapidly rising crime rate, recently characterized as "one of the terrifying facts of life, which we have come to accept as normal, and which we must not accept as normal."[1] Although the police can affect crime in a number of ways—both through prevention and active patrol—the identification and apprehension of offenders plays a critical role in the overall police–crime control mission.

Routine criminal investigation work can be an extremely frustrating task. Very few crimes present investigators with enough evidence to identify the offender rapidly. For any given lead, numerous time-consuming actions may be taken in attempts to generate additional information, with no assurance as to which ones will prove to be useful. Even after the suspect has been identified, the requirements of a lawful arrest and successful prosecution may entail many additional hours of effort to prepare the case.

When this study began, very little was known about the pattern of investigative activities followed across police departments, or the impact of these activities on solving crimes. Because reported crime and arrest data do not distinguish between the results of patrol activity and those of investigative efforts, little was known about investigative outputs. Also, the nature of investigative activity was thought to have changed as a result of court decisions severely limiting the interrogation of suspects[2] and warrantless searches. These changes have created a demand for more objective or scientific investigation techniques that do not infringe on the constitutionally protected rights of suspects. These were the factors that led us to undertake the research reported here.

Scope and Objectives

This book results from a two-year Rand study of police investigation practices, supported by the National Institute of Law Enforcement and Criminal Justice, Law Enforcement Assistance Administration, U.S. Department of Justice. The study's objectives were negotiated between Rand and the Institute, based on

---

1. Attorney General Edward H. Levi, *Los Angeles Times,* July 22, 1975, p. 1.

2. For a discussion of such practices, especially the so-called third degree, see Franklin (1970) and Hopkins (1972). (See bibliography for complete citations.)

questions raised by previous Rand work[3] and the Institute's policy interests. In general these objectives were

- To describe, on a national scale, current investigative organization and practices.

- To assess the contribution that police investigation makes to the achievement of criminal justice goals.

- To ascertain the effectiveness of new technology and systems being adopted to enhance investigative performance.

- To reveal how investigative effectiveness is related to differences in organizational form, staffing, procedures, etc.

The scope of this study is limited to police investigation of serious reported crimes—homicides, rapes, robberies, burglaries, larceny-theft, i.e., those crimes used by the FBI to establish the Crime Index.[4] Excluded from our analysis are misdemeanor offenses, which when reported to police receive little or no investigative attention. In addition, we have not been concerned with the enforcement of victimless crimes, such as narcotics, vice, and gambling. Although investigative effort is often directed toward curtailing this unlawful conduct, the nature of such work is sufficiently different from the investigation of victim crimes that it has been excluded from this study.[5] We have also excluded the investigation of organized crime, racketeering, or militant groups,[6] which is pursued by only a small number of departments, usually in cooperation with federal law enforcement agencies. This type of investigation involves surveillance and other intelligence-gathering activities to a unique degree.

Method of Research

The literature of the field was first surveyed to provide a background for our work. Since few data were available concerning the investigative function across

---

3. Greenwood (1970); Greenwood et al. (1976).

4. The offenses of murder, forcible rape, robbery, aggravated assault, burglary, larceny-theft, and auto theft are the subject of an index in the Uniform Crime Reporting Program, purporting to measure the rate and distribution of crime in the United States. These offenses were selected because of their inherent seriousness and/or because their incidence has presented a serious problem to law enforcement officials.

5. Traditional police investigation seeks primarily to identify and apprehend the offender. In drug and vice enforcement, by contrast, the emphasis is on detecting the crime and securing sufficient evidence to prosecute suspected offenders.

6. SLA, Weatherman, etc.

a broad spectrum of departments, a comprehensive national survey of all major police departments was designed, and the survey questionnaire was administered to every municipal or county police department in the country having 150 or more full-time employees or serving a jurisdiction whose 1970 census population exceeded 100,000. The questions covered such topics as:

- Department characteristics
- Deployment of investigators
- Status of investigators within the department
- Training
- Use of evidence technicians
- Organization and degree of specialization
- Evaluation criteria used by department
- Interaction with the prosecutor
- Case assignment
- Computer files used
- Crimes, clearances, and arrests

Most of the cities were contacted by mail, but in twenty-nine departments the instrument was administered in person. These latter cities were chosen both for convenience in location and because they had been identified by members of our advisory board[7] and other prominent police officials as having one or more interesting or particularly successful programs. These in-person visits provided extra information not asked for in the survey and enhanced our knowledge of the organization and day-to-day functioning of investigative units.

In response to the 300 questionnaires distributed, we received 153 replies for a 51 percent response rate—quite high, considering the many questionnaires with which police departments are routinely bombarded. Some variation was observed in the response rate according to the size of the department and its geographic location. Large departments responded more frequently than did small ones. Departments in the south central and western areas of the country

7. Cornelius (Neil) J. Behan, Chief of Personnel, New York City Police Department; James Fisk, Member of Los Angeles Police Commission; Thomas Hastings, Chief of Police, Rochester New York; Jerry Wilson, Former Chief, Metropolitan Washington, D.C. Police Department; Eugene Zoglio, Chairman, Department of Public Service, Prince George's Community College, Largo, Maryland; Raymond Sinetar, Head, Preliminary Hearing Division, Los Angeles County District Attorney's Office; Robert Hill, Deputy Chief of Police, Long Beach, California.

responded more frequently than did those in the northeastern part. Neither of these variables was thought to seriously bias our results since we were able to control for each one.

On the basis of the information collected, some of the 153 responding cities were selected for detailed study. In these cities we typically interviewed the chief or deputy chief in charge of investigation. Several days were spent with working-level investigators, discussing cases, observing procedures, and studying programs, activities, or problems unique to that department.

In some departments an effort was made to maintain contact with a few detectives over the entire course of the study in order to get a more representative view of their routine working environment. As our contacts and experience developed we began to act in some respects as members of the force—participating in field interviews, interrogations, squad meetings, meal and coffee breaks, and cruising the streets. Each day's activities were described in field notes which were used as references in preparing this book.

Data collected during these visits were of two principal types: (1) statistics prepared by the department for its own internal use or in conjunction with evaluation of certain special projects or programs; (2) data that we coded directly from departmental records, logbooks, or case files.

Table 1-1 lists the cities in which we collected special data samples, briefly describes the nature of the data, and indicates in which chapter(s) they are fully described and analyzed.

Organization of this Book

The remainder of the book is divided into four parts.

Part I: The Process Described (Chapters 2-4) is devoted to discussing the various activities which make up the investigative function, as well as suggesting methods by which such activities might be evaluated. In Chapters 2 and 3 we present a description of how investigations are typically conducted, including characteristics of the investigators, the procedures they follow, and their relationship to other police activities. Readers who may be familiar with only one department or with a few aspects of investigative work will be given a more systematic, realistic view of the investigative process.

Chapter 3 discusses various approaches to measuring investigation effectiveness, and Chapter 4 presents and synthesizes the information we obtained from our review of previous literature on the investigative function.

Part II: A National Survey of Investigative Practices (Chapters 5-7) reports on the responses to the questionnaire survey. Chapter 5 discusses the design and administration of the survey instrument, Chapter 6 is devoted to the descriptive results of the survey in terms of overall departmental characteristics, and in Chapter 7 differences among departments with regard to policies, resources used,

Table 1–1
Special Statistics and Data Samples Collected

Police Department	Nature of Statistics or Data Samples Collected	Chapter of This Book in Which Data Appear
Berkeley, Ca.	–Cleared and uncleared residential burglaries	10
	–Cleared robberies	9
	–Cleared cases (all crime types combined)	9
Kansas City, Mo.	–Detective case assignment file	8, 9
Long Beach, Ca.	–Cleared and uncleared residential burglaries	10
	–Cleared cases (seven non-robbery offenses)	9
	–Investigative strike force statistics	13
Los Angeles, Ca.	–Cleared robberies	9
	–Latent fingerprint processing statistics	10
Miami, Fla	–Cleared robberies	9
	–Latent fingerprint processing statistics	10
	–Investigative strike force statistics	13
Richmond, Ca.	–Cleared and uncleared residential burglaries	10
	–Latent fingerprint processing statistics	10
Washington, D.C.	–Cleared robberies	9
	–Latent fingerprint processing statistics	10
Anonymous	–Court disposition data from two prosecutorial jurisdictions	11
	–Victim survey	12

and operational characteristics are identified and then related to standard gross performance measures such as clearance and arrest rates.

Part III: The Process Evaluated (Chapters 8–13) presents a comprehensive description of the criminal investigation process (based on all data gathered in the course of the study) and an analysis of those issues that can be illuminated by quantitative evidence. In Chapter 8 we show in both qualitative and statistical terms how the efforts of investigators are distributed among the various activities in which they are engaged. The statistical data in this section come from the Kansas City Case Assignment File, which is also described. With the file we were able to discern how much time is devoted to different types of cases, how long cases are active, and on what activities the effort is expended.

In Chapter 9 we shift from investigation inputs to outputs and examine how cases are actually solved. We use a sample of cases selected from the Kansas City Case Assignment File, plus smaller samples drawn from several departments, to determine which activities are primarily responsible for the solution of various types of cases. This information provides a basis for making overall judgments about the effectiveness of various investigation practices.

Chapter 10 describes and analyzes a variety of approaches to collecting and processing latent fingerprints from crime scenes as an alternative technique for identifying suspects. Data are derived from case samples drawn from several departmental statistical records.

A different aspect of investigative performance is discussed in Chapter 11, which uses a small sample of robbery cases drawn from two different jurisdictions to examine the relationship between the thoroughness with which evidentiary facts are documented by the police and the eventual outcome of the case.

Chapter 12 analyzes the attitudes of victims toward various investigative strategies and the amount of feedback information they might receive, based on a small sample telephone survey. Chapter 13 describes and presents summary outcome data for two different types of investigative strike forces that deal with robberies and burglaries.

Part IV: Conclusions and Policy Implications (Chapters 14 and 15) presents a summary and synthesis of the overall findings of the study and draws policy relevant conclusions and recommendations.

A complete bibliography appears at the end of the book. Citations in the text mentioning only the author and date refer to this bibliography.

Part I

The Process Described

2

The Investigative Function

A primary objective of this study has been to develop a realistic description of the activities in which police investigators are routinely engaged. At its beginning we had considerable doubts about whether we could ever resolve the many conflicting views concerning what detectives really accomplish.

Stereotypes of the Investigator's Role

Three common stereotypes influence the public's perception of investigative effectiveness. First is the media image, which some detectives would claim for themselves while others would deplore it—the resourceful, streetwise cop, who always gets his man. Next is the historical stereotype, the image that old-timers on the force have of the detective's contribution to law and order. Finally, the critical stereotype—which recent objective studies have tended to develop. Some combination of these alternative stereotypes provides the basis for current investigative policies in most police departments today.

The media image of the working detective, particularly pervasive in widely viewed television series, is that of a clever, imaginative, perseverant, streetwise cop who consorts with glamorous women and duels with crafty criminals. He and his partners roam the entire city for days or weeks trying to break a single case, which is ultimately solved by means of the investigator's deductive powers. This image is the one that some investigators prefer—perhaps with a degree of sanitizing. They would concede that criminals are rarely as crafty or diabolical as depicted in the media, but may not quarrel with the media characterization of their own capabilities.

Some current investigative practices appear mainly as a means to preserve a media-like image or to give a victim the kind of services he expects largely because of that image. That is, fingerprint dusting, mug shot showing, or questioning witnesses are often done without any hope of developing leads, but simply for public relations.

The stereotyped images held by older police administrators are influenced by the special status that detectives once held in earlier times.[1] Not too many years ago various forms of illicit activity such as vice, gambling, prostitution, and

---

1. This brief historical account was compiled from information presented by Smith (1960), Fosdick (1921), and Franklin (1970).

speakeasies were much more openly tolerated by city governments than they are today. The existence of these illegal, but accepted, enterprises created problems for the city police. How could they keep such institutions under control without driving them completely out of business? The police dealings with these institutions were frequently carried on by detectives. The detectives ensured that the businesses were run in a somewhat orderly fashion and that "undesirables" who attempted to take part were driven out. By this delicate handling of a troublesome situation the detectives often won the favor of the business leaders and politicians connected with these activities. Such political connections made the detective a man of respect and influence.

Allowing these illegal enterprises to continue had special investigation benefits for the police. When serious crimes did occur or when public pressure was brought to bear on the police to deal with a particular problem, these illegal activities provided a valuable source of information to which the detectives could turn. Not surprisingly, thieves and con men would often be customers of the vice and gambling operations, or have close contacts with people engaged in such business. If the police really wanted information on a particular criminal activity, the detectives could turn to their contacts within the illicit activities and either solicit information as a favor or extort it by threatening the safety of the illegal operation. Thus the "effectiveness" of detective operations frequently depended on maintaining close contacts with a select group of potential informers.

Another role detectives played in addition to that of policing illicit activities was that of dispensing street-corner justice. A good cop was expected to maintain order without resorting to the courts. He did this by persuasion, and by threats, and by actual physical force, if necessary. Only in those instances where it was clear that his presence alone would not deter crime did he bring in a suspect for criminal proceedings.

Detectives played a prominent role in the exercise of this discretionary justice because they were less visible than a uniformed patrolman when it came to breaking down doors or pummeling offenders on the street. Because of their experience they were expected to be more diplomatic in handling these incidents—part of the detective's basic working knowledge included which individuals could be treated roughly without getting the department into trouble. The detectives who could handle or clear up delicate situations without causing a commotion were highly valued by police and city administrators.

Another method formerly available to help a detective close cases was the third-degree or the extended interrogation. *Miranda*,[2] increased enforcement of civil liberties, and the rise of community review boards put a limitation on this type of activity. It is no longer acceptable for detectives to arrest a suspect and keep him in custody simply for investigative purposes. The use of physical or psychological force in an attempt to extort a confession or to get information

2. The rights enumerated in *Miranda* v. *Arizona,* 384 U.S. 436 (1966).

about other suspects in a case is no longer permissible, under current due process requirements.

We have no empirical evidence concerning the results produced by these various techniques; therefore any comparisons between the effectiveness of historical and current approaches is purely speculative. However, it is obvious that investigators once possessed a number of investigative tactics that are no longer permissible.

A more critical stereotype of investigative effectiveness can be gleaned from a number of studies which attempt to analyze how detectives go about their work.

The earliest critic was probably Raymond Fosdick (1921). After visiting police departments in all of the major cities of the United States, he criticized detectives for:

- Lack of civil service standards in selection.

- Lack of training.

- Poor coordination with patrol operation.

- Lack of effective supervision.

- Lack of ordinary "business systems" for handling their administrative work.

In many departments, these criticisms are equally appropriate today. More recent analysts have argued that:

- Police agencies do not routinely collect and summarize data that can be used to determine the effectiveness of investigation activities. Clearance and arrest statistics in particular are unsuitable because they fail to distinguish outputs of investigative efforts from those of other units in the department. Clearance data alone are also extremely unreliable indicators of police performance because of their subjective nature.

- The solution rate of crimes assigned to detectives appears insensitive to the number assigned, implying that detectives can accurately predict which cases can be solved and work on only those, or that the cases solve themselves.

- A high proportion of cases are closed when a patrol unit makes an arrest at the scene of the crime.

- Investigators make scant use of indirect evidence such as fingerprints, toolmarks, etc.

Uncomplimentary views are also being espoused by a number of progressive police chiefs who have seen reforms and new initiatives take hold in every other area of policing, but find their detectives the last bastion of the status quo. In their departments, an appointment to the detective bureau is no longer viewed as the best path to promotion. In some departments (Los Angeles Police Department, for instance) an independent detective bureau no longer exists. Investigators are now assigned directly to a local operations commander.

Many of these chiefs are quite candidly critical of the old freewheeling detective style of operation. They see their detectives as simply trying to preserve the freedom and prerequisities of their jobs without making any efforts to adapt to the rapidly shifting community and legal climate in which they must work.

Current Investigative Activities

Since one purpose of this volume is to suggest possible changes in how future criminal investigations are conducted, the reader should be well acquainted with the current investigative process. We now turn our attention to providing a realistic perspective of current investigative activities.

A realistic view of investigative activities can most easily be portrayed by describing how a typical case is handled. We also present some variations that frequently occur in this typical pattern, as well as some departmental policies that govern how cases are handled. Finally, we discuss the supporting activities that police perform to increase the likelihood of identification and apprehension.

Incident Report and Preliminary Investigation

Most police cases begin with a citizen's telephone call to the department: a parent reports the rape of a daughter; a victim tells of an armed robbery; a couple complains of the burglary of their apartment, discovered on their return home. As a variant, a silent alarm may indicate that a burglary of a commercial warehouse is in progress. Or, a victim may appear at the station. Many of these calls will require a timely response to the scene of the crime or the location of the victim. In very few departments are detectives available for this action; in most, a patrolman is given the initial assignment. He responds to the location, lends appropriate assistance, and records an incident report that formally initiates the case. Providing aid to the victim and recording the incident report would typically consume about 40 minutes of the patrolman's time. His crime report would contain basic facts about the victim, the crime scene, and the offense, including the identity of witnesses made known to him. In most departments under most circumstances, the burden of the case will then shift to the investigative division.

As we have noted, some departments do assign greater responsibility to the responding patrolman for additional investigative effort or for further service to the victim. The patrolman may be expected to make inquiries of neighbors; to search for footprints, toolmarks, and fingerprints; and to summon an evidence technician if the presence of physical evidence appears to justify it. He may be expected to counsel the victim on protective devices and defensive tactics to minimize future loss and injury.

Whatever the extent of his responsibility, the final step for the patrolman is the completion of his crime incident report. Policy governing the thoroughness of this report varies widely from department to department—from a scant recitation of only the most central information at one extreme to an exhaustive recording of all relevant details at the other. In most departments the report is handprinted, then photocopied and distributed; in a few departments the patrolman is able to dictate his report by telephone to an automatic recording machine.

Screening and Assignment

Crime reports that accumulate through the night are distributed in the morning to the appropriate investigative units, chosen almost invariably on the basis of the unit's crime specialty or locality of responsibility. When a case contains several offenses of different types—e.g., both robbery and homicide—established department policy usually governs which unit is assigned the case.

Police departments may adhere to any one of several alternative policies to assign the crime report to a specific investigator once it reaches the investigative unit, provided it is not suspended for lack of sufficient information. If the detective squad—which may number as few as three or as many as twenty-five— has been organized in terms of crime specialties, the assignment of the case simply conforms to that organization. If there is no crime specialization within the investigative unit, the supervisor may be guided by a policy of assigning cases to balance current workloads among the detectives or to concentrate under one investigator the crime reports that fit a pattern. Or, the assignment scheme may be to give all cases arising within a specified period of time or in a given geographical area to one detective. Whatever the assignment policy, its effect is to add, on the average, one or two new cases per day to an investigator's load. But the actual increments are typically irregular—perhaps six on one day, then only one in the next two days. The assignment rate of serious crimes will be somewhat less, averaging perhaps ten cases to an investigator per month.

Follow-up

When the investigator receives a new case, his first job will be to compare it against the files. He will check to see if it is similar to any other recent cases.

He will log the case into any files he personally maintains. Any further steps depend on his workload and his own inclination.

At this point we can distinguish three different types of cases: those in which the next investigative steps are obvious, those that look routine and suggest no further action, and those that look unusually severe. The obvious cases are those in which a suspect is suggested by the victim, or the crime report indicates there is a witness who may have some additional information. They may also involve some special type of stolen property that will be difficult to fence. There may be a complicated fact situation about the way in which the crime was carried out, or some prior relationship between the victim, the witnesses, and the offender. The victim may have had a good look at the suspect, such as in a sex or robbery offense, and may indicate that he can identify the suspect if he sees him.

The procedure for handling the obvious cases is straightforward, although it may be time consuming. The victim or witnesses must be contacted and interviewed for additional information. Inquiries must be made at locations where special stolen property may be fenced. Mug shot photos are shown. A collection of photographs, including one of the suspect, must be assembled.

The handling of the common offense, without any leads, is also straightforward. After it is routinely checked against other cases, it may simply be filed without further inquiries. Perfunctory attempts may be made to contact the victim to see if he has any further statements to make.

In serious[3] cases without leads, special action may be taken to get the investigation under way. A wider search of the crime scene for evidence or weapons may be instigated. A canvass to determine if new witnesses can be located may be undertaken, or the victim's friends may be re-interviewed to determine if additional facts can be learned that were not covered in the initial report. Unless some obvious leads are developed, even serious cases will be dropped within a day or two under the press of new assignments.

For most investigators the first few hours of the day are devoted to office work, which includes reviewing cases, preparing reports, and attending meetings. Late in the morning they will move out to conduct interviews, interrogate suspects, or just cruise. Lunch is taken out of the office, usually at favorite hangouts. The afternoon is devoted to interviews or paperwork.

Interviewing witnesses is probably the most challenging task the investigator faces. In most cases the witness has already been interviewed by the reporting patrolman. The investigator's job is to elicit new facts or cast the old facts in a new light. In a large number of cases, especially those against the person, the victim and the offender may be acquainted. In such cases the victim or witness may be unwilling or afraid to give sufficient facts to implicate the suspect. Then it is the investigator's responsibility to convince the person that he should furnish the necessary information, or to establish that he may be protecting the suspect.

---

3. Seriousness is determined by the violence of the attack, the value of the loss, the status of the victim, or the publicity that the case attracts.

The task of inducing reluctant victims or witnesses to come forward with new information can often place the investigator in a compromising position where, if he pushes too hard, he is likely to receive a complaint from the citizen concerning his behavior. On the other hand, if he takes everything he is told at face value, he may not single out the cases in which the victim has been previously involved with the offender.

Most investigators we observed were extremely casual about recording the results of their interviews. Usually, nothing was written down at the time of the interview. The investigator simply travels around with the facts of a number of cases in his head. When he interviews a victim or a witness he uses the information to support a hypothesis he may have developed, or to suggest other things he might do. He rarely attempts to carefully analyze what has been said or to compare one set of statements by a witness against another at an earlier time. If he does take notes, they are usually on a scrap of paper in the case folder and usually involve an address, an alias, or a license plate. He seldom writes down a statement describing an interview or takes down responses from the witness. As an example, see Appendix G "Playing a Hunch."

Even when such notes are taken they are rarely made a part of the investigator's folder. They are simply used to get to the next step in the investigation and are then discarded. Only in homicide cases is one likely to see verbatim transcripts or interviews with witnesses.

One of the less demanding and more enjoyable activities of investigators involves comparing notes with their colleagues, either within the same squad or among different units. Most cases are depressingly routine, so when a truly unusual case occurs, or the detective finds something particularly interesting, he is eager to share it with his colleagues. Investigators seem to particularly enjoy looking over new suspects, weapons, and contraband that has been seized, or discussing novel MOs. Obviously, some of the information that results keeps them aware of what is going on in the street, but it also helps relieve the boredom of the regular routine.

When detectives from one unit visit another jurisdiction in the course of their duties, they will often take time to swap stories concerning recent crime patterns or procedural changes within their respective departments. In fact, many types of specialists, such as robbery or forgery investigators, belong to county or statewide organizations and meet for lunch on a regular monthly basis. At these sessions they compare notes among themselves and with representatives of industries that are particularly concerned with their crime types.

In Custody

If an offender has been arrested at the time the crime was committed, some departments require their investigators to assist in preparing the case for prosecution. Police departments vary greatly in the amount of effort devoted to such post-arrest investigations.[4] In some localities, the arresting patrolman retains the primary duty of supplying information about the suspect and the crime to the prosecutor. Here the detective's role is limited to relating these data to other offenses and clearing past crimes. In other jurisdictions the investigators prepare whatever detailed investigation report is required to serve the prosecutor's need for information about the suspect and the offense for which he has been arrested.

The difference in the investigator's role seems to be dictated by local custom, by the demands of the prosecutor, and by the time available between arrest and arraignment. A minimally adequate investigation can be best accomplished if the suspect is in custody and available to the detectives for at least one working day after his arrest. But in many jurisdictions this is impossible because of the immediacy of arraignment and a predetermined bail schedule.

There are also wide disparities among police departments in their application of the *Miranda* requirements.[5] The exclusionary rule causes some departments

---

4. Chapter 11 presents examples of these contrasting efforts and explores their implications.

5. Prior to any questioning of a suspect initiated by law enforcement officers, after a person has been taken into custody or otherwise deprived of his freedom of action in any significant way, he must be advised of the rights enumerated in *Miranda* v. *Arizona,* 384 U.S. 436 (1966). As typically phrased, the rights are as follows:

1. You have a right to remain silent.
2. Anything you say can and will be used against you in a court of law.
3. You have the right to talk to a lawyer and have him present with you while you are questioned.
4. If you cannot afford a lawyer, one will be appointed to represent you before any questioning, if you wish one.

Having given these rights, the police then usually ask the following questions to obtain a waiver of them:

1. Do you understand each of these rights as I have explained them to you?
2. Having these rights in mind, do you wish to talk to us now?

If the arrested person indicates in any manner that he wishes to consult with an attorney before speaking, there can be no questioning without violating his constitutional rights. The fact that he may have answered some questions or volunteered statements does not deprive him of the right to decline to answer any further inquiries until he has consulted with an attorney and then agrees to be questioned. Given a violation of the *Miranda* requirement, the prosecution may not use his statements at trial. On the other hand, inconsistent or contradictory statements obtained by such a violation may be used to impeach the defendant's testimony if he testifies. The arrested person does not have the burden of initiating a request for counsel.

The *Miranda* requirements are not met by a mechanical recitation of the warnings. Once the arrestee states that he wants an attorney, the interrogation will be wrongful if it proceeds before an attorney is present. One *Miranda* warning, adequately given, may be sufficient for later interrogations. The defendant may waive his rights, provided that the waiver is made voluntarily, knowingly, and intelligently. The fact that a defendant asked for counsel in prior interrogations, but did not assert the right during the session in which the incriminating statement was actually made does not constitute a waiver.

It is not established whether and to what extent the "fruit of the poisonous tree" doctrine is applicable to evidence derived from statements wrongfully obtained in violation of the *Miranda* requirements. Some courts have ruled that the testimony of a witness who was discovered solely through interrogation in violation of *Miranda* would not be excluded.

to exert little pressure on the suspect to make a statement. Others are not deterred by an expression of unwillingness to answer questions after the suspect has been warned of his right to remain silent and his right to the presence of an attorney. Even though the exclusionary rule precludes the use of information gained thereby in the pending prosecution,[6] these departments will continue to interrogate to learn about other crimes and to facilitate subsequent investigations. The pitfall here is that the defendant may reveal his involvement in a more serious offense for which the police would prefer that he be prosecuted, but since his disclosure would be tainted by a *Miranda* violation, the prosecutor would have the burden of proving that the evidence used in a subsequent proceeding did not result from the unconstituional interrogation.

Organization and Management of Investigative Units

Earlier we described the most common method of organizing and deploying investigative resources. It entails establishing a separate and distinct investigative unit outside the normal patrol chain of command. Within this unit, investigators specialize by type of crime; for example, crimes against persons and crimes against property in small departments, and homicide, robbery, burglary, auto theft, forgery, and juvenile in larger departments. Within these sub-units there may be further specialization by crime type (taxi robbery, bank robbery, motel and hotel robbery, etc.) or by geographic area. Cases resulting from reported crimes are automatically referred to the appropriate squad and investigator based on the type of offense reported and/or its location, depending on organizational structure.

This type of organization allegedly results in several deficiencies which a few departments have attempted to remedy through organizational change.

One claim is that the rigid separation between patrol and investigation results in duplication of efforts, lack of continuity in handling cases, and exclusion of patrolmen from potentially more satisfying and challenging activities. If the investigators require information which they believe may be available at the crime scene, and the patrolman has failed to include this information in his report, then the investigators often must repeat all of the work already performed by the patrolman in his preliminary investigation. If the patrolman has failed to record every significant piece of information available initially at the crime scene, potential witnesses or evidence can be completely lost to the investigator.

Another claim is that the traditional segregation of investigators from the patrol force results in a lack of cooperation and failure to share information. Thus, it is alleged that investigators hold themselves aloof, the patrol force doesn't know what to look for, and the detectives do not know what is happening on the street. In larger departments, it is alleged that the investigators lose touch

---

6. Statements obtained in violation of *Miranda* requirements have been held admissible for purposes of impeaching a witness. *Harris* v. *New York*, 401 U.S. 222 (1971).

with the different neighborhoods because they cover cases in different areas of the city and cannot build up informants or contacts in any one area. Finally, it is alleged that the traditional assignment of investigators to individual cases causes each man to be buried under his own caseload. The result: everything gets handled in a routine perfunctory manner. Opportunities for high quality[7] but time-consuming arrests must be foregone to keep up with the assigned caseload.

To overcome these alleged deficiencies, as well as to respond to new patrol concepts, a number of departures from the traditional organizational pattern have been tried. The most frequent variation found in the larger departments is separation by geographic district, usually involving coterminous patrol and detective boundaries. In this variation, some form of headquarters unit is often retained to handle the more serious or complex cases.

Another reform, motivated primarily by patrol considerations, is team policing. Under this concept detectives work directly with a team of patrolmen assigned to a specific area. The patrolmen and detectives are both responsible to a single team commander (usually from patrol) who (theoretically) controls all of the police resources in his team area. Still another more radical form embodies the concept of the patrolman/investigator in which the responding patrolman handles *all* aspects of the investigation for all but the most complex cases. The most complex investigations and the analysis of crime patterns may be handled by a few investigative specialists who also supervise the patrolmen/ investigators in their investigations. This form of organiztion has been practiced for many years in Berkeley, California.

Finally, another innovation employs the investigative strike force. Instead of investigating cases on an individual basis, the strike force deploys both investigators and patrolmen in specific high crime areas or against specific target crimes. Their objective is to have an immediate visible effect on the reported crime rate through deterrence and apprehension.

In the remainder of this section we describe four departments that embody various forms of these innovations and their apparent impact on the aforementioned deficiencies of more traditional organizations.

District Squads

Here we illustrate two organizational variants of the combined centralized/decentralized approach to investigation, as typified by the Washington, D.C., and Los Angeles police departments. The Metropolitan Police Department of Washington, D.C., utilizes the district form of organization to a limited degree. Although the city is divided into seven patrol districts, each with its own investigative

---

7. Offenders who commit serious felonies, or professional thieves.

squad, all of the more serious crimes are handled by the Central Investigation Division (CID). According to a general order of the department, CID handles all homicides and armed robberies, and all burglaries of over $1000. CID is organized in the traditional specialist fashion. Investigators work in pairs, and each is assigned his share of the caseload.

Citywide coordination of investigation is facilitated by daily staff meetings at which representatives from each district meet with CID to discuss ongoing cases. Another coordinating device is the daily lineup at which all suspects recently taken into custody are presented, along with their criminal history and a description of their current offense. All CID investigators and an investigator representing each district attend. Following the lineup almost every suspect is questioned by at least one group of investigators about particular cases in which the detectives are interested.

It is the policy of the Metropolitan Police Department that investigators stay out of the office unless they have some specific business to conduct there. Most of their time is to be spent on the street conducting investigations or responding to crime scenes.

Because of the CID/district separation of responsibility, several cars will frequently respond to a reported crime—a patrolman, his supervisor, CID detectives, and district detectives. Until some preliminary investigative work is performed, it is often not clear exactly who should take the case. If CID takes over, then no district investigator need be assigned.

The follow-up investigative policy in Washington requires that some minimal efforts be made on every case; e.g., to recontact the victim. If he or she cannot be reached after several calls, the case is then suspended. The preliminary report produced by the responding officer is usually quite brief, because it is asserted that there is constant pressure on patrol units from their supervisors to minimize the time devoted to such service calls so as to return to patrol. For this reason, preliminary reports of patrol officers have low credibility with the detectives, who tend to place scant reliance on the facts in these reports unless they have verified the information themselves.

The Los Angeles Police Department also operates on a decentralized basis. The city is divided into 17 areas, each with its own command and stationhouse. Each area maintains its own complement of patrol, investigators, vice, and juvenile officers. In contrast to Washington, the LAPD district investigators retain full responsibility for *all* crimes reported in their district. Central Investigation plays a much less pervasive role. In addition to maintaining surveillance over pawnshops and other such functions which are most appropriately performed on a citywide basis, Central Investigation only comes in on particularly difficult cases, and then only to assist the areas.

LAPD investigators are frequently at their desks. They respond to reported crimes much less frequently than do investigators in Washington. More reliance is placed on the patrolman's report, although the screening process by which cases are selected for follow-up investigation is about the same in both departments. In both cases, official departmental policies imply that every case will be investigated; in actual practice many routine cases are suspended after nominal, but fruitless, efforts to contact the victim.

The Robbery Detail in Central Investigation is made up of eleven men, divided into two- and three-man teams. Each team is responsible for monitoring cases in three or four areas. These investigators perform a coordination function, informing their areas of information developed elsewhere that may be useful in one of their cases. They will get involved in only the most serious cases when it becomes evident that one offender or group of offenders is implicated in a series of offenses or when a particular case becomes extremely involved. In time-consuming cases, where numerous people must be located and interviewed, their regular caseload prevents division investigators from giving the case adequate attention. This is where Central Investigation will step in to provide aid.

Also, when a suspect taken into custody appears responsible for a number of crimes across the city, Central Investigation will gather up all the cases and interrogate the suspect to establish whether or not he was in fact reponsible for those crimes.

Team Policing

Team policing has been or is in the process of being implemented in a number of the jurisdictions we visited. Here we describe the general concepts of team policing, as they affect investigation, and some variations in practice that we have observed.

The basic concept of team policing involves assigning complete responsibility for police service in a small geographic area to a team of police officers, commanded by a team leader. Using this pattern a city of several hundred thousand may be divided into six to ten team areas, with each area covered by a team of 20 to 40 police officers.

In practice, no department is ever completely decentralized in this fashion. Some functions are always retained in a headquarters unit—such as records, communication, etc. Investigations can go either way. All investigators can operate out of central headquarters, or they can be dispersed to the teams. The only city we observed in which the former option was being tested was Cincinnati. Most of its proponents tend to feel that team policing requires that at least some investigators be assigned to the teams.

In Los Angeles, each area commander has almost complete discretion in determining if his command will adopt team policing. If he decides to proceed, he has considerable latitude in deciding how the teams will operate. In one area, the investigators remained physically and organizationally segregated from the patrolmen on their teams. Although each detective is attached to a team for purposes of assigning cases, all detectives report to a single captain. The five or six investigators on each team specialize by crime type so that the assignment of cases becomes almost automatic once the category of crimes and location of occurrence are known.

This type of arrangement seems to negate many of the benefits that team policing is supposed to promote. It does not provide team leaders the flexibility to use their men in plainclothes or uniform as the situation demands, and it provides little opportunity for contact between patrolmen and investigators.

In another area of Los Angeles, all investigators, except Juvenile and Vice, were assigned to teams. They worked directly for the team supervisor. The investigators' desks were grouped by team around their supervisor so that there was considerably more contact between patrolmen and detectives. If the team leader was absent, the senior detective took his place.

Even in this mode we did not observe any instances in which men were shifted between investigative or patrol duties as the situation demanded. Investigators continued to specialize by crime types. Coordination of cases was provided by designating the senior investigator in each team as the coordinator for a particular crime type. He kept a record of all assignments for his type of offense and reviewed all potentially relevant material.

The city of Rochester, New York, is divided into three geographic areas for police administrative purposes. Since 1973, approximately half of each area has been policed by a Coordinated Team Patrol (CTP) while half is still policed by traditional methods. The objective of this split is to evaluate the benefits of team policing in each area of the city.

In areas not covered by CTP, all investigations are performed by a central Criminal Investigation Section (CIS). In CTP areas, CIS continues to handle all homicides, assaults likely to become homicides, first-degree rapes, auto thefts, and juvenile crimes. Vice and narcotics are also handled on a centralized basis. All other crimes are handled by detectives assigned to the CTP teams.

There do not appear to be any substantial differences between the operations of CTP or non-CTP detectives. In all areas of the city, patrolmen are responsible for conducting complete preliminary investigations on all but the most serious crimes against persons. In Rochester a crime report form is used to capture solvability factors that the detectives can use in determining which cases to follow up.

The principal difference between CTP and non-CTP detectives seems to be that the former are more responsive to the patrol's concerns, and there is more sharing of information. CTP detectives appear to work more at night or on weekends than their non-CTP colleagues.

The Patrolman-Investigator

Berkeley (California) has traditionally been recognized as having an innovative police department. In the past it has attracted officers with advanced education, some from the University of California School of Criminology at Berkeley.

Prior to 1972 Berkeley patrolmen were responsible for completely investigating any crimes to which they were dispatched. At present there is a greater degree of specialization. The patrol force is divided into five platoons—two platoons of investigators and three of patrolmen. On the day and evening watches both patrolmen and investigators are on duty. Investigators are dispatched to felony calls, and patrolmen to misdemeanors. Whoever is dispatched handles the case from initial response through to its eventual conclusion.

During the early morning watch (from 2 a.m. to 10 a.m.), only one platoon of patrolmen is on duty. They investigate all crime reported during this tour.

The investigators are supported and supervised in their investigative capacity by seven specialist details: one each for homicide, robbery, auto, forgery, theft, general works, and fugitive. Each detail is staffed by up to four men, at least one of whom carries the title of inspector, a grade that ranks in pay between sergeant and lieutenant. The seven specialist details are headed by a lieutenant and comprise the Inspector's Bureau. Together with the Juvenile Bureau, it constitutes the entire Detective Division.

Inspectors are charged with coordinating crime investigations within their specialty and maintaining liaison with neighboring departments. They review all investigators' reports and assign additional effort where they think it is needed. If a case becomes complicated or requires extensive efforts outside of the city, they will step in and take over; this is almost always the case for homicides. And because the inspectors are in the best position to detect *patterns* of crimes (those possibly committed by the same offender(s)), they usually take charge of such cases.

Under the original concept of the patrolman-investigator, every patrolman was supposed to participate in investigations. The current separation of the patrol force into patrolmen and investigators is a response to the department's finding that some patrolmen are either uninterested or incapable of producing acceptable quality reports. As inspectors supervise investigations through review of written reports, this places a particular emphasis on report quality.

Investigators spend most of their time on the street in civilian clothes and unmarked cars. They are assigned to beats that match those of the patrolmen, although each investigator may cover two or three patrol beats. When a felony is reported, the appropriate investigator is dispatched to respond. No patrol car is sent unless it is a crime in progress and backup cars are needed. Both patrolmen and investigators work alone.

When he arrives at the scene, the investigator completes a full preliminary investigation. If some leads develop, he continues to pursue them until the end of his tour or until he is interrupted by a dispatch to another crime scene; in the event the latter is a crime in progress, he will drop the investigation and proceed to the next call. Since most reports are of crimes that are already completed, this problem is not usually severe. When he is not on call the investigator cruises or works on his paperwork in the car.[8]

---

8. For a description, see "On Patrol," Appendix G.

In comparison with other departments, the inspectors function somewhat like senior investigators and somewhat like supervisors. They will enter a case to assist the investigator if his workload becomes too heavy, or if there are tasks that will take the investigator off his beat for an extended period of time. They take over every case that requires contacting sources outside of the city.

Pervasive Problems of Investigative Units

Our observations in police departments across the country disclosed a number of problems that consistently appear to hamper investigation effectiveness, regardless of any other features of departmental organization or practice. At this time we are not prepared to offer any easy solutions or even to declare that changes necessarily must be made. Our only present purpose is to point out the limitations that these problems create in regard to investigative units.

Sources of Information[9]

In the folklore of the "good old days" a detective was considered "as good as his information"—a direct reference to the fact that detectives were expected to cultivate a number of information sources within the community to whom they could turn for information on a serious case. During this earlier period, it was often considered acceptable or even fashionable for police officers and other public officials to deal with certain members of the underworld—particularly those involved in the more sociably acceptable crimes of vice, gambling, or selling alcoholic beverages. Moreover, policemen often lived in high-crime neighborhoods. As a result, police were often able to use these associations as sources of useful information in particularly serious crimes. After all, in many cases the offender might be one of the gambler's or bootlegger's best customers.

Community standards have changed considerably in their tolerance of this type of behavior. More concern is now expressed for the integrity of police agencies, and elimination of corruption is a primary concern of many police chiefs.

In most departments, applicants are screened to make sure they have no past or current connection with criminal elements. Police officers, both on duty and off, are expected to hew to the highest standards of personal morality and behavior. Many big city policemen have adopted suburban lifestyles, which make contact with criminal elements less likely when they are off duty. One result of these changes is that investigators have fewer opportunities to develop good informant contacts. The people they meet in the suburbs are not the kind who can help them learn who is trying to fence a particular piece of jewelry or who suddenly seems to have a lot of cash.

---

9. For one scenario on investigator interaction with an informant, see "Wheeling and Dealing," Appendix G.

Some departments have attempted to make up for this decline in cooperative informants by offering cash payments to people who provide usable information. The procedure for making such payments often requires that the
informant be identified to a supervisor (within the department) who controls the reward funds. Payment is usually made only if sufficient information is provided to make an arrest. Rewards tend to be in the $25 to $50
range.

The experience in departments that maintain such a system is that they get
very few takers. Twenty-five dollars is hardly worth being killed for. The offender
who is arrested is often able to deduce who set him up. Also, since the FBI is
able to offer much larger rewards, this tends to dry up some informant sources
of local police agencies.

The detectives' effectiveness in developing informants is more limited in
largely minority neighborhoods. In our observation, detectives seem to have
little contact with the minority community in which they work, especially in
neighborhoods heavily populated by minorities. Friendly contacts, other than
an occasional smile or wave, are generally limited to the established business
community. These businessmen are seen as one of the principal client groups to
be served by the police; they are the ones who are most frequently robbed and
who can be counted on to support the police.

Changes in acceptable standards of police behavior also seem to limit the
usefulness of another police practice intended to develop investigative leads—the
field interrogation. This aggressive patrol practice involves stopping pedestrians
or drivers of "suspicious" autos to determine their identity and what they are
doing.

Most police departments now severely restrict the conditions under which
such field stops can be made. Also, the person detained must be treated courte-
ously or the officers will be subject to an official complaint. For most patrolmen,
the potential risk of physical harm, and the likelihood of receiving a complaint
that will hurt their record, make field interrogation an action to be avoided. As
a result, the field interrogation files, in departments where they are maintained,
do not contain enough information to be of much help on current cases. Even
when pressure is placed on patrol units to make such stops, supervisors report
that there is a tendency to stop innocuous people rather than those who really
appear suspicious.

The foregoing discussion of factors explaining why certain information
sources needed for investigative work may be less available now than in the past
is not an evaluation of current and historical approaches. Our primary purpose
has been to suggest that the development and use of informants and aggressive
patrol tactics for solving serious offenses play a more minor role in modern
police work than was reported in the past.

Information Processing and Coordination

When a "squeal" came in over the telephone, the lieutenant at the desk wrote it down on a piece of paper and handed it to a detective. "Here Bill," he'd say, "look that up." Bill took the paper, put it in his pocket, and when the paper wore out the case was closed.

—Woods, *Crime Prevention,* p. 342.

Much of an investigator's time is involved in processing information already collected by him or others, rather than in attempting to gather new information. This is largely because the investigator's focus is on clearing cases rather than on arresting new suspects. Most detective clearances are achieved by linking a suspect already in custody to other offenses. Identifying these potential clearances involves comparing suspects in custody with the descriptions from other offenses. The principal linking factors in such clearances are descriptions of suspects and vehicles, weapons, MO, and stolen property.

Much manpower is devoted to recording and circulating among detectives the type of information described above. But very little assistance is provided to help process this information. Instead, each detective must develop his own system for trying to keep track of the huge volume of information that is potentially relevant to his cases. In only a few departments have procedures been established to automatically screen this information and suggest potential matches to the responsible detective. Much of the typical investigator's time is devoted to manually screening information which a computer or a lesser paid clerk could handle more expeditiously.[10]

This information processing usually involves data that someone else, usually a patrolman, has already collected. It is generally available to the entire department. Another class of information is that which has been collected for a particular case: the statements of witnesses, victims, and potential suspects; background information on all of the above; background or supplemental information on the location or execution of the offense; descriptions of investigation activities—both successful and unsuccessful.

In many police departments, investigators record only information that is absolutely necessary to justify the arrest of the suspect and to support a prima facie case. Additional information is considered extraneous or potentially damaging if it could be used to impeach any aspect of the case against the suspect.

As a result, investigators rarely take complete written statements or even careful notes, relying on memory or casual notes on scraps of paper. Fruitless investigative activities are rarely described. Investigation files are simply file

---

10. See "Administrative Details," Appendix G.

folders in which all the material pertaining to a particular case is loosely collected. In most departments, the investigation records of a case are of little use to a supervisor who is attempting to monitor cases or to another detective who must pick up the case if the original detective is not available. We have listened to tape recordings of informants describing cases where the detective, who is newly assigned to the case, does not know the identity of the informant nor his apparent reasons for talking. We have also examined voluminous files involving numerous statements by participants and witnesses in which it is impossible for the reader to identify the conditions under which the statements were taken.[11]

The prosecutor may lose the case when he is confronted with new information at the trial. For instance, the victim may fail to identify a suspect arrested near the scene, but may then identify him at a subsequent lineup. The earlier attempt at identification is not recorded but, of course, the defendant informs his attorney of this identification failure. This neglected piece of information provides the defense with a powerful impeachment weapon to use against the victim's subsequent identification, especially when it comes out by surprise.

Supervision

The achievement of manpower economy (in criminal investigation) will continue to wait upon the development of police administrators, and particularly detective administrators, who possess and exercise an active interest in the problems of management. Our cities attract and train many capable detectives, but thus far they have not often developed competent directors of criminal investigation.
—Bruce Smith, *Police Systems in the United States,* p. 123.

Most investigators receive little substantive supervision in the performance of their jobs. They must seek permission to take leave, spend money, or sometimes to use a vehicle; but rarely does a supervisor provide substantive advice on how to handle a case. They may be reprimanded for not getting a report in on time, but usually not for its substantive content.

This independence from direct supervision is a result of both tradition and the nature of their work. By tradition, detectives have been considered professionals—the elite of the department. The only men picked were those who were trusted to do their job. Such men did not need to be watched closely.

In many departments today,[12] the lieutenant or captain in charge of a detective unit may have considerably less experience in investigative work than

---

11. Many of these observations have been made by other observers, going back to Fosdick (1921).

12. The following material is based on consistent observations in approximately 10 major departments and roundtable discussions held with detectives from various departments over the course of the study. As such, the material represents extremely subjective views of the detectives with whom we spoke, and is not necessarily representative of situations in all departments.

his senior men have. The supervisor is often younger but has more formal education than the senior detectives. Often he will move to a new administrative position every few years as he progresses up the chain of command, while the detectives tend to stay in a given unit for five or ten years.

Given this pattern of personnel assignment, the supervisor is often a victim of the old detective mystique. When he comes into the unit he does not know precisely what his men are up to, and he is unlikely to make himself look foolish by asking. Also, he may be somewhat awed by the reputations of the senior detectives, as are most others in the department, and is loath to provoke their resistance by constraining their activities.

There is also a general feeling that detectives cut corners that their supervisors are not aware of. Harassment or pressuring of suspects, deals with informants, violation of departmental procedures, phony clearances, protection of influential citizens, or the "creation" of evidence may all be techniques that a detective feels called upon to use occasionally in carrying out his job. As long as the cases are adequately covered, the supervisor is rarely involved in these matters.

In evaluating the work of an individual detective, supervisors rely on a variety of criteria, often weighting or combining the criteria in a purely subjective fashion. All detectives are respected for solving big cases, keeping out of trouble, and acting with tact and diplomacy. Younger, less experienced detectives with big caseloads are expected to maintain an adequate clearance rate and to get their paperwork done. Older detectives are valued for their ability to handle sensitive or difficult cases.

In some instances, the end result of this professional distance between the young up-and-coming supervisors and the more experienced investigators is that the supervisors are unable to monitor closely the activities of individual investigators. Detectives, in such an arrangement, are left pretty much to determine their own way. The young lieutenant or captain is responsible for seeing that paperwork required by the front office is completed on time and handles the leave schedules and other routine personnel matters of his men. He may occasionally participate in an interesting or particularly important case. He may occasionally inquire to see if departmental standards of procedure have been followed. His desk will frequently be clean, or it may be covered with material relating to a special project on which he is working for his chief. His primary contacts with his men will be when he meets with them to pass on the word from above, or when he walks through the detective area to ask how things are going. The detective, on the other hand, decides how much effort to put into each case and how the case should be pursued.

3

Measuring the Effectiveness of Police Investigation

Although investigators can contribute in many ways to a police department's effectiveness, in this study we are concerned only with their role in criminal investigations. We therefore omit any discussion of the effectiveness of such activities as locating missing persons, establishing that suspicious events (e.g., unattended deaths) did not involve any crime, or conducting background investigations of persons applying for permits or employment of various types. However, in considering the productivity[1] of investigators, it must be taken into account that departments differ widely in the number of tasks of a noncriminal nature assigned to investigators, and the amount of resources actually devoted to criminal investigations may not be easy to determine from an organization chart.

In regard to criminal investigations, the objectives of a police department are primarily these:

- Deterring and preventing crime.

- Uncovering the occurrence of crimes.

- Identifying and apprehending criminal offenders.

- Recovering stolen property.

- Supporting the prosecution of arrested offenders.

- Maintaining public confidence in the police.

These objectives, which are basically compatible, are counterbalanced to a certain extent by several objectives of society as a whole that are shared by the police:

- Protecting the privacy and rights of individuals, including minimizing the extent of false arrest.

- Maintaining fairness and equity in the process of justice.

---

1. Productivity can be distinguished from effectiveness by the fact that it involves a comparison of what was accomplished with the resources required to accomplish it. For a complete discussion, see National Advisory Group on Productivity in Law Enforcement (1973).

- Performing the police function at a reasonable cost to the taxpayers (or balancing effectiveness against cost).

All of these objectives are common to the patrol function as well as to the investigative function, and indeed some of them may be accomplished better, or more efficiently, or to a greater extent by patrol officers (either alone or in interaction with investigators) than by investigators. Therefore, in assessing the effectiveness of investigators, it is important not to consider department-wide statistics related to these objectives as if they reflect only the activities of investigators. At a minimum, some effort must be made to sort out the contribution of investigators to any performance statistics that are calculated. In many instances, subtle judgments are required. For example, some arrests are made by patrol officers based on direct instructions from an investigator. These should not be excluded from measures of the contribution of investigators to apprehension rates, even though the arrest report may clearly identify the arresting officer as a noninvestigator.

It is extremely difficult to calculate numerical measures of the extent to which some objectives are accomplished. This difficulty may be due to conceptual problems (i.e., there is no agreement about how they might be measured), to the unavailability of suitable data, or to the magnitude of the data processing task that would be needed to calculate preferred measures even when data are available. For some objectives (i.e., crime deterrence and the fairness and equity of the justice process), all three of these problems arise.

In this study we have not resolved any of these problems, nor have we developed new measures of effectiveness that constitute theoretical advances in research. But we have collected some data relating to as many of the objectives as we found feasible, and when we could choose the form in which data were collected, our procedures were designed to produce the best measures of investigative effectiveness that could possibly be obtained under the circumstances. Finally, we have been careful not to judge any activities as unproductive when in fact they are primarily directed at objectives we were unable to measure. For example, time spent by investigators on crimes that are never solved is by definition not productive when clearances are used as a measure of performance, but there may well be some (unmeasured) deterrent value that justifies such investigations.

Performance Measures

In this section we shall discuss the measures of effectiveness actually used in this study and contrast them with traditional measures, where appropriate.

Deterrence and Prevention

To the extent that criminal offenders are aware that crimes they have committed are under investigation, the process of carrying out an investigation
(whether successful or not) presumably has in itself some deterrent value, even
though that is not its primary purpose. In the extreme, it must be assumed that
if no investigations were ever conducted, crime rates would increase, although
we have no way of estimating at what rate. This effect applies also to individuals
who have not committed crimes but who assume that, if they did, there would
be an investigation.

Here, deterrence arises from the fact that there is some chance that the investigation will lead to apprehension of the perpetrator. It is not known whether
cities with a high chance of apprehending perpetrators achieve a greater degree
of deterrence than cities with low apprehension rates, but most police officials
believe they do. Indeed, the *perceived* risk of apprehension is even more relevant
than the *true* risk in this regard, which serves as a justification in some quarters
for artificially inflated clearance rates (as discussed below).

Some activities of investigators are carried out specifically for their deterrent
or preventive value. This is particularly true for officers in the juvenile division,
who spend time counseling youths and their parents and conducting surveillance
of recreation centers and the like.

To measure the extent of deterrence would require carefully controlled
experiments, together with elaborate data collection instruments such as victimization surveys. Moreover, research would be needed to provide a detailed understanding of how crime rates vary with influences other than investigative practices.
For example, crime rates may be affected by *other* police activities aimed at
prevention or deterrence (such as reducing response time to crime-calls, changing
foot patrol or radio car patrol levels, educational campaigns aimed at hardening
crime targets), by private investments in security equipment and personnel, by
changing the speed and certainty with which offenders are convicted and the
severity of their sentences, and by a host of social, economic, and psychological
factors. Since even elaborate studies related to the deterrent value of police
activities (for example, the Kansas City experiment on preventive patrol, Kelling
et al. 1975) have been at best indecisive, the resources available to this project
were clearly inadequate to measure deterrent or preventive effects competently.
We have therefore omitted such measurements entirely and merely indicate the
circumstances under which our conclusions have been limited by such omission.
In some instances, we have indicated what changes occurred in *reported* crime
rates when a new form of investigative operation was instituted. However,
such figures are not intended to be definitive measures of the impact of the
change, since reported crime rates can be affected by changes in reporting
practices and other extraneous factors. This is discussed further in Chapter 13.

Uncovering Crimes

In this study we have focused primarily on investigative units whose function is to investigate previously reported crimes. The objective of uncovering crimes therefore plays a minor role, and we have not attempted to measure it.

Identifying and Apprehending Offenders

Clearance and arrest statistics have been traditionally used as measures of police effectiveness in "solving" reported crimes and apprehending suspects. The clearance rate, as usually defined and reported by police departments, is the number of cases cleared[2] in a period of time divided by the number of crimes reported to the police in that same period; it is usually reported by offense class. The arrest rate is the number of persons arrested in a period of time divided by the number of reported crimes. Both of these statistics suffer from inadequacy because crimes for which suspects are arrested during a given period of time are not necessarily crimes reported during the same period. For example, it is possible for three homicides to be reported in October and for four homicides to be cleared, which produces a homicide clearance rate of 133 percent for the month. Although this is entirely legitimate, it is not meaningful as a performance statistic. Even if only three homicides are cleared in October (yielding a 100 percent clearance rate), four suspects may be arrested, in which case the arrest rate is 133 percent.

Problems of definition also arise. A case is denoted as cleared when the police have identified a perpetrator, have sufficient evidence to charge him, and actually take him into custody. In addition, "exceptional" clearances may be recorded if some element beyond the control of the police precludes placing charges (e.g., the suspect has died or is being held for prosecution in another jurisdiction). Police departments (and units within a department) differ in their standards for when a case is recorded as cleared. In some departments, a clearance will be claimed only if an arrest is made for the instant offense. In other departments, additional clearances are claimed when the suspect arrested for one crime admits to committing other crimes, when the arrest for one offense leads to uncovering additional information (such as modus operandi) pointing to guilt in *other* crimes, or when the suspected perpetrator is known but not arrested.

For these reasons, the clearance rate is generally unreliable as a measure of effectiveness. Two previous studies have demonstrated the extent of this problem. Greenwood (1970) and Greenberg et al. (1972) showed gross disparities among police units in the way clearances are recorded. Greenwood demonstrated that the average number of clearances per arrest for burglary varied dramatically

---

2. The definition of "cleared" will be discussed below.

(from 1 to 20) across the 79 precincts of the New York City Police Department, depending on how frequently clearances were credited on the basis of modus operandi only. Among the six departments Greenberg studied, he found large variations in how the FBI "exceptional clearance" guidelines were applied. For example, in one department, 27 percent of the cleared burglary cases had been closed solely on the basis of the suspect's admission; in another department, such clearances were never based on this evidence alone.

From the viewpoint of gauging *investigative* effectiveness, another limitation is that neither the clearance rate nor the arrest rate reveals to what extent investigative, as opposed to noninvestigative, police efforts contribute to their overall level. Finally, it should be noted that neither of these statistics provides any indication of the overall *quality* of the arrest or clearance, or of the investigative contribution to the quality. Therefore, arrest rates may be misleading because they are not corrected if a charge is not filed by the prosecutor, or if it is filed initially, but later dropped or dismissed. And the clearance rate can be misleading because a crime involving multiple offenders can be "cleared" even if the police believe they know the identity of only one of the perpetrators.

Except for the issue of quality (which we discuss below), most of the disabilities of clearance and arrest rates can be eliminated by collecting data in an appropriate form. First, it is necessary to focus on a particular set of criminal incidents, rather than on a particular period of time. Next, the outcome of each case must be recorded in finer detail than as simply "cleared" or "not cleared." A suitable categorization is as follows:

- Cleared by arrest for the instant offense:
  - All perpetrators arrested
  - Some perpetrators remain unarrested

- Cleared by arrest for another offense, with identification as follows (multiple categories permitted):
  - Positive identification
  - Physical evidence
  - Confession
  - Possession of stolen property
  - Similar modus operandi
  - Other

- Cleared without an arrest:
  - Victim refuses to prosecute
  - Property recovered[3]
  - Other (died, held in another jurisdiction, etc.)

---

3. In some departments, an auto theft is recorded as cleared if the vehicle is recovered.

- Unfounded (i.e., no crime was committed)

- Not cleared or unfounded

Third, for cleared crimes it is necessary to record the role (if any) played by investigators in the clearance.

Once such information has been collected, it is possible to calculate *incident-oriented* statistics, which indicate the fraction of incidents that resulted in a given outcome. For example, it is possible to determine what fraction of robberies presented to investigators unsolved were subsequently cleared by an investigator-initiated arrest for the instant offense. Such a statistic is, first of all, relevant for measuring *investigative* effectiveness and, second, subject to less administrative manipulation than traditional clearance rates and is thus more comparable among departments.

For this study, we usually had to collect data appropriate for incident-oriented statistics by selecting samples of cases and reviewing case folders. However, we believe that police departments should be interested in such statistics for their own internal purposes and should review the possibility of calculating them whenever changes in information systems are contemplated. In particular, it is common for computerized arrest files to be separate from incident files, so that matching arrests to incidents is either prohibitively expensive or impossible. But if incident files are currently updated to indicate clearances, it is just as easy to update them with information about the arrest status of the case.

Assistance to Prosecutor

There is a body of opinion that holds that suspect identification and apprehension effectiveness are not validly weighed by arrest and clearance rates, because these statistics encourage poor arrests. The National Advisory Group on Productivity in Law Enforcement (1973) suggested measuring quality arrests by including only those arrests that pass the first judicial screening. Others hold that final dispositions in the courts are better measures of arrest quality. The quality of arrest clearly should be reflected, albeit only partially, in subsequent stages of case processing by the prosecutor, the defense, and the court. But factors associated with these agencies may also affect ultimate case outcome, such as the prosecutor's screening policy, the competency of prosecutors, defense counsel and judges, court delay and backlog, and so on.

For example, one prosecutor's office may adopt a policy of accepting and filing felony complaints only when the probability of conviction by a jury is very high—that is, a filing standard far in excess of probable cause is used. Another prosecutor's office may apply a probable cause standard in the filing decision. So, an arrest of moderate quality may be rejected by one prosecutor and filed by another. Thus, ultimate case outcome (rejection in screening, dismissal, acquittal, and conviction) and type and severity of sentence imposed are imperfect measures of investigative effectiveness. We do not know of any previous study that has succeeded in converting information about case disposition into a valid measure of the quality of investigative work.

In Chapter 11 we analyze, in a preliminary fashion, the relationship between post-arrest investigative thoroughness and case disposition in the courts. The measure of post-arrest investigative thoroughness (or arrest quality, if you will) we employ is the presence or absence of certain information, obtainable from the prosecutor's case file, that has been collected from crime and arrest reports and in police interviews of the suspect, victim, and witnesses at the time of the incident, at the arrest, and in the follow-up investigation. Of course, this measure of post-arrest investigative thoroughness is imperfect and only suggestive, because we do not attempt to discern the relative importance and contribution of the various information items to ultimate case disposition in the court.

Public Attitudes

An important output of investigative efforts is their effect on the public's attitude toward, and confidence in, the police, and their perceptions regarding their safety on the streets. Studies have shown that people's perceptions about their safety on the streets are not necessarily related to the true risks they face of being victims of crime. Such perceptions are also affected by the way in which crime information is treated and by public confidence in the police. Many police officials assert that the *appearance* of dedicated efforts on each case contributes positively to public confidence in the police. Even when a general public effect is discounted, extra investigative efforts (such as interviewing witnesses, dusting for fingerprints, neighborhood searches) are often used to placate particular victims rather than in hopes of solving the crime. Some police assert that the victim deserves extra attention because of his emotional trauma or property loss, regardless of the eventual outcome. This attitude is shared by the American Bar Association, as evidenced in their Project on Standards for the Administration of Criminal Justice. They recognize that one of the major current responsibilities of the police is "to create and maintain a feeling of security in the community."[4]

In this study we do not address the broad issues of what determines public attitudes toward the police and people's perceptions regarding their safety on the streets. Instead, we focus on one segment of the public (i.e., the victims of crime), and on one policy lever that could be employed by police to affect victim attitude (i.e., information feedback on case progress and outcome). That is, we

---

4. American Bar Association Project on Standards for Criminal Justice (1974), p. 15.

hypothesize that most victims, particularly the victim whose case has not been cleared by an arrest (for that crime), are largely unaware of police efforts and progress in their case, that they would welcome feedback on their case, and that such feedback would increase their confidence in the police. Many police officials share this view, at least for those cases in which the perpetrator is arrested and prosecuted; this hypothesis (among others) is being tested in an experiment, funded by the Police Foundation, and conducted by the Sacramento (California) Police Department. In addition to other ways of improving handling and treatment of victims, the department will notify victims at three points in their case: when an arrest is made, when prosecution commences, and at final case outcome.

But in the vast majority of cases, the case is either never cleared, or it is cleared but the police cannot or will not attempt to have the prosecutor press charges against the suspect for that crime. To our knowledge, there are few data on the relationship between victim attitude and case information feedback for these classes of victims. Therefore, in one city we conducted a small sample telephone survey of victims whose cases were uncleared, cleared by arrest, and cleared exceptionally. Information was collected regarding their knowledge of the progress and disposition of their cases; their desire for, and the importance they attach to, additional feedback; the nature of such feedback and their reactions to it; ways the police department should notify them; and whether such feedback would alter their confidence in the police department.

Other Measures of Effectiveness

The extent to which investigative activities impinge on privacy and other constitutional rights of citizens who come in contact with police is an important element of effectiveness, but we did not attempt to measure these impacts; rather, we treat them as factors to be considered when comparing the effectiveness of various modes of investigative activity, much as cost can be considered. To give a hypothetical example, if two investigative techniques are equally costly and equally effective, but only one of them involves field stops of nonsuspects, surveillance, and other infringements of privacy, then the technique without such infringements is the preferred one.

In regard to false arrest, it should be noted that the incident-oriented statistics described earlier give no credit whatsoever to an arrest that does not lead to clearing a crime. Therefore, using such statistics avoids counting such arrests as indicators of effectiveness. It may be argued that they should be counted negatively in some way, but we have not done so.

As mentioned earlier, the cost of an investigative activity is a factor which, when compared to effectiveness, gives an indication of productivity. We have not performed any cost analyses as part of this study; we have considered the number of investigators or investigative man-hours as suitable proxies for cost. This ignores any differences in pay scale among cities or among officers of various ranks within a city, but it is accurate enough in light of the uncertainties inherent in the effectiveness measures themselves.

4 Literature on the Police Investigation Process

Our review of the literature identified a number of titles that appear to contain worthwhile reading material for the student, police officer, supervisor, or administrator interested in the field of criminal investigations.

Criminal Investigation Textbooks

Although at first glance there appear to be a great many criminal investigation textbooks, a closer examination reveals that much of this material is insubstantial or outdated. At present only a handful of academically oriented textbooks pertain to the field of criminal investigation. O'Hara's *Fundamentals of Criminal Investigation* (1970) is the most widely recognized text used by police departments, although others such as Weston and Wells (1970, 1971) and Leonard (1971) are highly regarded. *Fundamentals,* first published in 1956, discusses the general nature of criminal investigation and outlines elements of proof for each major offense category. The latest edition includes a long excellent discussion about how to collect physical evidence from a crime scene and how to use the technical resources of a criminalistics laboratory effectively.

Despite its preeminence, however, the book has serious drawbacks, probably the most damaging of which is that it continues to promulgate the belief that investigation is an art and not a science. In the preface the author states: "The detection of crime is, after all, not a science but an art, whose secrets are not likely to be captured in any great part between the covers of a book." His adherence to the belief that routine investigations are more art than science encourages the idea that criminal investigation should be guided by individual intuition rather than by a rational and systematic method of inquiry. *Fundamentals* would have a more affirmative effect if it emphasized investigative methods that lifted the detective's performance from the realm of artistry and mysticism and that produced procedural rules enhancing police ability to identify criminal offenders.

O'Hara's statement that no normative criteria exist to judge the success or failure of an investigation may also be misleading, because police supervisors employ methods of evaluation daily. A discussion of the management and evaluation of detective activities would have been valued to both supervisors and investigators.

37

Despite its few faults, O'Hara's book stands well above other general investigation texts in terms of its concise yet comprehensive nature. As such, it appears to be an excellent treatise for introducing police personnel to the fundamentals of criminal investigation.

Textbooks of this general nature, which attempt to span the fundamentals of criminal investigation, are being published less frequently. As the detective function has become more specialized and investigation more complicated, textbooks have concentrated on a particular type of crime or a particular facet of the investigation. In fact, texts outlining how to conduct an investigation of homicide, rape, or traffic violations are plentiful. However, because departmental procedures vary regarding the investigation of particular crimes, most instructors we spoke with during the course of the study commented that such texts could only be used to augment departmental guidelines and training bulletins. Homicide texts, which are regarded as the most comprehensive and practical, are frequently used this way.

The dynamic nature of criminal law, embodying a steady stream of Supreme Court decisions adding or modifying rules of law, is understandably bewildering to the individual investigator. To translate judicial decisions into standard police operating procedures, lawyers have begun to write texts specifically directed toward the police investigator, especially regarding admissions, confessions, and searches. An example of such a work is *The Supreme Court and the Law of Criminal Investigation* (Nedrud 1969). For the law enforcement officer, the author contends, "This text can be considered his complete library." Although this claim is possibly an overstatement, the book does encompass two broad areas: Part A deals with Arrest, Search and Seizure, and Part B covers Confessions/Self-Incriminations. A concise summary of the law precedes each section, and cross-references are given to the cases in each. This combination gives the officer access to related cases that deal with the same legal principles.

The only difficulty presented by this and similar texts is their presupposition that the reader is versed in legal terminology. To the average police officer, such legally technical reading may be formidable. Nevertheless, this particular text gives an excellent treatment of the subject of custodial interrogation; it should provide an intelligent investigator with a rich source of information.

The majority of investigation texts are written by former police officers and reflect their biases. The practicality of procedures is usually not an issue, but such texts usually emphasize identifying and apprehending the suspect, while the police investigator's role in a criminal prosecution receives little or no attention. Few texts discuss in detail the steps used in the evaluation of evidence, the evidentiary factors directed by the prosecution, or how to prepare to testify under the scrutiny of cross-examination. This inattention to the "case preparation" function encourages investigators to accord it secondary importance. The effect is to unnecessarily hamstring or defeat prosecutions. To illustrate this point, one popular text states, "A criminal investigation is unnecessary when the offender is caught in the act." On the contrary, an investigation is necessary even though a perpetrator may be apprehended at the scene, and texts should instruct the officer on how to properly prepare and present the case for prosecution.

Overall, it appears that criminal investigation textbooks are becoming more specific in context, and as such should assist in developing more concrete guidelines and procedures for the individual investigator. However, because of the ever-changing nature of the relationship between technology, the law, and criminal investigation, other types of publications possibly hold more promise.

Articles

In the field of criminal investigation, where changes in technology and law can take immediate effect, material in textbooks may be out of date soon after it is published. By contrast, police periodicals could serve as a timely medium for communicating ideas, pertinent legal decisions, and techniques. Hundreds of police periodicals exist, some containing excellent and practical investigative materials, but few are regularly read by investigative personnel. The reluctance of the police, and particularly investigators, to read professional publications in part reflects their distrust of "theory" and underscores their continued reliance on trial-and-error street experience. Moreover, distribution of such periodicals in most police departments is woefully haphazard and inadequate.

An example of high-quality tutorial material that has appeared in relatively obscure periodicals over the years is a series of six articles written by Charles Samen and published in *Law and Order* (Samen 1971, 1972). Each article discusses a different aspect of major crime-scene processing (casting, corroborating evidence, developing invisible evidence, search patterns, and securing and sketching the scene). Written by a former detective, the articles discuss not only the latest scientific techniques, but also the practical problems that arise in particular types of evidence collection (e.g., protecting blood from contamination). Regrettably, such current and useful investigative material remains scattered among numerous limited-circulation periodicals; police personnel would benefit if this material were assembled into a single volume, indexed in depth, and kept current with regular supplements.

Police Training Literature

Possibly the largest single source of practical investigation literature is the abundant departmental training material existing across the United States, but because few police agencies allow their training bulletins to be copied and distributed elsewhere, this literature is seldom read outside of the preparing department.

Normally written by investigating officers, these training publications generally contain the most practical and easily understood information available. It seems paradoxical that they are the most poorly distributed.

An example of a useful, but poorly distributed, training bulletin is *Training Key,* published twice monthly by the International Association of Chiefs of Police (IACP). Each issue discusses basic procedures surrounding a single police activity; cumulatively, since the inception of this bulletin, nearly all facets of a police investigation have been addressed (e.g., preliminary examination, follow-up investigation, developing informants, the investigator's report, investigative resources). That investigators could benefit from a source of information such as this, which is constantly updated, is patent; but most police personnel are not exposed to it, except during an initial training session. At least one publication of this type ought to be currently routed to an investigative division to provide investigators easy access to information on the latest advances in techniques and technologies.

Previous Studies of the Investigative Function

Until recently there were virtually no analytical studies of the investigative function; the secrecy that surrounded the investigative function shielded it from objective research. However, in the late 1960s, the work of the President's Commission on Law Enforcement and the Administration of Justice broadened interest and prompted research in the investigative process. Despite the resource limitations of these research projects, their findings are significant contributions to a field in which almost no objective information was available until recently.

Under the auspices of the President's Commission, Isaacs (1967) examined a sample of cases from the Los Angeles Police Department to identify investigatory factors that contribute to the solution of crimes. In his sample of 1905 crimes, he found that 25 percent were cleared. Of these clearances, most involved a named suspect or an on-the-scene arrest. These data suggested a need both for fast response time to reported crimes and more investigation at the scene of the crime. Major questions were raised as to how detectives should be deployed. Isaacs characterized his analysis of police records as a "preliminary and exploratory analysis." His report revealed the paucity of information about methods of investigation.

In 1968, Greenwood analyzed New York City Police Department programs for apprehending serious criminal offenders (Greenwood 1970). He found that the probability of arrest was high for crimes against persons—homicide, rape, and assault—and low for crimes against property—robbery, burglary, and larceny. Most arrests for property crimes were made either at the scene of the crime or as a result of evidence readily apparent when the crime was reported. He compared the effectiveness of various modes of detective deployment, and as a means to

This unit employed some of the department's best investigators to perform intensive investigations of reported burglaries in specified areas of the city. Greenberg concluded as follows: The SEU prepared more comprehensive and better written investigative reports than did the regular force; it made neighborhood checks in 88 percent of its cases compared with 22 percent in normal practice; but it was no more successful in discovering physical evidence and witnesses or in making arrests than were regular units.

- *Investigators make scant use of indirect evidence.*

Each of six cited studies supports the proposition that, to make an arrest, police investigators rarely exploit other than the most direct types of evidence—apprehension at the scene, suspect named by the victim, street identification by victims or witnesses, etc. Concomitantly, the studies indicated that on-scene arrests were the most prevalent type of arrest in theft crimes, while follow-up investigations, which could involve significant proportions of investigative time, were almost entirely ineffective.

Isaacs (1967) noted both the frequency of fingerprint information at the scene of a burglary and the paucity of its use. Of 626 burglaries in Low Angeles, at least 43 percent indicated fingerprint evidence; yet only 5 percent of these cases had evidence booked.

In examining 61 solved cases in the Boston Police Department, Folk (1971) found that whereas detectives interviewed felt that informants were their most valuable asset in solving a case, in fact most cases were cleared on the basis of eyewitness evidence. Physical evidence was little utilized.

Parker and Peterson (1972) sought to demonstrate the availability of physical evidence at crime scenes both by observing the work of the Berkeley Police Department's evidence technicians in their crime scene searches and by making an independent assessment of what evidence could have been obtained. They concluded that 92 percent of 734 cases produced some usable evidence. Specifically, 41 percent contained fingerprint evidence. Twenty-two categories of physical evidence were said to be present—the occurrence rates ranging from 43 percent for tool marks, to 15 percent for cigarettes, to 5 percent for hair or blood. Notably, the crime laboratory received only one item of evidence on a robbery case during the period studied, and none for burglary, although the Berkeley Police Department handled 875 burglaries and 101 robberies during this period.

Greenwood's review of investigative reports in New York City (1970) disclosed that only 5 percent of the burglary reports listed any evidence and less than 1 percent of the robbery reports indicated evidence other than a named suspect or a physical description.

Greenberg et al. (1972) also found that physical evidence other than fingerprints was seldom used in burglary investigations. And those departments that collected fingerprints frequently did not process them. Greenberg felt that this meager utilization of physical evidence resulted in large measure from serious inadequacies in information storage and retrieval systems currently used to process physical evidence. He also reported that data on the involvement of informants in the cases he studied were totally absent, notwithstanding the police assertion that informants have been one of the most effective means of solving crimes. (Similarly, Feeney et al. (1973) found that in the reports of 646 robbery cases, only one tip, which was not even an identification, was mentioned.) Finally, Greenberg et al. (1972) concluded that the low "hit" rate in identifying stolen property by means of California's computer system (CLETS) derived from the poor quality of the descriptions given by victims of their stolen property. However, an analysis of his case sample discloses that even where property serial numbers or good descriptions were available, the probability of clearance was not affected.

In their examination of robbery cases, Feeney et al. (1973) discovered that the suspect was arrested by patrolmen near the crime or was known to the victim in more than two-thirds of the arrests. Physical evidence contributed to the arrest in only 7 percent of the cases. This study also disclosed that physical evidence by itself (possession of stolen property or weapon used) was never sufficient for the prosecutor to charge.

Greenberg et al. (1972) reported the impression that post-arrest interrogation has decreased because of recent court decisions, and thus has become a lost art. Feeney's data, on the other hand, showed that interrogation information was available for 52 percent of the suspects in custody, although confessions played a key role in only 3 out of 145 cases.

These findings from previous research served as a springboard for our study, directing us toward particular avenues of inquiry. If cases are solved largely on the basis of facts collected in the original crime report, then the quality of preliminary investigation and the interaction between patrolmen and investigators should affect the chance of successful solution. Supporting activities that tend to increase the investigator's ability to process and selectively sift through the reams of records pertaining to past offenses might also improve the likelihood of successful case solution.

These findings, along with our own early observations, provided a focus for much of our research. We set out to confirm or rebut the implication of low effectiveness in solving crimes resulting from many of these studies. If detective effectiveness could be shown to be low across various departments and crime types, we would attempt to explain why. If differences were found, we would attempt to isolate those practices, procedures, or equipment that seemed likely to enhance effectives. Two studies with similar motivations, by Bloch and Bell (1976) and Greenberg et al. (1975), were completed after our study. They will be mentioned in connection with our conclusions in Chapter 14.

Part II

A National Survey of Investigative Practices

5 Survey Design and Patterns of Response

Our survey was undertaken as one of the first steps in our study of the criminal investigation process. Its purposes were

- to obtain a descriptive portrait of the current organization and operation of investigative units,

- to identify particular aspects of organization or operation that were deserving of subsequent detailed analysis in the study, by virtue of their relationship to readily available performance measures, and

- to help the research team locate police departments having specified investigative practices, imaginative innovations that they viewed as especially successful, or unique data resources of interest for further analysis.

The limitations of a survey are particularly apparent in connection with measures of performance. We have already noted that the performance statistics commonly tabulated by police departments (such as arrest and clearances) are inadequate measures of investigative effectiveness, and yet it is not possible to ask departments responding to a survey to calculate statistics that they do not have. Therefore, the findings presented here in Part II are basically descriptive in nature, even when organizational characteristics of departments are compared with arrest and clearance rates. These comparisons, which for the most part reveal a lack of significant relationship where one might be expected, raise questions about investigative operations and about the crime reporting system itself that are explored in more detail in Part III: The Process Evaluated.

Survey Universe

In our survey we attempted to contact every municipal or county police department that had 150 or more employees (sworn plus civilian) at the end of 1972 or served a jurisdiction with 1970 census population over 100,000. This particular survey universe was selected for three primary reasons:

1. Since very small police departments have a limited number of choices as to how they will organize their investigative function, and a written report

47

describing these choices would be of little interest, we decided to establish a size threshold and survey only those departments that were above the threshold. The number of employees in the department is a reasonable measure of its size, and other measures (such as total budget) would have led to essentially the same survey universe.

2. The resources available for this study permitted a total of approximately 300 departments to be included in the survey. By inspecting available data sources (namely, the *Uniform Crime Reports* published by the Federal Bureau of Investigation), it was possible to determine that there were about 300 departments having 150 or more employees. Therefore, the threshold was set at 150 employees.[1]

3. Since some departments do not report their number of employees to the FBI, all departments serving a jurisdiction with population over 100,000 were included, so that we would be unlikely to miss any departments with 150 or more employees.

In most surveys, a fairly large universe of study is selected, and then only a small sample out of this universe is actually contacted to fill out the survey questionnaire. Such a design was not appropriate for our survey because we wanted to assure that *every* department that had innovative investigative organization, operations, or data files would come to our attention if it wished to respond to the survey. We therefore sent the survey instrument to all municipal and county police departments that met the size criteria mentioned above. State police departments, highway patrols, and special-district departments (such as park police) were the only ones excluded.

The resulting list, which is shown in Appendix A, consisted of 69 county police departments or sheriff's offices and 231 city police departments. This is a total of exactly 300 departments, which is somewhat accidental, since our selection criteria were merely intended to capture *approximately* 300 departments. In summary, then, we conducted a 100 percent survey of a universe consisting of *all municipal and county police departments having 150 or more full-time employees or serving a city with a 1970 census population over 100,000.*

Design of Survey Instrument

The survey instrument was prepared in two versions. One, reproduced in Appendix B, was designed for administration by mail. The other version was designed for administration by interview and captured substantially more detailed

---

1. The survey was designed in 1973, which is the reason for using 1972 data concerning the number of employees.

information. The first draft of the instrument was prepared in consultation with the entire staff of Rand's criminal investigation project and was reviewed by independent law enforcement experts and by the project's contract monitors at the National Institute of Law Enforcement and Criminal Justice. After revision, the next draft was pretested with the cooperation of four city police departments and one county police department. These departments suggested changes for purposes of clarity and indicated the time required to answer various questions. This led to further revisions and the omission of certain questions of marginal interest that were difficult or laborious to complete.

This third draft was further modified by Rand's Survey Research Group for ease of administration and keypunching. This entire process required approximately two months' elapsed time. The final version was submitted to the Office of Management and Budget for approval, a process that required several additional months. The OMB-approved version is the one shown in Appendix B.

Administration

This survey was conducted during the first half of 1974. A total of 29 questionnaires were administered through on-site interviews by members of the Rand staff. The criteria used to select these departments included proximity to one of Rand's offices, a reputation for effective or innovative investigative methods, or known availability of special data-collection procedures that might be suitable for analysis by the project team. All but one of the departments that we contacted to request cooperation with an on-site interview agreed to participate in the study.

The remaining 271 departments were contacted by mail addressed to the chief (by name, where known). The mailed packet contained the survey instrument, a cover letter with attachments explaining the study and confidentiality conditions (Appendix C), and a postcard (Appendix D) permitting the chief to indicate whether his department would respond, and by what date. If no postcard was received after a short period of time, a follow-up letter (Appendix E) was sent. The postcards were useful in permitting us to remind departments to return their questionnaires, if they had already indicated they would cooperate, while avoiding a second contact with the remaining departments.

For readers interested in survey design, we make the following observations. The use of a follow-up letter, which is known to be good practice in surveys of all types, again proved its value in this case by increasing the response rate by about one-quarter. Use of the chief's name on the envelope, rather than simply a title such as "Chief of Police," proved to be important by virtue of the absence of any responses from those few departments where the name of the current chief was not known to us. Indeed, some of these departments indicated on their postcards that they would not respond because we had not bothered to find out the name of the chief.[2]

Some negative consequences, however, resulted from using the names of addressees, in that turnover among police chiefs is fairly rapid, and in some cases we used the name of the current chief's predecessor. This led to exasperated communications or, worse, transmittal of the packet to the ex-chief. Problems with the U.S. Postal Service or internal mail delivery led to approximately five cases known to us in which the questionnaire never arrived at our offices.[3]

Processing of Returned Surveys

All completed questionnaires were reviewed and edited for keypunching. In addition to correcting obvious errors and omissions, this process involved establishing codes corresponding to responses in categories labeled "other (specify)," coding the information initially provided in the form of an "organization chart" with counts of manpower assigned to each organizational unit, and transcribing answers that were textual in nature. The coding sheet used to count the number of officers assigned to specialized investigative functions, as opposed to generalized, is shown in Appendix F. The material entered on this sheet was captured from respondents' answers to Question 24 of the survey instrument shown in Appendix B.

Additional Sources of Data

We asked the FBI director, Clarence Kelley, whether he would assist this study by providing a computer-readable tape of all information reported to the Uniform Crime Reporting Section by departments in our survey universe, and he agreed to do so.

---

2. The fact was that we had made a considerable effort to search for names of appropriate addressees, using publications of organizations of sheriffs and police chiefs together with recent newspaper articles. However, we had not considered the matter to be of sufficient importance to contact the remaining departments by telephone, a step we would recommend to others undertaking similar surveys in the future.

3. Difficulties such as these are inherent in any large mailing, and we apologize to any department that finds itself listed as a nonrespondent in Appendix A but believes that it either did not receive the survey packet or actually did respond.

This data tape contained information for 1972 concerning estimated population in the department's jurisdiction, number of employees, and the usual FBI categories of reported crimes, arrests, and clearances.[4] This information was available to us for 296 of the 300 departments, whether or not they responded to the survey.[5]

In addition, for city police departments certain demographic data were obtained from standard statistical sources for the year 1970. These included minority population, median family income, measures of poverty levels, and police budget information. These data permitted comparison of respondents with nonrespondents to determine potential survey biases. Corresponding data for county police departments could not be collected because in many cases a county agency does not serve the entire county, but rather covers whatever part is not otherwise served by municipal departments. Without a completed survey form, we were unable to determine what part of the county was involved.

---

4. The FBI collects data for the following categories of crimes, which are given uniform nationally recognized definitions:

1. Homicide and nonnegligent manslaughter
2. Forcible rape
3. Robbery
4. Aggravated or felonious assault
5. Burglary
6. Larceny of $50 or over
7. Auto theft

(The above are known as *Index crimes*.)

8. Larceny under $50
9. Manslaughter by negligence

(These two, together with all Index crimes, constitute *Part I crimes*.)

10. Several other categories known collectively as *Part II crimes*.

For Part I crimes, the FBI collects information on the number of crimes and attempted crimes *reported* to the police, the number *unfounded* (upon investigation it is found that no crime was attempted or committed), and the number *cleared*. The number of arrests in each category is also collected for both Part I and Part II crimes. In this book, we use the term "reported crimes" to refer to the number remaining after unfounded crimes are subtracted out.

5. The Uniform Crime Reporting system is fairly complex, with some departments reporting directly to the FBI on a monthly basis, others on an annual basis, and still others reporting to regional systems for transmittal to the FBI. The data tape sent to Rand was intended to coalesce information from these various sources but was nonetheless incomplete in regard to clearance data.

Response Rate

The total of all departments from which complete responses were received, either by interview or by mail, was 153, or 51.0 percent of the total.[6] The response rate for counties (44.9 percent) did not differ significantly from the response rate for cities (52.8 percent).

While this response rate may be considered rather high, compared to mailed surveys in general, it is not so large that the possibility of significant bias in the findings can be excluded. However, because we collected a variety of data about the entire universe of interest, not just those that responded to the survey, it is possible to describe the types of departments that are overrepresented or underrepresented in the survey data. These facts can then be kept in mind when interpreting the findings.

One of the more important biases present in the data is that large departments were more likely to respond to the survey than small departments. This pattern, which was nearly identical for counties and for cities, can be observed by comparing response rates with a number of different variables, such as population of the jurisdiction, area of the jurisdiction, number of sworn officers, number of total employees, budget of the police department, and crime rates per population, all of which are interrelated.

We illustrate this pattern for two of the variables. Table 5-1a shows that among the 75 departments whose jurisdictions have the smallest population (i.e., the lowest quartile), the response rate was 42.2 percent, while for the largest 75 cities or counties, the response rate was 62.7 percent, which is significantly higher. In table 5-1b, we see that departments having the highest crime rates per population were more likely to respond than the others, which tells us approximately the same thing as table 5-1a, since small cities in general have lower crime rates.

A second bias is that departments whose reported clearance rates are very low were less likely than other departments to respond to the survey. Again, this pattern was consistent for cities and counties and for a variety of different clearance measures. We illustrate it in table 5-2 by showing the variation in response rates with clearance rates for Part I crimes, and with clearances per police officer. This pattern appears to be independent of the one noted earlier, as the group of departments with low clearance rates included both large and small jurisdictions.

By far the strongest variations in response rate were related to the region of the country in which the department is located. For this purpose we defined

---

6. Some of the responses from pretest departments were not complete because of changes we made in the questionnaire. These departments are nonetheless listed as respondents in Appendix A, so that the total number of responding departments as shown in the appendix is 156.

regions according to standard Census Bureau categories, as shown in table 5-3. The response rates were as follows:

South Central . . . . .76.9 percent
West . . . . .60.0 percent
North Central . . . . .49.2 percent
South Atlantic . . . . .45.7 percent
Northeast. . . . . .36.4 percent

Table 5-1
Variations in Response Rates

a. By Size of Jurisdiction		*b. By Part I Crime Rate*	
Population[a]	Response Rate (%)	Crimes per 100,000 Population[a]	Response Rate (%)
Lowest quartile (25,000–94,000)	42.2	Lowest quartile (1,000–3,800)	42.8
Second quartile (94,000–135,000)	37.6	Second quartile (3,800–5,400)	46.9
Third quartile (135,000–250,000)	59.9	Third quartile (5,400–6,840)	47.6
Highest quartile (over 250,000)	62.7	Highest quartile (6,840–11,560)	65.0

[a]Estimated 1972 resident population.   [a]FBI data for 1972.

Table 5-2
Variations in Response Rate by Reported Part I Clearances

Clearance Rate[a]	Response Rate (%)	Clearances per Policeman[b]	Response Rate (%)
Lowest quartile (5–14%)	39.4	Lowest quartile (1.2–3.1)	34.9
Second quartile (14–18%)	54.4	Second quartile (3.1–5.6)	43.7
Third quartile (18–26%)	54.6	Third quartile (5.6–8.3)	61.1
Highest quartile (26–47%)	54.6	Highest quartile (8.3–24.0)	63.3

[a]Number of Part I crimes reported to the FBI as cleared in 1972 divided by the number of Part I crimes, expressed as a percentage.

[b]Number of Part I clearances reported in 1972 divided by the number of sworn officers in the department.

Table 5-3
Composition of Geographical Regions[a]

Region	State	
Northeast	Connecticut	New York
	Maine	Pennsylvania
	Massachusetts	Rhode Island
	New Jersey	
South Atlantic	Delaware	Maryland
	District of	North Carolina
	Columbia	South Carolina
	Florida	Virginia
	Georgia	West Virginia
South Central	Alabama	Mississippi
	Arkansas	Oklahoma
	Kentucky	Tennessee
	Louisiana	Texas
North Central	Illinois	Minnesota
	Indiana	Missouri
	Iowa	Nebraska
	Kansas	Ohio
	Michigan	Wisconsin
West	Arizona	New Mexico
	California	Oregon
	Colorado	Utah
	Hawaii	Washington
	Nevada	

[a]Only those states that include a department in the sample universe are listed.

Thus the East Coast departments were less likely to respond than any of the others, and South Central departments were most likely to respond. To exclude the possibility that response rates were influenced by a nonrandom choice of departments which were visited by Rand staff members, the rates were calculated for unvisited departments separately. This did not affect the relative rankings of geographical regions in the list above. In fact, the visited departments were concentrated on the East and West coasts, and no South Central departments whatever were included in the first wave of site visits which were for the purpose of obtaining the information related to this survey. We are unable to draw any direct inferences as to why the response rates were lower on the East Coast, since every such department that we contacted directly to arrange a site visit was fully cooperative with the research team and provided all information requested, even of a confidential nature.

The totality of information available to us regarding respondents and nonrespondents would have permitted establishing a sampling weight for each responding department in the analysis. However, as will be seen, the characteristics that were related to response rate did not show important correlations with other items studied, except in the case of geographical region. Moreover, since geographical region is not in itself a causative factor in determining investigative effectiveness of a department, but is simply a proxy for other less easily measurable characteristics, we took the approach of tabulating other variables against region rather than applying a sampling weight. Because no clearly identifiable subset of the departments had a response rate under one-third, it may be assumed that no particular type of department is severely underrepresented in the data.

6

Descriptive Results from the Survey

In this chapter we summarize the answers given to questions on the survey questionnaire. For clarity of presentation, we shall use certain terminology in describing investigators and their units.

The term *detective* will be used to refer to a sworn officer who has a special title that is presumably related to investigation. Although many departments do call these officers "detectives," other titles such as "inspector" or "investigator" apply in some locales. The term *detective* does not include supervising officers in investigative units who perform primarily administrative functions. However, it may include some officers who do not actually perform investigations, although they have the appropriate title. For example, a detective may be assigned to a planning unit or to protect the chief of the department during public appearances.

We will use the term *investigator* to refer to any sworn officer who is assigned to a unit having investigative duties. This term includes those detectives who are assigned to investigation, patrolmen who work in plainclothes for investigative units, and supervising officers.

A *specialized* unit is one that has responsibility for investigating certain types of crimes, but not all crimes. For example, a homicide squad is a specialized unit, although, as we shall see below, it is not the most common specialized unit for a department to have.

Overall Departmental Characteristics

Table 6-1 shows general characteristics of the surveyed departments and their jurisdictions; these relate to all operations of the departments (not just the investigative function). The median identifies the point at which half the departments were higher and half lower. Where county and city medians were similar, they have been consolidated into a single figure.

Aside from pointing out the wide range of types of departments included in the survey, table 6-1 also reveals that there is no "standard" or "average" amount of activity or performance by police departments in relation to arrests and clearances. There is a ratio of over 50 to 1 between the highest and lowest number of arrests per police officer per year. Moreover, some departments claim a clearance rate for Part I crimes that is over 50 percent.

57

Table 6-1
Departmental Characteristics

Characteristic	Lowest	Median for Counties	for Cities	Highest
Population of jurisdiction (estimated 1972)	25,402	190,500	148,000	7,890,000
Area of jurisdiction (square miles)	3	769.5	52	20,000
Part I crimes per 100,000 population (1972)	1,069	3,945	5,839	15,736
Number of employees (sworn and civilian)	132	372	300	35,262
Number of officers (1973)	96	255		30,881
Percent of employees sworn	45	82		100
Total budget (FY 73)	$993,000	$5,288,000		$1,029,800,000
Salary budget per officer (FY 73)	$7,000	$15,000		$27,000
Part I arrests per offense (1972)	0.074	0.172	0.182	0.383
Part I arrests per police officer (1972)	0.3	4.1	6.1	16.1
Total arrests per police officer (1972)	1.5	19.7	29.1	80.6
Part I clearances per offense (1972)	0.048	0.162	0.188	0.541
Part I clearances per arrest (1972)	0.38	1.00	1.08	4.04

We examined the reported clearance rates to see whether departments claiming a high rate happened to have an unusual mix of crime types,[1] but this was not the case. Ordinarily a department that reported a high clearance rate for one type of crime also had a clearance rate well above average for the other types.

Table 6-1 also helps illuminate the remarkable variation in departmental policies regarding when a crime is counted as cleared. In general, one would expect the average number of clearances per arrest in a department to be approximately 1.0. The reason for this is as follows. In a large number of cases, a single arrest would clear exactly one crime. However, in some cases more than one person is arrested in connection with a single crime, or a person is arrested but no crime is cleared. These instances would tend to cause the average

---

1. For example, most departments have a homicide clearance rate well over 50 percent.

clearance/arrest ratio to fall under 1.00. In the opposite direction are instances where one arrestee is connected with several crimes, which tend to push the average clearance/arrest ratio over 1.00. If instances of both types are about equally common, the clearance/arrest ratio would be around 1.00, which is the case for the "median" department. But as can be seen from table 6-1, the department with the lowest clearance/arrest ratio (0.38) actually averages 8 arrests for every 3 crimes cleared, while the highest department claims 4 clearances per arrest, on the average.

Whether these extreme variations are to be attributed to differences in stringency of departmental regulations regarding what constitutes a clearance or to inadequacies in the crime reporting system (e.g., some cleared crimes never get recorded as cleared), they do add to the evidence indicating the futility of attempting to measure effectiveness using reported clearance rates.

The information given in table 6-1 was determined from data provided by survey respondents and also from independent sources. The survey responses served mainly to correct errors or to fill in gaps from elsewhere. For example, some departments that do not send uniform crime reporting data to the FBI (or failed to do so in 1972) nonetheless responded to our survey. In a few cases the FBI data were erroneous, usually because the counts represented a period of time longer than the year 1972. However, in the vast majority of cases, the data for 1972 provided to us in 1974 were identical to the FBI data or differed only in that the number of crimes listed as cleared or unfounded had been updated slightly, reflecting more recent developments.

The remaining items discussed in this chapter refer primarily to information available from the survey, and the reader may wish to consult Appendix B for the exact wording of questions.

Resources Devoted to Investigative Function

The responses to our survey showed that departments in all cities with a population of over 250,000 and in 90 percent of the smaller cities gave a special title to officers assigned primarily to investigative duties. On the other hand, some of the responding counties, including 10 percent of the larger county departments, have no distinct title for persons assigned to investigation. Overall, in responding departments an average of 14.5 percent of their sworn personnel were detectives, with over half of the departments falling within the range of 11 to 18 percent. The maximum for city departments was 31 percent detectives; at the lower end of those departments that specially designate investigative positions, three departments reported that only 6 percent of their force were detectives.

By considering investigators rather than detectives, the picture of the amount of resources devoted to the investigative function is about the same, but increased by three percentage points. Thus, on the average, 17.3 percent of sworn officers work in investigative units, with half of all departments falling in the range from 14 to 20 percent. Nearly all the nondetectives assigned to investigative units were not involved in investigation of reported crimes. Namely, they were primarily in juvenile squads, vice and narcotics units, identification sections, etc.

Less than half of all departments indicated that they had any civilians assigned to the investigative function. Excluding evidence technicians, these tended to be few in number, almost always under ten. In the cities visited by Rand staff, the few civilians who were assigned to investigative duties were either criminalists, attorneys, or physicians.

In all of the county departments that responded to the survey, every one of their detectives was assigned to an investigative unit. (This was determined by summing the number of detectives listed for each unit.) While the pattern in most cities was similar, with at least 95 percent of detectives assigned to investigation, there were a few notable exceptions. Some 7 percent of cities had fewer than 80 percent of detectives assigned to investigation, and one city, the lowest, reported that only 55 percent of its detectives were assigned to investigation.

Organization of the Investigative Function

The level at which investigators are placed within the organizational hierarchy of the police department varies according to local custom and the policies of the police chief. In some departments all are under the single command of the chief of detectives, reporting directly to the chief of police. In other departments, detectives may report to the operational commander responsible for a specific area of the city. In such cases, investigative activities will usually be divided between these geographic commands and a headquarters unit responsible for providing certain specialized services to the entire city. In response to our survey, 28 percent of the cities reported they maintained separate geographic commands, as did 61 percent of the counties. As table 6-2 shows, the majority of these departments maintained four or fewer such separate commands, with the highest being 73 in New York and the next closest 22. Of the departments with geographic commands, 63 percent located all investigators at a central headquarters; 22 percent had investigators operating primarily from the local district stations; the remaining 15 percent placed a small portion of the investigators in the districts, while the majority remained at headquarters. In a few departments, experimental programs of investigative decentralization put investigators under a team commander responsible for both patrol and investigative operations in a team policing area.[2]

2. The Rochester, New York, team-policing experiment, with patrol officers and detectives working as a unit, may have produced significant improvement in clearance rates for certain property crimes, according to program evaluation conducted by the Urban Institute. Results of the study can be found in Bloch and Ulberg (1975).

Table 6-2
Number of Geographical Subdivisions
(Precincts, Divisions, Districts, Etc.)

Number of Subdivisions	Number of Departments	Percentage of Departments
None	99	64.7
2–4	29	18.9
5–10	20	13.1
11–20	3	2.0
Over 20	2	1.3

Recent increases in caseload volume and the size of investigative units have prompted many detective bureaus to change from an organization of generalist-investigators to one of crime-specialists, whose individual activities concentrate on one particular category of crime. Only 7 percent of the cities and 17 percent of the counties responding to our survey operated along the full generalist concept with no specialized units whatsoever. When specialization appeared in small departments, it might be simply according to "crimes against the person" and "crimes against property." In larger departments, specialization might possibly separate the offenses of homicide, assault, sex crimes, burglary, robbery, auto theft, and fraud—sometimes with further specialization, e.g., robbery separated into bank, taxi, and liquor store robbery. In some departments where specialization is not formally recognized on the organization chart, detectives will still specialize by informal agreement. (See p. 63 and Chapter 8 for details.)

In the vast majority of departments investigators work singly, as opposed to in pairs. The pattern of paired investigators appears to be primarily restricted to the Northeast, although 30 percent of the departments in the center of the country also have some or all of their investigators working in pairs.

Investigator Status

Traditionally, detectives have had an elite status in the police department. Their pay was higher, their hours of duty were more flexible, their supervision was more permissive, uniforms were not worn, and the work was regarded as inherently more interesting than routine patrol.[3] Albert Seedman, former Chief of the New York Police Department Detective Bureau, described New York City detectives as follows:

---

3. The historical difference in status has prompted some departments to make patrol duty more attractive to the better police officers. In some instances, this policy has been sufficiently successful that recruiting for the detective division has become difficult, particularly in departments in which patrol officers are on a four-day week and detectives must work five.

True, they were an elite force. Since the turn of the century, the second-floor squad room in each precinct house has been the exclusive domain of detectives who went up and down the stairs without so much as a nod to the uniformed desk man on the ground floor.[4]

To qualify for an investigator position, an officer must typically have served at least three to four years on patrol or as a uniformed investigator assigned to the detective division. Our survey responses indicated that in 60 percent of the departments, officers are assigned to investigative positions without civil service rank or tenure and can be returned to the patrol force at the pleasure of the chief. The departments in which investigators have civil service rank are primarily in the North Central and South Central regions.

The selection process can involve some form of civil service test, nominations by previous supervisors, or subjective evaluations by investigative supervisors. Whatever the formal criteria, detective supervisors have traditionally exercised considerable discretion in selecting personnel. In police departments historically marked by corruption, the strategic advantage of being a detective often caused heavy political pressure to be applied on the selection process. More recently, under the aegis of Affirmative Action programs intended to give minority group members an equal chance at career progression, the procedures for selecting and assigning new detectives are becoming considerably more formalized and objective.

Training

In a majority of departments, training for detective work is limited to on-the-job experience accumulated during an apprenticeship. Although most formal recruit training programs (93 percent of responding departments) give some attention to the investigative function, this coverage is limited to the basic material that a patrolman needs to know in conducting his preliminary investigation. More than half of the departments responding to the survey stated that they maintain no training program designed to assist the newly appointed investigators. Where there were such programs in existence, a 40- or 80-hour course was the norm, with one department reporting that it operated a 12-week training course for new investigators.[5]

Periodic refresher courses are offered by over 70 percent of responding departments, although the frequency and content of such courses varies significantly. In five departments investigators were required to attend weekly training sessions, while another 11 departments held such sessions at least every six

---

4. Seedman and Hellman (1974), p. 434.

5. Chapter 4 reviews some of the training materials currently in use.

months. The most common pattern, however, was annual training sessions or "training as needed," for example when an investigator was promoted or changed specialties. In addition, some of the larger departments have recently instituted management courses for investigation commanders.

Most detective units are manned only during regular working hours—8 a.m. to 5 p.m., five days a week. However, many departments keep several investigators on duty at all times so that investigation may begin immediately when a serious crime is reported.

Assignment of Investigators to Individual Units

We found that on the average, 78 percent of investigators were assigned primarily to investigation of reported crimes. The remaining 22 percent were in vice and narcotics units, internal inspection, missing persons, intelligence, organized crime, surveillance, and the like. Here there was a fairly substantial variation, with one department assigning only 35 percent of its investigators to handling reported crimes.

In one-quarter of the departments, investigators were merely separated into a "crimes against persons" unit and a "crimes against property" unit. While we have counted these as "specialized units," they represent a very modest form of specialization and could perhaps be included in a semigeneralized category. However, in many instances investigators within such units specialized in a particular subclass of crimes, such as robbery and assault, which is not the case in the few departments that reported their investigators had no specialties at all.

The prevalence of particular specialties was very similar for cities and counties and is shown in table 6-3. There are few surprises here, especially in regard to the fact that most departments have units specializing in juvenile crime and in vice and/or narcotics. Indeed, the surprise may be that a considerable number of departments operate without specialists in these fields. In regard to organized crime intelligence units, either a department had a special unit that engaged in this activity, or in most cases there was no indication whatsoever from the department's table of organization that any investigators were concerned with organized crime.

Among crimes that are ordinarily reported by the public, auto theft and burglary were most likely to have specialists assigned. In addition to the general burglary squads shown in table 6-3, 7 percent of the departments had separate residential and commercial burglary units. The next two categories in the table—homicide, and checks, forgery, and bunco—are evidently examples of crimes requiring lengthy investigations and specialized knowledge. However, over two-thirds of all departments did not have special units assigned to these crimes.

Specialties that do not appear in Table 6-3 were present in fewer than one-fourth of the departments. These included fugitives and missing persons,

Table 6-3
Typical Specialized Units

Type of Unit	Departments Reporting They Had Such a Unit (%)	
	Cities	Counties
Juvenile	73	61
Vice/narco (either separate or together)	50	50
Organized crime	41	43
Auto theft	40	39
Burglary	33	42
Homicide	33	35
Checks, forgery, bunco	30	33
Internal inspection	29	29

robbery, and sex crimes. A complete list of the specialized units that were found in more than one or two departments is given on the coding sheet in Appendix F. A small number of departments engaged in "super specialization," so that one investigator might be assigned to a class of crimes such as "safecracking in jewelry stores."

The average number of specialized units in cities was 4.8;[6] in counties, 5.0.

Practices for assigning cases to investigators covered a wide range, as shown in table 6-4. This question was intended to determine how the case was assigned to a particular individual after it was assigned to a unit. Therefore, in principle, the fact that the unit might consist of specialists in a particular crime type should not play a role here. Nonetheless, the predominant method of case assignment was by specialty of the investigator, indicating perhaps that specialties are more finely divided than would be indicated by the titles of units themselves.

Evaluation of Performance

Responding departments were asked to specify the importance to them of various ways that the performance of investigative units could be monitored. The responses in order of ranking were as follows:

Success in a major investigation . . . . .mostly "very important"
Supervisory review. . . . . .72% "very important"
23% "important"

---

6. In New York City, over 1,000 investigators assigned to special units were aggregated together into a category labeled "other," so the number of specialized units in New York is not included in this average.

Table 6-4
Method for Assigning Cases to Investigators

Method	Percent of Departments
According to specialty of investigator	45
By rotation as assigned by supervisor	17
By strict rotation	15
According to specialty and assignment by supervisor	7
By specialty and geography	7
If incident occurs during assigned time period	5
Geography only	2
All others	2

Clearance statistics. . . . ."very important"
Arrest statistics . . . . .mostly "important"
Caseloads. . . . ."important"
Property recovered . . . ."important"

Eighty-five percent of departments stated that they use statistics regarding prosecution of cases for evaluation of units, but our experience in visited cities is that these are often found difficult to interpret for evaluation purposes. Only 50 percent of departments said they used court conviction statistics in the same way, presumably reflecting the fact that conviction data are not available in a timely fashion or are difficult to obtain in a form that reflects back on investigative units' performance.

A large number of departments (60 percent) stated that their evaluations are in some degree based on an audit, which we defined as "detailed follow-up investigation of randomly selected cases." Our intent was to refer to a practice whereby a sample of cases that have already been investigated and are currently inactive is reinvestigated by someone else. While we have observed such a practice to exist in some large departments, our experience leads us to doubt that 60 percent of all departments undertake audits, and therefore there is some possibility that this question was misinterpreted.

Among measures of quality that were listed in the category "other," some of the most interesting were reported by departments that have formal procedures for observing and rating the practices and behavior of investigators during interviews, interrogations, and lineup, or that encourage supervisors to take note of the performance of the investigator as a witness in court. In addition, a few departments stated that the number of "cases unfounded" would count favorably in evaluating the quality of a unit.

Reorganization

The rapid state of flux in investigative organization is evidenced by the fact that nearly half of the responding departments indicated that there had been a significant reorganization of their investigative units during the two years prior to the survey. However, the lack of coherent impressions as to how investigative effectiveness can be improved is revealed by the fact that for each department making a specific change, there were usually one or two departments making changes in the opposite direction. Thus, some departments had decentralized their investigative units while others had centralized. Some had introduced specialization while others had generalized. The primary types of changes that were not counterbalanced by opposing changes elsewhere were (1) establishment of proactive and surveillance units, and (2) assignment of greater investigative duties to patrolmen.

Supporting Activities

In addition to the efforts of the investigators themselves, there are a number of other significant expenditures of resources within most police departments to aid investigation tasks. This section describes the most prominent of those activities.

Patrol Investigation

Unless detectives are kept cruising and are available to respond to reported crimes, the first contact with the victim will be made by a patrol unit. The amount of effort the unit devotes to the handling of the crime call can vary significantly, depending on the policy of the department. In some departments any investigation work is exclusively within the province of the investigators. The patrol officer simply notes down some basic facts about the crime and then turns the case over to the investigators. His or her only additional role might be to secure the crime scene if an extensive search is expected. Fifty-eight percent of the surveyed departments reported operating in essentially this manner.

In the remaining 42 percent, patrol officers have been assigned some or all of the duties traditionally reserved for investigators. Most frequently, the patrol officer conducts an extensive preliminary investigation at the time he takes the incident report. This consists of identifying and interviewing all available witnesses, in addition to the victim, and checking for any signs of physical evidence.

The results of this preliminary investigation can then be used by the detective supervisors to determine whether further investigation should be pursued. In some departments, the initial crime report is designed to guide the patrol officer in answering those questions that will help detectives make this judgment. The essential elements on which the detectives determine whether or not to pursue a case have been called "solvability factors"[7] Many cases are closed with no further effort, on the basis of the patrolman's work.

In most departments, where the patrol officer is responsible for some investigations, this role is restricted to specified crime types, usually minor offenses, but often including burglary. Other crime types assigned to patrol-men for investigation in only one or two departments were as follows: all crimes on the night tour, larceny, auto theft, assault, sex crimes, accidents, hit-run, and vandalism. Investigators retain responsibility for the more serious felonies. In 11 percent of responding departments, the patrol officers conduct all preliminary investigations. Finally, in an additional five departments in our survey, the patrol officers have been assigned all investigative responsibilities. They carry out all investigative functions, taking the preliminary report through to case closing. ("On Patrol," in Appendix G, presents the typical day of a patrolman/investigator.)

Interaction with Other Criminal Justice Agencies

Practices regarding who in the department seeks a criminal complaint from the prosecutor or court varied widely. Some 17 percent of departments have a specially designated liaison officer who handles all or some of this function. In only 11 percent of departments would the arresting officer invariably obtain the complaint. In 41 percent of departments the investigating officer would always seek the complaint. In the remaining departments the practice varied, usually by crime type or time of day. For example, in some jurisdictions it was possible to obtain a court complaint at night or on weekends when investigators were not on duty, in which case the arresting officer would handle this.

The role of the prosecutor's office in criminal investigations varied greatly among jurisdictions. In some, the prosecutor has his own investigative staff and actually conducts some investigations independent of the police. This was the case in three-quarters of the cities and counties that responded. The prosecutor in such jurisdictions may also monitor closely the progress of the police department's investigations in serious cases. In other jurisdictions it would be most unusual for the prosecutor to enter into the investigative process in any way, either before or after an arrest.

---

7. For example, the Rochester Police Department has patrolmen use a checklist describing information which if present is likely to lead to the successful completion of the case. A certain number of solvability factors must be present before the case is assigned for follow-up investigation. The checklist is based on the work of Greenberg et al. (1972, Chapter 2).

The survey showed that the prosecutor was *always* involved in investigating prior to an arrest or advising whether to arrest as follows:

Homicide. . . . . .25% of cities and counties
Official misconduct . . .20%
White collar 7%
Drugs 4%
All others. . . . . .uncommon

The prosecutor would *never* be involved prior to an arrest as follows:

Homicide. . . . . .10% of cities and counties
Robbery 28%
Theft/burglary 26%
Drugs 17%
Official misconduct . . .21%
White collar 19%

The practice of having police department employees staff the prosecutor's investigative units is rather uncommon. Only six departments reported they provided all of the prosecutor's investigative personnel; this is 5 percent of prosecutors' offices that have investigators. Another 18 percent of such prosecutors' offices had some police officers assigned to the staff.

We inquired as to what fraction of felony arrests are screened out by the prosecutor without drawing of an affidavit or formal complaint. Those departments that had no data on this and provided an estimate[8] responded predominantly "less than 5 percent." Departments having data responded mostly "5–20 percent," although a few of these also responded "under 5 percent." In addition, there was a substantial group (15 percent) responding "20–50 percent," and four departments reported that over 50 percent of their felony arrests are screened out by the prosecutor.

Evidence Collection and Processing

In recent years, many departments have developed a category of specialists called evidence technicians who are specially trained and available to go out to crime scenes and collect physical evidence. Eighty-seven percent of departments in our survey reported that they had such specialists. In 50 percent of the departments these were exclusively sworn personnel; in 9 percent they were all civilians; the rest were mixed. In those departments having evidence technicians, they

---

8. Nearly three-quarters of departments did not record (or tabulate) such data.

accounted for about 2.4 percent of the total force. Although most departments reported that fingerprint checks were "usually" or "always" made, we observed considerable variation in the pattern of their use. ("Playing a Hunch," in Appendix G, presents one such example.) In some departments, evidence technicians are reserved for only the most serious crimes, such as homicides, and they are rarely called out for burglaries. In the lesser cases patrolmen are expected to collect any clearly visible evidence themselves.

The typical pattern was to rely on the patrolman's judgment whether or not physical evidence could be collected. If the patrolman reported that some evidence might be available at the scene, an evidence technician would be dispatched, when available, to make a search. This meant that the evidence technician usually received a number of assignments at the beginning of the day and took each in turn. This method relies on the victim's not disturbing critical areas of the crime scene.

The most intensive use of evidence technicians occurred when they were kept immediately on-call, available to respond at the same time as the reporting patrolman. In these cases the patrolman and the evidence technician work together, the patrolman interviewing victims and witnesses, the technician checking the scene.

Reported practices in regard to frequency of evidence checks are summarized in table 6-5, which gives the percentage of departments reporting that an evidence check is "always" made. In general, very few departments stated that an evidence check was "never" made, except in the case of ordinarily inapplicable categories, such as checking for tool marks at the scene of robberies. Fingerprint checks, in particular, were said to be made "usually" or "always" by practically all departments in all crime categories. For example, in the case of residential burglaries, only 4.2 percent of departments indicated that fingerprint checks were never or rarely made. In light of the Parker and Peterson (1972) study of individual departments' practices in regard to collection of fingerprint evidence, many of these responses appear to be wishful thinking.

Once the evidence technician has collected any usable evidence, it is turned over to other specialists in the department for analysis. In all crimes but homicide, the only physical evidence utilized is almost exclusively fingerprints. Parker and

Table 6-5
Percentage of Departments Reporting Evidence Check
Always Made

	Type of Evidence			
Crime Type	Finger-prints	Tool Marks	Chemical	Shoeprint/ Tire
Homicide	81	54	61	52
Residential burglary	43	47	9	26
Commercial burglary	68	66	14	40
Robbery	55	41	18	43

Peterson found that blood, tool marks, clothing, and paint residues are sent to crime lab for analyses in fewer than one out of 300 other offenses. Fingerprints are routinely collected for between 10 to 60 percent of all offenses, depending on the effort devoted to collecting them. These prints are sent to finger print specialists who check them for quality and perform any searches required.[9]

Information Systems and Reference Files

Criminal investigation consists largely of assembling the necessary pieces of information required to establish the identity of a suspect, according to the standards and procedural guidelines established by the courts. Detective specialization is thought to facilitate this process by allowing the investigator to concentrate his attention on a particular category of crime. The more familiar the investigator becomes with the modi operandi (MOs) of frequent offenders, the more likely he is to establish relationships between an arrested offender and other past crimes.

To cope with this information-processing workload, all departments have established some basic set of information files. New information comes into the files, primarily from incident of arrest reports, usually provided in the form of a carbon copy of a report designed for some other purpose. Lack of dedicated clerical help and a lack of streamlined input procedures often make these files cumbersome to use, and suggest that important data are often missed. The most frequently encountered files are described in general below. Detailed examples of some types of files will be given in Chapter 10.

Incident File. Reports of all recent unsolved crimes are usually sorted and assembled by crime type. They may also be broken down according to such factors as the race of the offender (white robbers) or the specific target of the attack (liquor stores).

Known Offender File. Most departments attempt to keep track of known offenders, those previously arrested, who reside in their jurisdiction. These files usually contain the suspect's description, modus operandi characteristics, and statements concerning his previous criminal record. They may be further categorized according to special crime types or a particular section of the city. Such files are not only helpful because police personnel can use them to familiarize themselves with local recidivists, but because they provide a starting point for selecting mug shots to show victims.

---

9. More detailed information about the collection and processing of physical evidence is given in Chapter 10.

Mug Shot Files. Mug shots are used in conjunction with the known offender file to help a victim identify a suspect whom he had observed. The quality of photographs ranges all the way from the small black-and-white to high-quality color slides. Some departments have their mug shot files organized by crime type, race, skin tone, and height of the suspect so that with a basic description the victim can be shown a selected subset of the total files. In some departments, a computer is programmed to select only those photographs that fit a suspect's description.

Fingerprint Files. The fingerprints of all arrested persons are always maintained by police departments. In addition to an "arrestees' fingerprint file," departments frequently have separate fingerprint files for recidivist offenders. Both of these files are searched to establish the true identity of a person, and/or to match a lifted latent print with those of a suspect.

Advancing technology has made possible the development of computerized fingerprint systems, and experimental programs are under way in several police departments. The promise of these computerized systems lies in their capacity for rapidly matching latents from a crime scene with those of a suspect.

Every department that had obtained a computerized fingerprint retrieval system made specific reference to the system as an innovation it would recommend to others. Many provided, in addition, detailed descriptions of the process by which prints are microfilmed or stored on computer cards, coded, identified, and rapidly accessed. One department also stores palm prints in this fashion.

In only one case, New York City, did the computer system actually examine the physical image of the fingerprint and process it in some way. In all other departments, prints could be accessed only by knowing the name or other identifier of the individual whose prints were stored, or by sorting on previously coded print characteristics. In general, the effort required to prepare the files for these systems was substantial, and a staged approach was used—such as beginning with prints for robbers and then moving on to forgers, sex offenders, and burglars.

Computerized modus operandi (MO) files. These files were mentioned favorably by departments that have them. These systems store characteristics of crimes and perpetrators and permit rapid searches of large files to determine a series of crimes that may have been committed by a single person. While the intent of such systems is to assist in identification of a suspect in cases where other leads fail, the predominant favorable comment had to do with clearing a number of crimes committed by a suspect already in custody. In some departments, the MO file is checked by clerks even before a crime report reaches the investigators, so that he has whatever added information can be obtained from the file in hand at the start of his investigation. This procedure is part of the process of "case enrichment," to be described in the next subsection below.

Intelligence Files. Some departments maintain intelligence files in which they attempt to keep up-to-date information on suspected offenders, including the suspect's associates, a description of the cars he is using, places he is frequenting, and his activities. Data are input from routine detective activities or by special surveillance units.

Field Interrogation Files. Many departments maintain special field interrogation files in which they input information from each patrol field stop concerning the location of the stop, the identity and description of the person, and the vehicle they are using if one is involved. These field interrogation files can later be used to determine if a suspect has been observed in a given area or to determine what suspects have been frequenting a given neighborhood.

Stolen Property File. Most departments maintain some form of stolen property file in which they list descriptions or serial numbers of property that has been taken in property offenses. These files may also be tied into state or national networks and may be used to check on suspicious property found in the custody of suspects or in swap meets and pawnshops.

In our survey 56 percent of the departments reported access to computerized files containing crime reports, arrest reports, and monthly FBI statistics. Twenty-six percent had access to computerized court dispositions, and only 15 percent had computerized known offender files. Fingerprint and mug shot files were computerized in only 4 percent of the departments.[10]

Table 6-6 shows the prevalence of computer-readable files about which we specifically asked on the survey instrument. Table 6-7 lists files mentioned by departments in the category "other." Not shown in the tables are various motor vehicle and traffic files mentioned by a large number of departments.

Just half of the departments indicated that they kept some sort of file (manual or computer-readable) that collects together in one place all the following information about a reported crime: (1) crime report, (2) whether an arrest was made, (3) whether cleared, (4) whether prosecuted, and (5) court disposition.

Special Projects and Innovative Programs

During the past few years, significant amounts of federal and foundation funding[11] have been made available for innovative programs in an attempt to upgrade

10. Descriptions and preliminary analyses of three systems—New York's Latent Fingerprint System, Los Angeles's Field Interrogation System, and Indianapolis's Pawned and Stolen Property System—were prepared by Eugene Poggio of The Rand Corporation, Santa Monica, California. This material was not included in the present book because of its specialized nature and lack of conclusive results.

11. The funding for the majority of experimental investigation projects has come from the Law Enforcement Assistance Administration (LEAA), established as a result of the Omnibus

Table 6-6
Availability of Computer-Readable Files

Type of File	Percentage of Departments with Access to Computerized File
Crime reports	56
Arrest reports	56
Monthly FBI statistics	56
Hot car	40
Court dispositions	26
Known offender	15
Modus operandi	13
Sex offender	10
Organized crime intelligence	10
Fingerprints	4
Mug shots	4

the quality of police performance. Although most of these funds have been spent on patrol or community service functions, a small percentage has been devoted to the investigative area. Responding departments were asked whether they had any innovative investigative programs or policies showing enough promise that other departments should know of them. Forty percent responded that they did, and an even larger number indicated that other departments' responses to this question would be of interest to them. In the remainder of this section we will describe the type of innovative projects most frequently encountered.

Case Screening

Many departments traditionally devote some minimal investigative effort to every reported felony. In others, the selection of cases to pursue is left to the individual investigator's discretion. Recent studies, which have attempted to identify those factors most frequently found in cleared cases,[12] have led some departments to use so-called "solvability factors" when formally screening cases

---

Crime Control and Safe Streets Act passed by Congress in 1968. One of the objectives of this Act was to "encourage the development of new methods for the prevention and reduction of crime, and the detection and apprehension of criminals." The Act created the LEAA in the U.S. Department of Justice. At the state level, the Act was to be administered by State Criminal Justice Planning Agencies (SPAs). Planning grants were earmarked for the establishment of SPAs, with each of the latter being charged with developing a comprehensive plan for reducing crime throughout the state, and allocating the resources in conformity with it. As evidenced by the programs included in this survey, some of these funds have gone into the police investigation area.

12. See Greenwood (1970) and Greenberg et al., Vol. IV (1972).

for assignment. In such departments,[13] the patrolman's preliminary investigation is focused on the existence of these solvability factors.[14] When the report is turned in, it is checked by a screening unit for the existence of solvability factors. If none are present the case is filed without further effort, possibly with an information copy going to detectives. If solvability factors are present, the case is then assigned to investigation for follow-up work. Use of such solvability factors can cut the burglary investigation caseload to about 20 percent of the total reported cases.

In this connection, one department specifically noted the importance of sending a form letter to those crime victims whose cases are "screened out." The letter was said to be well received, eliminated a "great deal of unnecessary legwork," and provided the victim with information about what to do if there were any new developments in the case that he knew of.

Use of Information Systems

A novel type of information processing known as case enrichment was found in a few departments.[15] In this process, the regular incident report compiled by the responding patrolmen is enriched by other data available from departmental fields. In actual operation these incident reports are sent to the case enrichment unit at the same time they are sent to the detectives. The case enrichment unit checks the data in the incident report against such files as field interrogations, modus operandi, or known offenders, and forwards any results to the detectives to provide them with additional leads.

A related category of innovation was computerized case management systems that keep track of the current status of each case, times at which progress reports or court appearances are scheduled, and the investigator(s) assigned. These permit rapid "flagging" of cases that are failing to progress as expected for any reason and institution of timely corrective action.

Technical Resources

Several departments mentioned the establishment of a mobile evidence technician unit, its expansion, or purchase of improved equipment as having a favorable

---

13. These departments include Fremont and Long Beach, California; Cincinnati, Ohio; DeKalb County, Georgia; and Rochester, New York.

14. These factors include locating a witness to the crime and finding out whether a suspect can be named, located, described, or identified. Other items include license plate number and presence of significant MO or physical evidence.

15. Examples of recently installed systems that have components to aid investigators are the PATRIC system in Los Angeles; CRIME in Oakland, California; ALERT in Kansas City, Missouri; DATUM in Paterson, New Jersey; and GATCHA in Miami, Florida.

Table 6-7
Additional Computer-Readable Files Available
in One or More Departments

Investigators' activity records
Field interview cards, suspicious persons, suspicious vehicles
Arrest warrants
Wanted persons
Escapees, fugitives, missing persons
Registered informants
Index to polygraph records

Offender files
    Nickname, alias, monicker
    Rap sheets, criminal history
    Known drug offenders
    Known alcohol beverage law violators
    Known robbery offenders
    Known burglars
    Known safe men
    Known juvenile gangs, motorcycle gangs
    Known gamblers
    Suspect-offense cross index
    Peculiarity traits

Crime-specific files
    Selected case histories
    Handwriting samples
    Check cases
    Check classifications
    Fraud cases
    Gambling cases
    Subversive activities

Location-specific files
    Bars and restaurants
    Burglary incidence
    Known narcotics sales
    Known gambling

Files related to stolen property
    Identification numbers inscribed on property
    Lost or stolen property
    Pawn tickets
    Scrap metal sales
    Bicycle registrations
    Stolen guns

Weapons
    Permits, registrations, and sales of guns
    Ballistics file

impact on investigations. New designs of mobile vans were frequently mentioned, along with sophisticated equipment such as gas chromatography. A few departments were training their mobile evidence technicians in the use of polygraphs.

Tape recorders are being used by police investigators in a variety of ways. For example, in the Berkeley (California) Police Department, the patrolmen-investigators record all of their reports on tape, which are subsequently transcribed by clerical help.

In Cincinnati, Ohio, it is routine procedure for the investigator to record all of the statements made by the suspect in the course of questioning. The following advantages were noted by Cincinnati police officers.

- Statements can be replayed to the suspect in case of doubt about what was said.

- The recording can contain the reading to the suspect of his rights.

- There is no need to wait for a stenographer (in fact, a suspect can confess in the privacy of a jail cell if he so desires).

- It is easier to refute charges of intimidation because voice inflections on the tape would tend to indicate whether coercion was taking place (for increased credibility they do not stop the tape during the recording of a statement).

- It is easier for supervisors to determine whether a statement should be used for multiple case clearances.

The principal disadvantages of using tapes are the problems of purchasing and maintaining equipment. Tapes also must be stored for a long time and must be protected from theft and alteration.[16]

In Washington, D.C., all police lineups are photographed and tape-recorded. The department also has plans to begin videotaping lineups.

One department described a "Talking Rogue's Gallery," in which a slide projector is combined with a tape player. Color photographs of suspects can be shown at the same time as a 35-second recording of the suspect's voice is played. This system was claimed to improve the accuracy of identifications by victims and witnesses.

Crime Prevention

A large number of community-oriented projects were mentioned in the category of crime prevention. These included programs to encourage citizens to mark their property, "secret witness" programs in which newspapers and radio stations provide means for anonymous tips regarding the perpetrators of crimes, reporting of all auto thefts on a local radio station, and advising members of the public how to improve the security of their homes and businesses.

---

16. Bloch and Specht (1973).

In one city persons who, by the nature of their jobs (e.g., bank employees), are likely eventually to be the victims of a crime or a witness were being trained by the police on how to behave in such situations. Another city purchased portable burglar alarms and installed them in crime-prone establishments, moving them from time to time. The details of these programs varied from city to city, but the general concept of community-oriented crime prevention was being tried in most reporting jurisdictions.

The second major group of activities labeled "crime prevention" involves proactive activities by police officers, usually in plainclothes. Dressed in "modern style," driving types of cars ordinarily not purchased by police departments, and mixing with the criminal element, these officers concentrate on immediate detection of crime and arrest of perpetrators. Since our study focuses primarily on investigation of crimes after they are reported, we have not attempted to summarize the vast variety of operations of this type. However, the frequency with which such efforts were mentioned by survey respondents indicates that they consider them to be important contributions to investigative effectiveness. A few examples from selected cities will be described in Chapter 13.

Property Marking

Many departments actively encourage citizens to put identifying numbers on all of their valuable property—usually their drivers' license numbers. Although such programs are largely thought of as having deterrent value, they can, in principle, also aid in the identification and recovery of stolen property.

Civilianization

Civilians can assist investigators by searching for and providing background information in specific cases; this pattern was found in Oakland and Miami. Clerical help in report writing is provided in New York, Long Beach, Berkeley, and other cities. Civilian employees are also often responsible for notifying witnesses of the time of their court appearance and may even be dispatched to provide transportation for the witness. In Miami, all physical evidence is collected and analyzed by civilian evidence technicians. In Cincinnati, Ohio, civilians notify witnesses of court appearances, handle telephone calls, and serve subpoenas.

Legal Aides

Police departments across the country are recognizing the importance of having police investigations properly prepared for court presentation. To this end, several departments are beginning to employ legal staff to assist the police in case preparation. The largest effort of this type that we encountered was undertaken in 1973 by the Dallas Police Department. Six attorneys are assigned to the department on a full-time basis, and each attorney is responsible for reviewing all of the felony prosecution reports in his legal area of expertise (e.g., homicide, robbery). Subsequent to this reviewing procedure, the attorney

1. Sends the case to the prosecutor for filing, or
2. Returns the case for further invesgation, or
3. Refuses to file a case if there appears to be insufficient evidence or no case.

In addition to reviewing cases before filing, the attorneys also review all cases that are "no billed"[17] or dismissed after indictment. They reexamine such cases to detect any developing trends that may have caused excessive no bills or dismissals and that could be attributed to police error. These trends are then examined by the training classes conducted by the attorneys.

Statistics gathered by the attorneys for evaluation purposes show that they have been very successful in reducing the no bill and dismissal rates. In the first year of the project, 29.4 percent of the cases were no billed, and 13.2 percent of those were attributable to police error. During the second year 17.8 percent of the cases were no billed, and only 6.2 percent were due to police error.

---

17. Grand jury refuses to indict or prosecutor refuses to charge.

7

Relationships Among Department Characteristics

In this chapter we compare the arrest and clearance rates of the departments that responded to our survey with other characteristics of the departments. This constitutes a cross-sectional correlational analysis, with most of the data from the years 1972–73. The purpose of this analysis was to identify patterns of relationships deserving of detailed exploration in subsequent stages of the study. However, this purpose was not fulfilled, as we found no strong and consistent patterns that have operational significance for the organization of the investigative function.

This finding does not necessarily mean that there is no difference in effectiveness among various investigative practices, but rather that clearance and arrest rate statistics for departments as a whole may be inadequate to reveal whatever differences do exist. Our results add evidence to the observation, noted in Chapter 3, that such statistics are inappropriate measures of *investigative* effectiveness.

One warning in advance about interpretation of relationships showing statistical significance: When a large number of variables are compared with each other and a standard of significance at the 0.05 level is used, as we shall do in this chapter, then somewhere around 5 percent of all relations can be expected to be statistically significant even if the variables are unrelated.[1] While we will point out the ones that were statistically significant, it can happen that they appeared through statistical accident. Therefore, it is not appropriate to consider each statistically significant relationship as if it were meaningful, but rather to see whether coherent *patterns* of relationships emerge. Examples of coherent patterns are relationships that emerge as significant for both clearance rates and arrest rates, or that appear in a similar form for several different types of crimes or types of departments.

Methodology

In accordance with definitions given in Chapters 3 and 5, the number of crimes reported by a department as cleared in each FBI crime category for the year

---

1. Because the comparisons are not all independent, the expected figure would not be exactly 5 percent.

1972 was divided by the number of crimes reported[2] in the category for 1972 to calculate a *clearance rate*. Similarly, the number of arrests in each category was divided by the number of reported crimes to give an *arrest rate*. The categories were also aggregated into crimes against persons (homicide, rape, robbery, and felonious assault), crimes against property (burglary, larceny, and auto theft), and total Part I crimes, and clearance and arrest rates were calculated for the aggregates also. Finally, the number of clearances in each category was divided by the number of arrests to give a *clearance/arrest rate*. The ranges of these variables are of some interest in themselves and are shown in table 7-1. The data in this table refer to the entire survey universe, not just the departments that responded to the survey. In interpreting the table, it is important to realize that the department which happened to be "lowest" in one category is unlikely to be "lowest" in another one, and therefore it is not correct to compare statistics down each column as if they referred to a single department.

The calculated clearance and arrest rates were compared with nearly all other departmental characteristics for those departments that responded to the survey. The comparisons were made by means of correlations and multiple regressions in cases where the departmental characteristics could be described numerically. These statistical procedures are designed to reveal linear relationships among variables, but they can also detect monotonic relationships that are not linear. When significant relationships were observed, correlations for other characteristics were controlled for variations in the characteristics known to be significant.

To observe nonmonotonic relationships, two techniques were used. First, graphs of relationships were produced. Second, clearance and arrest variables were grouped according to the value of the variable, and the grouped variables were cross-tabulated against other variables describing department characteristics. For descriptors of department characteristics that were nonnumerical, cross-tabulation alone was used to determine whether significant relationships were present. A standard of significance at the 0.05 level was used in all cases. The analysis was performed using a collection of computer programs known as the Statistical Package for the Social Sciences (SPSS).

General Characteristics of Departments

The data showed that three department characteristics having no direct relationship to the organization of its investigative function are strongly correlated with arrest and clearance statistics: the *size* of the department, the *region* of the country in which the department is located, and its crime *workload* (number of

---

2. Unfounded crimes were excluded in the count of reported crimes.

Table 7-1
Crime, Clearance, and Arrest Statistics for 300 City and County Departments[a]

Statistic	Lowest	Median	Mean	Highest
	Part I Total			
Offenses per 100,000 population	1,070	5,448	5,590	13,946
Arrests per offense	0.07	0.180	0.191	0.44
Clearances per offense	0.05	0.185	0.204	0.54
Clearances per arrest	0.38	1.065	1.133	4.04
Arrests per policeman	0.30	5.652	5.757	16.15
Clearances per policeman	1.28	5.713	6.292	23.92
	Part II Total			
Arrests per policeman	1.22	21.185	23.122	75.39
	Murder			
Offenses per 100,000 population	0.48	8.867	11.384	55.09
Arrests per offense	0.07	1.001	1.166	7.00
Clearances per offense	0.33	0.895	0.876	1.50
Clearances per arrest	0.16	0.874	0.897	2.67
Arrests per policeman	0.002	0.047	0.063	0.47
Clearances per policeman	0.003	0.042	0.050	0.19
	Rape			
Offenses per 100,000 population	1.6	26.6	30.0	123.0
Arrests per offense	0.06	0.462	0.512	2.00
Clearances per offense	0.13	0.559	0.580	1.18
Clearances per arrest	0.36	1.139	1.436	8.50
Arrests per policeman	0.004	0.062	0.076	0.30
Clearances per policeman	0.003	0.074	0.091	0.28
	Robbery			
Offenses per 100,000 population	3.9	165.3	235.1	1,240.2
Arrests per offense	0.11	0.343	0.390	2.00
Clearances per offense	0.07	0.307	0.335	0.87
Clearances per arrest	0.24	0.846	0.959	4.74
Arrests per policeman	0.004	0.319	0.383	2.64
Clearances per policeman	0.02	0.254	0.319	1.71
	Felonious Assault			
Offenses per 100,000 population	6.2	189.6	245.3	1,300.3
Arrests per offense	0.06	0.474	0.527	1.80
Clearances per offense	0.13	0.644	0.639	1.04
Clearances per arrest	0.45	1.224	1.680	9.76
Arrests per policeman	0.03	0.442	0.600	6.69
Clearances per policeman	0.03	0.598	0.777	3.24

Table 7-1 (continued)

Statistic	Lowest	Median	Mean	Highest
	Burglary			
Offenses per 100,000 population	237.4	1,493.2	1,634.2	5,519.0
Arrests per offense	0.04	0.142	0.154	0.44
Clearances per offense	0.03	0.161	0.192	0.59
Clearances per arrest	0.30	1.106	1.360	5.08
Arrests per policeman	0.06	1.147	1.302	5.51
Clearances per policeman	0.22	1.323	1.645	8.28
	Larceny			
Offenses per 100,000 population	306.7	2,680.1	2,767.5	7,680.8
Arrests per offense	0.04	0.178	0.184	0.50
Clearances per offense	0.04	0.162	0.176	0.46
Clearances per arrest	0.23	0.966	1.091	4.23
Arrests per policeman	0.16	2.558	2.916	13.22
Clearances per policeman	0.22	2.516	2.885	11.73
	Auto Theft			
Offenses per 100,000 population	2.1	483.7	668.0	3,763.9
Arrests per offense	0.005	0.160	0.378	32.25
Clearances per offense	0.004	0.164	0.190	0.798
Clearances per arrest	0.03	0.929	1.130	11.32
Arrests per policeman	0.005	0.404	0.492	2.82
Clearances per policeman	0.007	0.449	0.515	2.26

Source: FBI data for 1972.

[a]All departments with 150 or more employees or a jurisdiction with population over 100,000.

crimes per police officer). Each of these characteristics was found to have an influence that is independent of the effect of the other two.

The size of a department can be measured by many different variables, among which are the number of employees, the number of sworn officers, the number of investigators, the annual budget, and the population of the jurisdiction served by the department. While these variables are by no means synonymous (because, for example, some departments have substantially more police officers per 1,000 population than other departments), a high value for any one of them was found to be related to a large number of clearances per arrest. Thus, in general, large departments tend to claim more clearances for each arrest than small departments. This relationship was found for nearly every category of crimes considered.[3]

---

3. In this instance, as in several others that follow, statistics for the crime of homicide did not follow the general pattern. This is primarily because clearance rates for homicide are high in most departments.

There are several possible explanations for this observation. First, it may be that small departments count crimes as cleared under more restrictive circumstances than those permitted in larger departments. Second, it is possible that small departments make more unfruitful arrests (i.e., arrests that prove to have been unrelated to any crime) than large departments do, or that they are more conscientious about recording such arrests when they do occur. Finally, the differences could be unrelated to actual practices but simply reflect differences in record-keeping. (For example, to record a crime as cleared may require retrieving the original crime report and updating it in some way. This may be easier to accomplish in large departments with computer-readable crime reports than in small departments with manual files. Keeping an accurate count of the number of arrests is easier, because an arrest form is filled out for each person arrested.) The data available from the survey are inadequate to distinguish among these possible explanations.

Despite the fact that clearance/arrest ratios were generally higher in large departments than in small ones, there were no consistent variations in arrest rates or clearance rates (i.e., the number of arrests or clearances per crime) among departments according to their size.

The variations in arrest and clearance statistics according to the region of the country in which the department is located were even stronger than the variations according to the size of the department. In fact, they were the strongest relationships found in this cross-sectional analysis. Departments located in the South Central states[4] reported substantially higher numbers of clearances per arrest (averaging over 1.5) than departments in other areas. Departments in the Northeast and the West were lowest in this regard (under 1.0). As a consequence, the rankings of departments by region according to arrest rates were as follows:

Northeast (highest)
West
South Atlantic
North Central
South Central (lowest)

But the rankings by clearance rates were almost exactly reversed:

South Central (highest)
North Central
South Atlantic
Northeast
West (lowest)

---

4. See table 5-3 for composition of regions.

This observation clearly illustrates the futility of attempting to use either arrest rates or clearance rates as measures of performance for comparing police departments. Evidently it is impossible that departments located in the South Central portion of the United States are at the same time the best in the country and the worst in the country, but interpreting arrest and clearance rates as performance measures appears to lead to this conclusion.

To compare arrest and clearance statistics with crime workload, several measures of workload were used: the total number of Part I crimes per police officer; the total number of crimes against persons per police officer; and, for clearance and arrest statistics for a particular crime type, the number of crimes of that type per police officer.

Regardless of the particular measure used, the same patterns were observed. First, for every crime type the arrest rate was found to be significantly lower in departments with high crime workload than in cities with low workload. When this relationship was inspected in greater detail, it was found that the number of arrests per police officer increased nearly (but not quite) in direct proportion to workload until a certain threshold of workload was reached.[5] Beyond this threshold, increasing workload was associated with much smaller increases in the number of arrests per police officer. The thresholds were at approximately 35 Part I crimes per police officer per year and 3.5 crimes against persons per police officer per year. These thresholds are fairly high, as only about 20 percent of departments had greater workload levels.[6]

These findings are consistent with the assumption that a city can increase its number of arrests or decrease its crime rate (or both) by increasing the size of its police force, but the effect of added resources would be greatest for cities above the threshold. However, since the data are cross-sectional, they do not prove these hypotheses are true.

In regard to clearance rates, the data showed that departments with high crime workload tend to claim more clearances per arrest than cities with low crime workload. As a result, clearance rates are less sensitive to workload than arrest rates. Although clearance rates for every crime type were found to decrease with increasing workload, the decreases were not significant for some types of crimes. These relationships are summarized in table 7–2.

Because the general department characteristics of size, location, and crime workload were found to be correlated with arrest and clearance rates, these three variables were controlled in our analysis of other department characteristics.

---

5. More precisely, there was a linear relationship between arrests per officer and crime workload, up to the threshold, but the intercept of the straight-line fit was at a positive value of arrests per officer. As a result, the relationship between arrest rate and crime workload cannot be linear.

6. After 1972, crime rates in the United States have generally increased. Since we did not perform any longitudinal analysis, we do not know whether the thresholds also increased or remained at the same levels.

Table 7-2

Correlations: Workload vs. Arrest and Clearance Rates

	Correlation (Significance)		
Variable	*Part I Crimes per Police Officer*	*Crimes Against Persons per Police Officer*	*Number of Crimes in Question per Police Officer*
Homicide arrest rate	-0.01 (n.s.)	-0.03 (n.s.)	-0.19 (.013)
Homicide clearance rate	-0.11 (n.s.)	-0.25 (.002)	-0.24 (.002)
Rape arrest rate	-0.35 (.001)	-0.24 (.002)	-0.38 (.001)
Rape clearance rate	-0.25 (.002)	-0.11 (n.s.)	-0.21 (.006)
Robbery arrest rate	-0.27 (.001)	-0.42 (.001)	-0.44 (.001)
Robbery clearance rate	-0.14 (n.s.)	-0.26 (.002)	-0.33 (.001)
Assault arrest rate	-0.20 (.011)	-0.39 (.001)	-0.48 (.001)
Assault clearance rate	-0.11 (n.s.)	-0.09 (n.s.)	-0.05 (n.s.)
Crimes against persons			
Arrest rate	-0.21 (.007)	-0.45 (.001)	
Clearance rate	-0.10 (n.s.)	-0.12 (n.s.)	
Burglary arrest rate	-0.16 (.029)	-0.20 (.011)	-0.19 (.013)
Burglary clearance rate	-0.16 (.037)	-0.19 (.018)	-0.15 (.042)
Auto theft arrest rate	-0.13 (n.s.)	-0.22 (.005)	-0.20 (.011)
Auto theft clearance rate	-0.07 (n.s.)	-0.11 (n.s.)	-0.08 (n.s.)

n.s. = not significant.

This means that the effect of size, location, and crime workload on each department's arrest and clearance statistics was estimated by means of a linear fit to the data,[7] and then the difference between the department's actual statistic and this estimate was compared with other characteristics of the department.

One such characteristic, which again is unrelated to the investigative function, is the total salary budget of the department divided by the number of police officers. This variable captures both the pay scale of police officers and the amount of support given to them in the form of civilian personnel. The data showed that high values of this variable were associated with higher numbers of arrests per police officer and lower clearance rates for crimes against persons. Arrest *rates* were not found to be related to this variable. This mixed pattern does not present any apparent interpretation, other than the fact that higher pay levels do not purchase higher arrest and clearance rates.

The relationships between general department characteristics and arrest and clearance rates are summarized for convenience in table 7-3.

---

7. For this purpose, "region" was arbitrarily converted into an integer variable, with the order determined by the preceding analysis: 1 = West, 2 = Northeast, 3 = South Atlantic, 4 = North Central, 5 = South Central.

Table 7–3
Relationship of General Characteristics to Arrest and Clearance Rates

Characteristics	Relationship

Size of department:
    Population of jurisdiction
    Number of sworn officers
    Number of investigators
    Budget of department
	More clearances claimed per arrest in all categories.

Region of country	Arrest rates increase in the order South Central, North Central, South Atlantic, West, Northeast. Clearance rates decrease in almost the same order.

Crime workload:
    Part I crimes per officer
    Crimes against persons per officer
    Homicides per officer
    Etc.
	Arrest rates decrease in all categories. Clearance rates decrease in most categories.

Salary budget per officer	Clearance rates decrease.[a] Arrests per police officer increase.[a]

[a]Controlled for size, region, and workload.

Investigative Resources

As we have already noted, there are not very large variations among departments in the fraction of the force assigned to investigative units. For this reason, the crime workload of investigators is highly correlated with the overall crime workload. Therefore, a comparison of arrest and clearance statistics with the crime workload of investigators would reveal the same patterns as shown in table 7–3 for overall workload. If one envisions that nearly all arrests and clearances are produced by investigators, so that patrol officers are irrelevant in this regard, then the patterns can be interpreted as showing the effect of workload on investigators' outputs.

However, as we show in Chapter 9, patrol officers actually make a major contribution to arrests and clearances, so that the appropriate analysis involves comparing these statistics to the number of crimes per investigator while controlling for the number of crimes per police officer. Mathematically, this is the same as comparing arrest and clearance statistics with the percentage of the force assigned to investigative units, holding overall workload levels constant.

When processed in this fashion, the data showed a significant relationship between the relative amount of resources devoted to investigation and the number of arrests and clearances per police officer, but with one exception, arrest and clearance *rates* were not related to investigative resources. More precisely, departments with a higher proportion of investigators have more arrests and clearances per police officer per year in nearly all categories. But this effect is not strong enough to lead to significant increases in arrest and clearance rates for any crimes other than burglary. In the case of burglary, clearance rates were significantly higher in departments with a relatively large fraction of the force assigned to investigation, but burglary arrest rates were not. Thus, if the total number of officers in a department is kept constant, while a greater or lesser portion of them are assigned to investigative duties, we cannot assert that there will be any important change in overall arrest and clearance rates. This observation is concisely summarized in table 7-4, along with the other relationships that will be discussed below.

Organizational Variables

The survey asked the extent to which patrol officers perform investigative functions. The data showed that in departments where patrolmen have major investigative duties, the number of clearances claimed per arrest is lower than in other departments for most crimes against persons, especially robbery. This finding appears to indicate that investigators make a greater attempt to associate suspects in custody with other crimes than patrolmen do, but they do not succeed in arresting a larger number of perpetrators.

In regard to specialization of investigators, the data did not reveal any significant relationship between the overall commitment of the department to specialization (i.e., the fraction of investigators in specialized units) and arrest or clearance rates, when all other relevant variables were controlled for. However, for the specific crimes of burglary and robbery, the data showed that departments having such a specialized unit have lower arrest rates for the crime in question, with no effect on clearance rates. While these findings are not very decisive, they do indicate that specialized units cannot be expected to produce substantially better arrest and clearance rates in the crime categories on which they specialize.

The amount of training in investigation given to newly recruited patrol officers or newly appointed investigators was not found to be related to arrest or clearance rates, while the amount of refresher training was related to increasing clearance rates, but not arrest rates.

Departments in which investigators work in pairs had lower numbers of arrests per officer than those in which they work singly. Since we did not collect data permitting a comparison of the quality of arrests produced by solo and paired investigators, this finding must be interpreted with caution. The practice of pairing investigators, which is common only in the Northeast, is nonetheless brought into sufficient question that further research appears warranted.

Table 7–4
Relationship of Department Characteristics to Arrest and Clearance Rates

Characteristics	Relationship (controlled for size, region, and workload)
Percentage of force in investigative units	Higher numbers of arrests and clearances per police officer. Higher clearance rates for burglary but not other crimes. No relationship to arrest rates.
Investigative role of patrolmen	Fewer clearances per arrest for robbery and for total crimes against persons. No relationship to arrest rates.
Percentage of investigators in specialized units	No significant relationships, but every arrest and clearance rate decreased as the percent specialized increased.
Unit specializing in homicide	No relationship to homicide statistics.
Unit specializing in robbery	Lower arrest rate for robbery; number of clearances per robbery arrest increased.
Unit specializing in burglary	Lower burglary arrest rate; number of clearances per burglary arrest increased.
Unit specializing in auto theft	No relationship to auto theft statistics.
Civil service rank for investigators	None.
Detectives work in pairs	Lower arrests per police officer. Lower arrest rate for auto theft.
Amount of investigative training for recruits.	None.
Amount of training for new investigators	None.
Amount of refresher training for investigators	Clearance rates (but not arrest rates) higher for crimes against persons, especially robbery.
Emphasis in evaluation on:	
Supervisory review	None.
Audit	Higher auto theft clearances.
Arrest statistics	Fewer arrests for homicide without a clearance.
Clearance statistics	Clearance rates for all crimes higher, robbery significantly so; arrest rates unaffected.
Caseload	Lower burglary arrest and clearance rate.
Success in major investigations	Lower burglary clearance rate.
Property recovered	None.
Prosecution statistics	Lower arrest rate for homicide.
Court dispositions	Fewer arrests for homicide without a clearance.
Percentage of employees civilian	Lower arrest rate for rape.
Role of the prosecutor in investigations	None.

Among the other policies for management of the investigative function that were covered in the survey, none appears to have a sizable effect on arrest or clearance rates and therefore the potential value of these policies to a department must be judged by other criteria.[8] It is interesting to note that departments placing emphasis on clearance rates for evaluation of units do indeed have higher clearance rates. One possible interpretation is that this reflects pressure on investigators to clear crimes under questionable circumstances. But another is that departments with high clearance rates are proud of them, and therefore reported on the survey that they place emphasis on clearances.

Role of the Prosecutor

Prosecutors' policies for screening out felony arrests (as reported by the police departments) varied substantially by region, as shown in table 7-5.

The role of the prosecutor in affecting performance levels of investigators could not be clearly discerned in the survey data (table 7-4). One would think that if the prosecutor insists on making a judgment about whether an arrest should be made prior to the arrest, or if he will be involved in the investigation after the arrest, fewer arrests would be made that do not lead to clearing a crime. But the data did not show this to be the case. If the *police department* reviews prosecution and court statistics for evaluation purposes, then some care appears to be exercised in making homicide arrests.

Table 7-5
Percentage of Departments
Reporting Prosecutor Rejected
20 Percent or More of Felony
Arrests

Region	Percent
West	37.8
South Central	30.0
North Central	13.8
South Atlantic	6.3
Northeast	0.0
Overall	18.3

8. Some "significant" findings in table 7-4 that appear to be statistical accidents are (1) the relationship between audits and auto theft clearances and (2) the relationship between civilianization and rape arrests.

Evidence Technicians

A reasonable hypothesis is that departments with heavy commitment to mobile evidence technicians would report higher levels of evidence collection than those that use few such technicians. With minor exceptions, this was not found to be the case. To examine this relationship, we categorized the commitment to evidence collection in two ways. First, the total number of evidence technicians (sworn plus civilian) was expressed as a percent of the total sworn force of the department. These percentages were divided into the following categories having roughly equal numbers of departments:

- no evidence technicians

- some, but under 1.5 percent

- 1.5–2.5 percent

- 2.5–3.5 percent

- over 3.5 percent.

Second, the number of evidence technicians was expressed as a ratio to the number of investigators, and these ratios were similarly grouped.

A typical tabulation is given in table 7-6, which compares the reported degree of collection of fingerprints at homicides with our first measure of commitment to evidence technicians. There is no systematic pattern in the figures, much less statistical significance. A similar result was found for our second measure of evidence collection. Moreover, there was no relationship tween commitment to evidence technicians and checks for tool marks, chemical

Table 7-6
Percentage of Departments in Category
Reporting Check for Fingerprints
"Always" Made at Homicides

Commitment to Evidence Technicians[a]	Percent
No evidence technicians	80.8
Under 1.5%	76.0
1.5–2.5%	85.7
2.5–3.5%	73.1
Over 3.5%	88.0
All departments	81.3

Note: No statistical significance on this table.

[a]Percentage of sworn force.

analysis, shoeprint-tire casting, and all other types of evidence mentioned in connection with homicides.

Since in general a considerable effort is devoted to evidence collection in cases of homicide, this finding might have been anticipated. However, there was a similar lack of relationship in regard to the reported degree of evidence checks at residential burglaries and commercial burglaries. In regard to robberies, some significant relationships were found.

The robbery data showed no difference for checking on fingerprints or chemical analysis, but there was a significant pattern for tool marks and shoeprint-tire casting (table 7-7). Departments with a sizable commitment to evidence technicians were found to be more likely to make tool mark and shoeprint-tire checks at robberies. This tends to indicate that departments with evidence technicians will make a thorough search for all types of evidence even if they are unlikely to apply to a particular crime.

Now it may be claimed that the purpose of evidence technicians is not to collect *more* evidence, but to collect *better quality evidence*. This hypothesis, if true, should reveal itself in comparisons with the fraction of arrests rejected by prosecutors and in clearance and arrest rates. However, none of these relationships indicated the anticipated patterns.

The relationship of evidence technicians to cases screened out was essentially random, as shown in table 7-8. In fact, 27.3 percent of departments with a heavy commitment to evidence technicians had over 20 percent of felony arrests screened out by the prosecutor, and this was approximately the same as for departments with no evidence technicians.

The commitment to evidence technicians was also compared with the various clearance rates discussed previously. Measures of commitment to evidence technicians were calculated as percentage of the force, ratio to investigators, and

Table 7-7
Percentage of Departments in Category Reporting
Evidence "Usually" or "Always" Checked
at Robberies

	Percent	
Commitment to Evidence Technicians[a]	Tool Marks	Shoeprint-Tire
No evidence technicians	38.5	30.8
Under 1.5%	29.1	37.5
1.5-2.5%	35.7	50.0
2.5-3.5%	48.0	40.0
Over 3.5%	44.0	60.0
All departments	38.8	44.1

[a]Percentage of sworn force.

Table 7-8
Percentage of Departments in Category Reporting Indicated
Level of Screening

Commitment to Evidence Technicians[a]	Percentage of Felony Arrests Rejected by Prosecutor		
	Under 5%	5 – 20%	Over 20%
No evidence technicians	38.1	33.3	28.6
Under 1.5%	54.5	31.8	13.6
1.5–2.5%	58.5	24.4	17.1
2.5–3.5%	60.9	21.7	17.4
Over 3.5%	45.5	27.3	27.3

Note: No statistical significance on this table

[a]Percentage of force evidence technicians.

actual count of technicians. (In this case there was no need to group the measures of commitment into categories as shown in the preceding tables.)

Simple correlations were calculated, and also correlations that controlled for other departmental characteristics. With two exceptions, no relationships were found between evidence technicians and clearance or arrest rates. These two were sufficiently unusual and inconsistent that they may be viewed as statistical accidents. (We refer here again to the fact that *some* relationships will be found significant if a large number of statistical tests are performed.) These were: (1) the fraction of homicides leading to an arrest was *lower* in departments with many evidence technicians than in those with few (but the same pattern did not appear in homicide *clearance* rates), and (2) the fraction of auto thefts leading to an arrest was *higher* in departments with many evidence technicians (also not appearing significant for clearance rates). These were the only significant relationships in a long list that included burglary clearance rate, burglary arrest rate, robbery clearance rate, etc.

We also compared reported frequency of performing evidence checks in homicides, burglaries, and robberies with the clearance and arrest rates for the corresponding crimes. As we mentioned above, these reported evidence checks are essentially independent of the number of evidence technicians. Again, only two inconsistent relationships were found: (1) homicide arrest rates (but not clearance rates) were *lower* in departments reporting high levels of checking chemical analyses at homicides, and (2) robbery arrest rates (but not clearance rates) were significantly *higher* in departments reporting collection of shoeprints and tire castings at robberies.

For emphasis, we list the relationships that proved to be nonsignificant for burglaries:

burglary arrest rate or clearance rate	vs.	reported frequency of fingerprint checks at burglaries
burglary arrest rate or clearance rate	vs.	reported frequency of tool mark checks at burglaries
burglary arrest rate or clearance rate	vs.	reported frequency of chemical analysis at burglaries
burglary arrest rate or clearance rate	vs.	reported frequency of shoeprint and tire casting at burglaries

The analogous relationships for homicide and robbery were also insignificant, with the exceptions noted above.

In summary, the data did not reveal any meaningful and important impacts of evidence technicians on reported qualities of evidence collected or on clearance, arrest, or prosecutor rejection rates.

City-County Differences

It should be noted that although all processing of the survey data was carried out separately for city and county police departments, under the assumption that they would be substantially different in many regards, the actual distinctions were quite minor and have been mentioned in the text wherever appropriate.

Part III

The Process Evaluated

8

The Daily Routine

Because investigators have considerable autonomy in determining how they will spend their working day and are not subject to hour-by-hour supervision, we felt it would be useful if our research could explore their daily routine. Such information might assist in developing rational methods for allocation of investigative personnel. In addition, as we shall see, information concerning the activities of investigators helps explain some of the performance patterns that will be described in subsequent chapters of this report.

Several methods were used to collect information for our study of the daily routine of investigators. First, Rand's research team spent many weeks "working" with selected investigative units or investigators as they engaged in their usual tasks and, to the extent that it was possible to do so without interfering, asked questions about the purpose of various activities and the investigators' implicit priorities that caused them to choose one activity over another. These researchers were not engaged in a time and motion study and did not collect any quantitative information about the number of minutes spent on particular tasks, but their observations help provide concrete examples that illuminate patterns found from other sources of data. While there may be some doubt that investigators who are being followed by a researcher will engage in the same activities as they would when unobserved, the wide range of activities actually observed suggests to us that only a brief familiarization period, lasting about a day, intervenes before observed investigators return to their usual patterns. This is a common experience in other types of participant-observer studies.

A second source of data was provided by the numerous case folders that were reviewed by the research team for other purposes of this study. In many instances, these records provided a complete history of the activities engaged in during a particular investigation, and they were summarized to provide case examples. Such information, however, is limited in that it gives no indication of how investigators' time is spent on activities not directly related to individual cases.

The third source of data was a computer-readable case assignment file maintained by the Kansas City (Missouri) Police Department. The availability of this file was discovered by the research team during the course of the survey that is described in Chapters 5, 6, and 7. All quantitative information in the present chapter was derived from analysis of this file; however, the illustrative examples that we use to interpret the data have been drawn from observations and case histories collected in departments other than Kansas City. This form of presentation

97

was adopted so as to protect the anonymity of investigators, victims, and suspects described in the case examples.

Kansas City Detective Case Assignment File[1]

Since 1971 the Kansas City Police Department has operated a system whereby detectives enter information about their daily activities on printed cards which are subsequently keypunched and processed by computer. Summary reports are produced by the department on a monthly and quarterly basis. These describe, for each investigator and for each unit, the number of hours spent on various activities, the number of cases handled, and the number of arrests and clearances produced.

The main purpose of this system is to provide statistical information for administrative and analysis purposes. It was also hoped that the system would prove useful for evaluating and monitoring the performance of detectives and their supervisors, but this purpose has not been fulfilled.[2] In rare instances of serious neglect of duty, unattended, data from the case assignment file have been used by the department as documentation during disciplinary proceedings. However, data from the computer system merely confirmed a problem situation that was already apparent to unit supervisors; it did not bring about the initial recognition of the problem.

Where there is no serious neglect of duty, it is apparent that activity data are not very useful for evaluative purposes. For example, a detective may work on only one or two cases during a particular month, but the possible explanations for such a situation may be either positive or negative. The supervisor may have given him responsibility for a sensitive or complex investigation, or the detective may have been appearing daily before a grand jury, or, at the other extreme, he may have been wasting most of his time on unimportant matters. Only his supervisor would know which explanation applies, and he would be familiar with the circumstances whether or not he received a computer printout.[3]

---

1. The description of this file given here may not be adequate for readers who are interested in the possibility of installing a similar system in their own department. Further details will be provided on request. Please address all inquiries to Dr. Jan Chaiken at The Rand Corporation, Santa Monica, California, not to the Kansas City Police Department.

2. The system is also intended to be used for self-evaluation. The instruction manual includes the following statement: "The monthly printout sheet, when reviewed by the individual, will keep him abreast of his total activity. It will emphasize his strong points, and if deficient in some area, allow him the opportunity for self-initiated improvement." Whether the system has been beneficial in this regard is not known to us.

3. Although we have criticized the lack of participation by supervisors in making tactical investigative decisions, it is true that most supervisors keep informed of what their men are doing, by general category of activity—i.e., court appearances, patrol, etc.

Many departments (over half of those responding to our survey) require that investigators complete some form of activity log, and a few of them convert the logs to computer-readable form. However, we did not encounter any other files that were as suitable for the purposes of our research as the Kansas City file, which contains a wealth of details and has been in use for several years, during which time various editing and quality-control programs have been developed. We are indebted to Chief Joseph McNamara for agreeing to provide us with access to this file. In accordance with our request, the department sent us a copy of all records for a one-year period: May 1, 1973, to April 30, 1974.

Organization of the File

Each detective in Kansas City, except those in the vice and narcotics unit, has a number of blank Case Assignment Cards on his desk. An example of such a card is shown in figure 8-1. These are filled out under one of the following circumstances:

1. The detective has spent a half-hour or more investigating a particular case.[4]
2. The detective has spent a half-hour or more in a specific investigative activity that is not related to a case, e.g., surveillance, checking crime-prone locations.
3. The detective has been assigned to a noninvestigative duty, e.g., presenting a speech at a high school.

The detective records the amount of time spent[5] on each of the following activities (some of which are indicated by the headings on the Case Assignment Card):

Interrogation (i.e., questioning a suspect)

Interview (i.e., questioning a nonsuspect)

Arraignment

Report (i.e., writing)

Arrest (processing)
   Adult
   Juvenile

---

4. A "case" may be a reported crime, a reported incident that is not necessarily a crime (e.g., a missing person), or an investigation initiated by the department.

5. Detectives in the Missing Persons Unit record only the *number* of activities in each category, not the time spent, and therefore we were unable to analyze the activities of this unit.

FORM 390 P. D.
REV. (9-71)

CASE ASSIGNMENT CARD

NAME OF COMPLAINANT/VICTIM/SUSPECT/ETC.

1. UNIT	2. CASE NUMBER		3. OFFICER'S SERIAL #	4. DATE	5. INTERROGATIONS		6. INTERVIEWS		7. ARRAIGNMENTS		8. REPORTS	
	TYPE	NUMBER			NUMBER	TIME	NUMBER	TIME	NUMBER	TIME	NUMBER	TIME
1	2	3–8	9–12	13–18	19 – 20	21 – 23	24 – 25	26 – 28	29 – 30	31 – 33	34 – 35	36 – 38

9 ADULT ARRESTS		10. JUVENILE ARRESTS		11. SURVEIL./CRIME PREVENT		12. ADMINISTRATIVE		13. OFFENSE CODE	14 OFF STAT	15 UNIT CRED	16. RECOVERED PROPERTY VALUE
NUMBER	TIME	NUMBER	TIME	CODE	TIME	CODE	TIME				(NEAREST DOLLAR) $
39 – 40	41 – 43	44 – 45	46 – 48	49	50 – 52	53	54 – 56	57 – 58	59	60	61 – 65

17. JUDICIAL ACTIVITY *		18. CRIME SCENE TIME	19. OVERTIME	20. SUPERVISOR'S SERIAL #	21. WARRANT STATUS (CHECK ONE)	22 OFFICER'S TIME AVAIL (SUPV.'S USE ONLY)
CODE	TIME				( ) INVESTIGATED – A ( ) CLEARED BY ARR. – B ( ) RECALLED – C	
66	67 – 69	70 – 72	73 – 75	76 – 79	80	PUNCH IN COLS. 72-75

Figure 8–1. Information Card Used for Kansas City Police Department File

Surveillance[6]

Crime prevention[7]

Judicial
    Court time
    Extradition
    Processing a warrant
    Obtaining a search warrant
    Obtaining an arrest warrant
    Subpoenas
    Prosecutor's conference
Crime scene investigation

Administrative
    Desk assignment
    Assistance to outside agency
    Speeches
    Special assignment

The amount of time spent is to be recorded to the nearest half-hour. In the event that several activities collectively consume a half-hour, the time may be recorded under any one of them, while the entry labeled "number" will indicate that the activity took place. It should be noted that the list of codable activities, while quite extensive, does not include every possible activity of a detective, and therefore there is no requirement that the sum of the hours shown on Case Assignment Cards for a given day should equal the total hours worked by the detective. The file is not used for any payroll purpose.

In addition to the information concerning the amount of time spent on each activity, the Case Assignment Card gives the identifying number for the case in question (if any), the officer's serial number[8] and unit, the date, and the type and status of the case (if any). The *type* of the case is coded into one of 109 categories (e.g., auto theft, burglary at a service station), which we collapsed into 52 categories for purposes of analysis.[9] The *status* of the case (if it is a crime) is coded as one of the following:

---

6. Includes attempts to locate (ATL) a witness or suspect as a separate code.

7. In this category, the type of location is coded.

8. In the copy of the file provided to Rand, serial numbers of officers were scrambled in a consistent fashion, so that we could tell which cases a particular officer worked on, but we would not be able to identify him.

9. Both the categories used by the department and the ones adopted for this study are shown in Appendix H, table H–1.

Cleared by arrest

Exceptional clearance

Unfounded

Reclassified

Leads exhausted

Warrant issued

Pickup issued

Inactive

Active

When a crime is declared cleared, the unit taking credit for the clearance is indicated on the card. This may be either the Patrol Bureau or one of the organizational units of the Investigative Bureau of the Kansas City Police Department:

Crimes Against Persons Unit

Crimes Against Properties Unit

General Assignment Unit

Youth and Women's Unit

Missing Persons Section

At the end of each month a special Case Assignment Card is filled out for each officer by his supervisor. This indicates the number of hours worked by the detective during the month.

Processing the File

The records provided by the Kansas City Police Department were separated into two categories according to whether they did or did not have a case number on them. Records without a case number represent administrative time, surveillance, crime prevention checks, work on warrants, and youth contacts where no crime is involved. Records representing case work were further divided into: "old" cases—reported before May 1, 1973, and "new" cases. The reason for this separation is that the file presumably did not contain the complete history of activities on "old" cases, but only whatever work was done after May 1.

To describe the activities involved in each type of crime, we needed to look at incidents for which we had as complete a history as was possible. This means that we could not look at incidents reported near May 1, 1974, because some of the activities on these cases would have occurred after the end of the file. By analysis of the records, we found that it was extremely rare to have any activity on a case after five months had passed. Therefore, by focusing on cases that began in May-November 1973, we could be confident that we had the "complete story" on these cases, with rare exceptions. All the results based on this file refer to the period May-November 1973, which will be referred to as the "study period."

An important step in our study was to construct a single record for each "new" case worked on[10] beginning in the study period. This *incident record* summarized the information contained in *all* the records in the department's file for that incident. Typical information on the incident file is:

- Date crime was reported.[11]

- Date detective first worked on the case.

- Date of arrest or clearance by arrest, if any.

- Date case was suspended.[12]

- Date of last activity on case.

- Number of dates the case was "worked on."

- Which units worked on the case.

- Number of officers working on the case.

- Crime type as first reported.

- Crime type at the end.

- Total time spent on each activity before date of clearance by arrest (if any) and beginning with the date of clearance.

- Unit(s) claiming credit for clearance.

- Outcome of case.

Validity

Some facts about the data in this file must be kept in mind when interpreting the summarized statistics.

---

10. A case is said to be "worked on" if there is at least one Case Assignment Card in the file with that case number. This means that at least a half-hour's time was spent on the case by an investigator.

11. This was determined by finding the highest case number "worked on" on each date.

12. In this analysis, we designated a case as "suspended" if 30 days passed without any activity on the case.

1. We do not know whether the officers are conscientious about reporting accurately how they spend their time, or whether they keep in mind "how it will look" on the monthly departmental summaries if they record certain types of activities.
2. Some case-related activity presumably takes place in blocks of less than a half-hour and therefore goes unrecorded.
3. If a detective spends an entire day in court and does not come to his office, he may or may not ever fill out a Case Assignment Card indicating this activity.
4. The file was found to be characterized by various keypunching errors. If an incident number is mis-keypunched, so that activities are logged against the wrong case, peculiarities of the following types can occur:
   - It appears that one detective classifies the case as a safe burglary while another classifies it as a rape.
   - It appears that the case was cleared a month before the incident occurred.
   - It appears that the only work done on a homicide was one hour, and this took place several months after the crime (i.e., one activity among many on a homicide is shown with the wrong incident number; this incident number appears to be a homicide when in fact it is not).

If the date is mis-keypunched, it can appear that the perpetrator was arraigned before he was arrested. If the crime code is mis-keypunched, then activity on a case of a runaway can appear to be activity on a homicide. Through the use of various editing techniques, we attempted to eliminate errors that could seriously affect general observations about the data, but some may have escaped our attention.

How Detectives Spend Their Working Hours

We classified detectives in Kansas City into groups according to the unit they worked in during the study period and the mix of cases they worked on. Table 8-1 shows how the working hours of detectives in each group were broken down among case work, other time shown in the file, and time not accounted for. The column labeled "case work" includes all the categories of activities listed above, if they were related to a case.

The data show that about 56 percent of the average detective's time is accounted for in the file as case work. To this we must add some allowance for possibly unrecorded court time and brief case-related activities, such as telephoning a victim, issuing a pickup notice, and so forth. A reasonable estimate, then, is that about 60 percent of a detective's time is spent on case work. This agrees well with our observations in other cities.

Table 8–1
Breakdown of Total Working Hours of Detectives
(Percent of time on each activity)

Unit	Case Work	Adminis-trative	Surveillance, Crime Prev., Warrants, Youths	Not Recorded in File
Crimes against persons	57.4	2.7	2.4	37.5
Homicide squad	53.7	3.1	2.8	40.4
Robbery squad	54.2	2.2	3.4	40.2
Sex crimes squad	70.0	2.7	0.1	27.2
Crimes against property	54.7	24.2	0.3	20.8
Auto theft squad	44.6	39.8	0.5	15.1
Residential burglary & larceny squad	59.7	14.4	0.1	25.8
Residential burglary specialist	63.2	13.8	0.1	22.9
Residential burglary/larceny	43.3	17.2	0.1	39.4
Nonresidential burglary squad	59.3	11.5	0.3	28.9
Safes specialist	64.4	10.5	1.5	23.5
Commercial burglary specialist	56.6	12.2	0.1	31.1
Others	60.7	11.0	0.1	28.1
General assignment	51.4	10.6	2.0	36.0
Arson specialist	65.5	4.3	0.3	29.9
Fraud/forgery specialist	45.5	13.3	0.1	41.1
Fraud/bunco specialist	48.5	10.8	0.1	40.6
Shoplift, pickpocket specialist	58.6	8.3	6.5	26.6
Youth and women's	58.0	27.2	5.1	9.8
All units together	55.7	13.8	1.9	28.6

Source: Kansas City Case Assignment File, May–November 1973.

Having made a slight adjustment in our estimate of the amount of case work, this leaves about one-fourth of a detective's time devoted to activities that do not fall into any of the categories permitted on the Case Assignment Card. Some of this is undoubtedly slack time, and is particularly apparent in the case of units such as homicide and robbery that are manned during nights and weekends so that detectives can respond rapidly to the scene of crimes. If no incidents happen to occur at night, the detectives cannot engage in alternative investigative activities.

Other non-case work activities (that may fall either into the "not recorded" column or the "administrative" column) include reading teletype messages and driving to court or locations where victims and witnesses can be interviewed. In our observations in several departments, automobile theft investigators were found to spend considerable amounts of time traveling to various places in and out of state to bring back arrested car thieves. They also check out car wash places, junkyards, and other auto-handling establishments to make sure that all is in order and to check for stolen autos listed on the "hot sheet."

Many forgery/fraud units are charged with issuing permits to people who want to solicit funds for whatever purpose or engage in such activities as door-to-door selling. Licenses are issued by the detail after an investigation, which is a search of available records. Not all persons with criminal records are automatically excluded from receiving licenses; it all depends on their record and on what license they seek.

Also, such details may receive numerous telephone calls each day from citizens who ask for advice, such as: "They charged me so much to fix my car and it doesn't run, what should I do?" Or "I was offered or told such and such, what do you think?"

For additional examples of non-case work activities, see the section "On Patrol" in Appendix G.

The specific types of activities that are recorded as "administrative" average some 14 percent of detectives' time in Kansas City, as shown in table 8-1. The exact amount varies by the type of unit, from a low of 3 percent in the Crimes Against Persons Unit to a high of 27 percent in the Youth and Women's Unit. These are primarily activities such as entering information into computer systems, assisting other agencies in the same jurisdiction or elsewhere, meeting with community groups, manning a desk at headquarters to which members of the public come for advice or records, and the like. As in many types of organizations, the most experienced and capable of the detectives are often most burdened with administrative activities. A composite example from our observations is given in the section "Administrative Details" in Appendix G.

In sum, then, we find from both the data and observations that detectives are not involved in a single-minded pursuit of solutions to crimes; rather, they spend some 40 percent of their time in an interruptible fashion on other activities. Every unit experiences "hot cases" from time to time that require the full attention of all the detectives and provide memorable moments in the detective's career, but the usual day involves many routine tasks. As we continue with our analysis of the data, this conclusion will be reinforced.

Mix of Cases

The data from Kansas City show that investigators tend to specialize in particular types of crimes. Table 8-2 shows the percentage of case work time spent on each type of crime and indicates why we have classified detectives into the categories listed in table 8-1. While the figures are specific to the organizational structure adopted in Kansas City, we can point out several observations that are general in their applicability.

First, we can see that homicide detectives have a wide range of responsibilities and in fact spend only half their case-related time on actual homicides. This is because the detail and precision required by most departments for a homicide

Table 8-2
Breakdown of Time Spent on Cases
(In percent)

Homicide Unit	
Homicide	51.2
Aggravated assault	26.6
Dead body	7.3
Common assault	6.4
Suicide	1.1
All other	7.4
Robbery Unit	
Robbery	69.9
Homicide	16.9
All other	13.2
Sex Crimes Unit	
Rape	66.9
Felony sex	10.7
All other	22.3
Auto Theft Unit	
Auto theft	85.4
Other auto crimes	8.7
All other	5.9
Residential Burglary and Larceny Unit	
Residential burglary sepcialist	
Residential burglary	79.2
Miscellaneous burglary	9.0
Larceny	7.9
All other	3.9
Residential burglary and larceny (mixed)	
Residential burglary	40.5
Miscellaneous burglary	6.5
Larceny	39.0
All other	14.0
Commercial Burglary Unit	
Safes specialist	
Safe burglary	29.3
Commercial burglary	15.4
Residential burglary	12.9
Miscellaneous burglary	32.7
Larceny	8.5
All other	1.2
Commercial burglary specialist	
Commercial burglary	27.9
Residential burglary	14.0
Miscellaneous burglary	44.4
All others	13.7
Other detectives in commercial burglary unit	
Burglary	43.0
Larceny	51.4
All other	5.6

Table 8–2 (continued)

General Assignment Unit	
Arson specialist	
Arson	70.2
Bombing	3.9
All other	25.9
Fraud, forgery specialist	
Fraud/embezzlement	25.4
Forgery/counterfeit	45.4
All other	29.2
Fraud, bunco, larceny specialist	
Fraud/embezzlement	39.3
Bunco	10.2
Other larceny	30.7
All other	19.8
Shoplift, pickpocket specialist	
Shoplift	41.5
Other larceny	45.6
All other	12.9

investigation are much greater than for any other type of crime; therefore, any incident that might possibly become a homicide must be treated from the beginning as if it were a homicide. Otherwise it will later be impossible to reconstruct the necessary details. Thus, cases of aggravated assault in which the victim may die are usually handled by homicide detectives, and in some departments they are assigned all aggravated assaults.

Another category shown for the homicide unit is "dead body." In most jurisdictions there is a requirement for unattended deaths to be investigated by the coroner, medical examiner, or police, with the details varying according to the legislation. From the point of view of the homicide unit, there is a danger that a reported "dead body" may subsequently prove to be a homicide, and therefore the detectives are engaged in frequent, but brief, investigations to determine whether there is any indication of foul play. The situation in regard to suicides is similar.

A second general observation from table 8–2 is that whether or not a unit appears to have a specialized function, the detectives within the unit will tend to develop particular types of crimes on which they focus. Thus, the General Assignment Unit in Kansas City, which might be thought to consist of generalist investigators, is actually a mixture of specialists whose crime types do not belong in any other identifiable category.

Workload

Nearly all investigators we have interviewed pointed out to us the enormous workload of cases they had to handle—not as a complaint, but rather as a fact of life. Rarely did we hear that a detective's workload constituted an excessive burden to him. More typically, we might be shown a pile of fifty or so folders representing "active" cases on an investigator's desk, but when a lull in the immediate activity occurred it became readily apparent that the investigator had nothing particular in mind that he wished to do on those cases. The cases were "active" primarily in the sense that they had been assigned to the investigator and were unsolved. They might also be "active" in the sense that the investigator is attempting to recall some of the details of the crimes in the event that similar incidents occur again or the perpetrator is subsequently arrested. But they are not "active" in the sense that any work is being done on them. We call such cases "suspended."

The fact is that many suspended cases never receive any more attention from an investigator than a cursory reading of the crime report, or perhaps a thorough reading and a telephone call. In other words, certain cases are selected for inattention from the start, while other cases are worked on. As mentioned in Chapter 6 some departments have adopted case screening procedures designed to identify those cases that should be worked on because of the presence of "solvability factors." But when such procedures are not used, the detectives make such judgments themselves.

The data from Kansas City confirm and illustrate these observations. In table 8-3 we show, for several crime types, the percentage of cases that detectives worked on during the study period.[13] The figures show that only homicide and rape (and suicide, because it is potentially homicide) are invariably worked on. A few other types of crimes that are universally regarded as serious are worked on in over 60 percent of cases, but many types more likely than not receive less than a half-hour's attention from an investigator (thereby counting as not "worked on"). Since the bulk of crimes fall into these latter categories, well under half of all reported crimes receive any serious attention by an investigator.

The net result is that the average detective does not actually work on a large number of cases each month, even though he may have a backlog of hundreds or thousands of cases that were assigned to him at some time in the past and are still theoretically his responsibility. Table 8-4 shows the number of worked-on cases per detective per month in the various units of the Kansas City Police Department. Some cases are handled jointly by two or more units and have been counted in the workload of each unit in this table. Even so, the number of worked-on cases per detective is generally under one per day, with the exception of the Missing Persons Unit. Of course, some cases involve the work of more than one detective, so the figures in the table are not representative of the number of cases the average detective pays attention to. But if we imagine that each case is assigned to a particular investigator as his responsibility,

---

13. These percentages could not be calculated for all crime types, because the categories used to classify the crimes in the Case Assignment File do not always coincide with categories of reported crimes.

Table 8–3
Percentage of Reported Cases
Worked on by Detectives

Type of Incident	Percent
Homicide	100.0
Rape	100.0
Suicide	100.0
Forgery/counterfeit	90.4
Kidnapping	73.3
Arson	70.4
Auto theft	65.5
Aggravated assault	64.4
Robbery	62.6
Fraud/embezzlement	59.6
Felony sex crimes	59.0
Common assault	41.8
Nonresidential burglary	36.3
Dead body	35.7
Residential burglary	30.0
Larceny	18.4
Vandalism	6.8
Lost property	0.9
All above types together	32.4

Source: Kansas City Case Assignment
File, May–November 1973.

the table shows the average number of cases that an investigator would be responsible for and work on in a month.

Working on Cases

In many departments, arrestees for serious crimes are processed by investigators. This means that investigators necessarily have some work to do on all cleared crimes, and in the case of arrests made by patrol officers, they have little choice about the timing of this activity. By law they are required to complete the processing within a specified period of hours or days.

Other crimes are reported to the investigator with such strong leads that the investigator is nearly compelled to pursue them. An example would be a crime report that gives the name and address of the perpetrator. Such crimes are very likely to be cleared, and then the investigator has additional work to do.

Among the remaining crimes, the investigators choose the ones they will work on by considering both the seriousness of the crime and whether sufficient leads are present to indicate that the chances of clearing the crime are high. As a result, work on cases by investigators has two important characteristics.

Table 8–4

Average Number of Worked-on Cases Per Detective Per Month

Unit	*Number of Cases*
Crimes against persons	9.2
Homicide	11.2
Robbery	7.7
Sex crimes	6.2
Crimes against property	16.9
Auto theft	19.5
Nonresidential burglary	9.4
Residential burglary/larceny	22.9
General assignment	18.6
Incendiary	7.8
Forgery/fraud/bunco	10.4
Shoplifting/pickpocket	20.9
Youth and women's	26.0
Missing persons	88.4

Source: Kansas City Case Assignment File.

Note: A more detailed version of this table appears as table H–2 in Appendix H.

First, the majority of crimes that an investigator works on are cleared, and second, most of the time spent on cleared crimes occurs after the arrest is made.

These two facts are illustrated from the Kansas City data in tables 8–5 and 8–6. Table 8–5 shows the percentage of worked-on crimes that are cleared and, where data were available, compares this with the overall clearance rate for the crime in question. Even for types of crimes with a low clearance rate, the data show that about half or more of the crimes that detectives work on are cleared.[14]

Table 8–6 shows the length of time, in man-hours, that cases of various types received during May-November 1973 in Kansas City.[15] These figures reveal that more time is spent on cleared cases after the arrest than is spent producing the clearance. This is true for almost every type of crime if the detective makes the arrest; and for most types of crimes it is also true that even if a patrol

---

14. In Kansas City the detectives have a special incentive to enter a card for a cleared crime into the case assignment system (thereby causing it to be counted as "worked on"); they will not get credit for the clearance on the monthly statistical report unless they do so.

15. Although the crimes are organized in table 8-6 according to the unit ordinarily assigned such a crime, the man-hours include all time spent on the case by all detectives in all units. A breakdown of case time according to the activity engaged in by the detective is given in Appendix H, table H-4.

Table 8–5
Clearance Rates for Worked-on Crimes

Crime Type	Percent of Reported Crimes Cleared	Percent of Worked-on Crimes Cleared
Homicide	78.1	78.1
Robbery	29.7	47.4
Sex crimes	51.2	55.8
Other crimes against persons	27.7	53.4
Auto-related crimes	22.4	29.5
Nonresidential burglary	21.8	60.1
Residential burglary	15.1	50.2
Larceny	2.3	41.5
Other property crimes	(a)	62.0
Vandalism	4.2	62.7
Fraud/embezzlement/bunco	(a)	55.4
Juvenile crimes	(a)	73.7

Source: Kansas City Case Assignment File, May–November 1973.

Note: A more complete version of this table appears as table H–3 in Appendix H.

[a]Data not available.

officer initially makes the arrest, the detective spends more than his typical pre-clearance time.

Moreover, for every type of case except bank robbery (an unusual crime in that the FBI has concurrent jurisdiction), the amount of effort devoted to cleared cases prior to the arrest is less, on the average, than the amount of effort devoted to those uncleared crimes that are worked on. The difference is statistically significant (at the 0.05 level) for the majority of crime types. We conclude, then, that detective work is not characterized by hard work leading to case solutions. If this were so, the more effort that was devoted to a case, the more likely it would be to be cleared. On the contrary, the data suggest that the cases that get cleared are primarily the easy ones to solve, and most of the investigators' work is a consequence of the fact that an arrest has been made.

Cases that fall in the uncleared category may involve lengthy investigations for several reasons. First, the detectives may have "solved" the case in some sense but are frustrated in their attempts to arrest the perpetrator. An example from our observations follows.

The bank teller noticed R long before he approached her with the .38 revolver partially hidden under a magazine. His unkempt bushy hair caught her attention as did a white patch over his left eye, apparently quite recently affixed; he "had a medicine smell about him." For the past 20 minutes he had been pacing back and forth among the various lines, trying to catch the quickest one to a teller. At times he would stop his furious pacing and step outside, where a man collecting for charity observed both his pacing the street and then placing a call in a nearby phone booth.

Finally reaching the teller, R asked for $4400 in traveler's checks. As she drew out a box of checks, he pulled his gun, warned her not to sound any alarms, and disappeared with the checks.

Without the alarm sounded, no surveillance photographs were made, and an additional camera was malfunctioning. However, a trail of clues was left behind which made identification relatively simple. Both the FBI and the University City Police worked together on the case.

The traveler's checks were numbered, and the bank had a record of these serial numbers. When R tried to cash a check in Las Vegas the next day, he signed his real name, most likely because he would have proper identification to show if asked. The casino manager grew suspicious, and R disappeared, leaving the manager with the check, which was forwarded to the FBI. The FBI ran a handwriting check on this signature compared to that of R's driver's license (pulled by the University City Police). They matched.

Although no usable fingerprints were found in the bank, there were good prints in a nearby telephone booth. These prints matched with army prints of R in FBI files.

Local investigators in the meantime ran a check of local hospitals and clinics, asking if someone with the robber's description received treatment. This venture proved unsuccessful; hospital personnel refused to cooperate. They did not have the time, and besides, they did not want to be involved.

Fortunately, their cooperation was not necessary. Witnesses identified R from his driver's license photograph, and the FBI obtained a warrant for his arrest.

Two weeks after the crime, however, R was in Mexico City, cashing checks.

A second type of investigation that may be lengthy but does not lead to a clearance involves cases where no crime was actually committed. These investigations are often characterized by complex and conflicting evidence, eventually resulting in the conclusion that the crime is unfounded. Such cases are particularly prevalent in the auto theft and sex crimes unit. In some cases the "victim" may be seeking revenge. In automobile theft cases, frequently the investigator goes on a wild goose chase because the car reported stolen was not actually taken unlawfully. Instead, cars reported stolen are often vehicles repossessed for nonpayment of installments, with the owner reporting them stolen just to make trouble. Also, many owners forget that they authorized others to drive their car, or cars are destroyed for the purpose of insurance fraud.

Finally, there is the investigation that is simply unfruitful:

When Bettina S. failed to return from work at her usual hour, her lover K reported her missing to the Campus City Police Department. Her bullet-riddled body was found the next day at the edge of a forest adjacent to a highway, by a man walking his dog.

Table 8-6
Number of Man-Hours of Detective Work

Crime Type	All Cases[a] (avg. time)	Uncleared Cases[a] (avg. time)	Cleared Cases			
			No Initial Patrol Arrest			Initial Patrol Arrest (avg. time)
			Avg. Time Before Clear	Avg. Time After Clear	Total	
Crimes against persons	5.4	8.4[b]	4.6	8.8	13.4	7.9
Homicide	144.6	212.3[b]	46.2	117.5	163.7	27.3
Aggravated assault	5.9	5.2[b]	2.4	5.4	7.8	4.7
Common assault	3.6	3.0[b]	1.6	3.1	4.7	2.8
Rape	20.2	16.3	13.6	15.2	28.8	12.8
Felony sex crimes	7.7	5.8	3.8	6.1	9.9	5.9
Robbery						
Bank	13.2	4.3	10.9	13.1	24.0	4.3
Residence	11.4	10.1	6.3	9.7	16.0	4.3
Taxicab	7.0	4.4	2.6	5.4	8.0	14.9
Concealed weapon	3.6	3.9[b]	0.0	2.0	2.0	3.5
Commercial	13.2	10.2[b]	7.3	12.9	20.2	19.0
Pursesnatch	5.5	4.1[b]	1.1	3.9	5.0	7.8
Strongarm	8.3	6.7[b]	1.7	7.3	9.0	9.3
Outside/street	7.6	5.9	2.3	6.3	8.6	9.3
Miscellaneous	10.2	10.0	2.0	9.3	11.3	9.6
Suicide	5.5					
Dead Body	5.2					
Kidnapping	10.0	6.3	3.4	12.6	16.0	(c)
Shootings	7.9	7.5			(c)	8.5
Crimes against property	5.4	4.6[b]	2.4	5.7	8.1	7.9
Auto theft	4.2	2.9[b]	1.8	7.3	9.1	6.7
Auto accessories	3.7	2.7[b]	1.2	3.3	4.5	4.4
Theft from auto	2.9	2.3[b]	0.7	2.3	3.0	3.4
Other auto	2.3	1.8	0.3	6.1	6.4	(c)
Burglary						
Safe	18.3	18.0	13.7	12.7	26.4	9.7
Residence	6.8	5.4[b]	2.1	6.6	8.7	7.6

Commercial	9.8	9.4[b]	3.9	7.4	11.3	8.7
Miscellaneous	10.5	9.4[b]	3.8	7.0	10.8	12.6
Larceny (all except below)	6.3	4.9	2.9	8.9	11.8	5.0
Larceny bicycle	3.5	2.8[b]	0.8	3.6	4.4	3.8
Larceny commercial	4.9	2.9	1.9	4.9	6.8	4.9
Crimes assigned to general assignment unit	5.3	4.5	2.6	5.5	8.1	4.3
Destructive acts						
Arson	10.1	10.8[b]	4.4	5.8	10.2	6.3
Destruction of property	5.3	5.2	2.1	4.8	6.9	4.1
Bomb or threat	4.1	4.4	0.0	3.6	3.6	(c)
Fraud and larceny						
Fraud/embezzlement	6.0	5.0[b]	2.8	6.0	8.8	5.2
Forgery/counterfeit	6.7	4.5	3.6	6.6	10.2	7.0
Extortion	10.8	9.7			(c)	(c)
Larceny by decit	9.8	(c)			(c)	(c)
Larceny other	6.2	6.0[b]	1.3	5.9	7.2	5.8
Bunco	8.3	8.1	3.4	6.7	10.1	4.6
Shoplifting	4.3	4.9[b]	1.2	4.7	5.9	3.3
Execute warrants	2.7	2.6	0.8	4.5	5.3	2.2
Crimes assigned to youth-women's unit	3.4	3.3[b]	0.4	3.4	3.8	3.0
Trespassing	3.3	2.9[b]	0.0	3.3	3.3	3.4
Disorderly conduct	2.7	3.0[b]	0.0	2.3	2.3	2.9
Incorrigible	2.9	2.7[b]	0.3	3.4	3.7	2.2
Protective custody	2.5	2.4[b]	0.4	2.6	3.0	2.0
Possess drugs	5.1	9.4[b]	0.5	3.9	4.4	3.4
Miscellaneous youth	4.0	4.5[b]	0.8	3.7	4.5	3.0
Miscellaneous women's	2.9	2.4	0.3	3.2	3.5	2.4

Source: Kansas City Case Assignment File, cases received during May–November 1973.

Note: Uncleared cases account for 40.2% of all detective casework time; cleared crimes account for 12.4% before clearance, 47.4% starting with clearance.

[a] Includes only cases on which detectives reported some time worked.

[b] Time spent on uncleared cases is significantly higher than time spent prior to clearance on cleared cases with no initial patrol arrest.

[c] Insufficient data.

Because of certain circumstances under which they lived together, Homicide suspected K. He denied the crime, and after interrogation bragged to a friend that "there is one clue the police don't know about." Several days later, K flunked the polygraph test as he was asked certain questions about the murder. Two weeks later, K presented a life insurance claim on Bettina S., who had stipulated in a letter one month before her murder that the proceeds should go to K and not her son, as originally arranged.

Although Homicide is convinced of K's guilt, as yet there is no court admissible evidence. What they do have is a case file that includes detailed photographs of the crime scene and of the woman lying where she was found, extensive photographs about and reports of the autopsy, and reports of ballistic experts on the type of gun that killed her. All in her neighborhood and who may have had contact with her were questioned and the interviews recorded. The crime scene was thoroughly examined by evidence technicians. Currently, all leads are exhausted and Homicide is waiting and hoping that the murder gun is found.

In sum, then, the time spent by investigators on case work falls primarily into two categories. Some investigations are lengthy but do not result in a clearance. Others lead to a clearance after a small amount of work but entail substantial efforts by the investigator once the crime is cleared. Some activities involved in the latter type of work are illustrated by the following example from our observations.

The ruse was an old one. Two black males captured an appliance delivery truck by pulling alongside the moving vehicle and indicating to the driver that his rear door was open. When the driver and his helper stopped to check the door, the suspects pulled guns, made them drive to some unknown location to unload the merchandise, and then drove the victims around for a while before releasing them and fleeing with the truck.

After being assigned to the case, Detective Dick and his partner interviewed the victims, who described one hijacker as wearing tennis whites, having a prominent scar on his left leg, and carrying a sawed-off shotgun with a red stock. As was department policy for hijacking and shooting cases only, lengthy and detailed statements were taken from each victim by Dick and his partner. The statements were carefully typed by the detectives as the victims recounted the events of the crime. Since the men and goods had been transported over state lines during the course of the robbery, the FBI was called in. The only help they provided was a helicopter for Dick and his partner to search for the alley where the merchandise was unloaded, to no avail.

The second day after the crime, an alarm was sounded on the stolen vehicle. When found, the vehicle was processed by the local crime laboratory, but with negative results since it had already been stripped by juveniles in the area. The latent prints lifted were not sufficient for identification purposes.

But for chance, the case would have ended here. Instead, several months later, a patrolman spotted a reported stolen automobile being driven down a highway. He stopped the car and as part of district policy he performed a complete inventory of its contents. Upon finding a sawed-off shotgun in the back seat, the patrolman requested a robbery cruiser; Dick happened to be in it.

When he saw the car's contents—tennis whites and a shotgun with a red stock—he remembered a similar MO, although he could not pinpoint the case until he went back through his records. One suspect matched the description given by the victims of the robbery/kidnapping.

The next day, the suspect's mug shot was one of a series of ten shown to the victims; he got one positive identification and one "possible." On a hunch, he showed the mugs to a robbery victim from another case and got another positive ID. At this time the case was cleared.

Although intuition tells that this case would quickly move to a just ending, this was far from what actually happened.

Local procedure requires a judicial order if the suspect is to appear in a lineup. A lineup was scheduled to take place in four days; the victims took time off from work to come down to headquarters to make the identification. But everyone was at the lineup but the suspect; the wrong man had been sent over from the jail.

After several days and much aggravation, another court appearance had to be scheduled in order to hold another lineup. However, the order was never given.

On the day of the preliminary hearing, Dick went to court and requested the case jackets on all the cases; only one was available—that for unauthorized use of a motor vehicle. Although Dick and his partner spent the whole day searching for them, the case jackets on the more serious crimes—armed robbery and kidnapping—were lost or stolen, either intentionally or accidentally by someone inside or outside the system.

Although Dick wanted to appear before the Grand Jury the following day to explain the situation, he was told that he could not be scheduled for a week. By the time Dick appeared before the Grand Jury, the defendant was out on bail and could not be found; the subpoena ordering his appearance for a lineup could not be served.

Over the next weeks, several robberies following the now familiar MO were committed. During their daily morning briefing about all suspects in custody, Dick arranged for mug shots of X to be shown. By chance several days later, X was spotted by two detectives cashing personal checks in a bank; they remembered him from mug shots.

X was again taken into custody and another lineup scheduled. During these events, Dick was on vacation. Paperwork about the lineup had been left on his desk, where it remained untouched until Dick came back to work a week after the scheduled lineup, for which, needless to say, no victims showed since none were notified.

After further administrative wrangling and stops and starts, the lineup was finally held. There had been only three victims to schedule for the aborted lineup three months earlier; now there were seventeen! Of these, over a half showed, with five positive IDs. With the D.A.'s insistence on exact identification ("it looks like the offender" will not do), Dick worries if his case will stick. In the meantime, X has shaved off his beard.

Duration of Cases

While the preceding example describes a case in which some sort of activity by an investigator took place sporadically over a period of several months, such cases are the exception rather than the rule. The vast majority of cases that a detective works on are handled in the course of a single day, after which they are either cleared or suspended. Only a few types of crimes fail to follow this pattern: homicide, rape, safe burglary, commercial robbery and forgery/counterfeiting.

We have already seen in table 8-6 that the number of investigative man-hours devoted to crimes other than those just listed is quite small in Kansas City, averaging under five man-hours for those that are actually worked on. Table 8-7 indicates that these hours are not spread out over a long period of time, but are concentrated in the first day or two after the crime is reported. Over 86 percent of cases are suspended by the end of the first week.

Concluding Remarks

The investigator's daily routine cannot be characterized as devoted primarily to piecing together clues for the purpose of solving crimes. For the most part he operates in a reactive mode, responding to externally generated events that require an action on his part. Administrative activities, service to the public, and other work not related to cases consumes nearly half of his time.

A large number of incidents come to his attention, but many of them receive little or no work and simply sit on his desk constituting part of his caseload. If an arrest has already been made, or it is apparent from the crime report that a limited amount of work will result in an arrest, then the case is pursued and most of the work involves post-arrest processing, writing reports, documenting evidence, and the like. A small number of cases are pursued simply because of their seriousness or importance, but it does not appear that the chances of clearance are enhanced in proportion to the amount of work. Further elaboration and explanation of this phenomenon will appear in Chapter 9.

Table 8-7
Length of Time Before Case Was Suspended[a]

Item	Average (days)	Percent Active						
		One Day	2-7 Days	1-2 Weeks	2-4 Weeks	4-8 Weeks	8-12 Weeks	12-16 Weeks
All cases together	3.8	72.7	14.9	5.2	4.7	2.3	0.2	
Homicide Unit								
Homicide	18.0	0.0	38.2	21.8	18.2	12.7	7.3	1.8
Aggravated assault	3.4	61.1	28.4	5.2	4.3	0.9		
Suicide	1.1	92.0	8.0					

Item	Average (days)	Percent Active						
		One Day	2-7 Days	1-2 Weeks	2-4 Weeks	4-8 Weeks	8-12 Weeks	12-16 Weeks
Robbery								
Bank	2.7	63.6	27.3	9.1				
Commercial	8.0	47.1	24.2	10.3	12.1	5.4	0.9	
Residence	3.9	57.8	26.5	7.2	7.2	1.2		
Outside-street	5.1	56.7	21.3	12.1	6.7	3.3		
Strongarm	5.9	52.7	24.8	10.1	8.5	3.9		
Pursesnatch	5.2	54.1	21.6	16.2	5.4	2.7		
Miscellaneous	5.1	55.6	22.2	9.9	11.1	1.2		
Sex Crimes								
Rape	9.4	36.7	34.3	10.9	7.7	8.5	1.6	
Felony sex crimes	5.5	51.8	27.7	8.0	8.0	4.5		
Kidnapping	6.0	38.5	38.5	7.7	7.7	7.7		
Auto								
Theft	4.7	69.6	13.5	5.5	7.4	3.9		
Accessories	4.4	76.0	6.2	7.0	8.5	2.3		
Nonresidential Burglary								
Safes	9.4	40.5	24.3	10.8	10.8	13.5		
Miscellaneous	6.4	59.1	17.2	8.6	10.5	3.9	0.5	
Other commercial	5.5	62.2	15.7	10.9	7.8	3.0		
Residential Burglary & Larceny								
Residential	4.5	65.2	18.6	7.2	5.9	2.9		
Larceny	5.1	64.5	18.2	7.3	4.9	4.7		
Incendiary								
Arson	5.9	51.3	26.3	13.2	6.6	1.3	1.3	
Forgery, Fraud, Bunco								
Fraud/embezzlement	6.1	52.9	25.2	9.8	6.8	4.5	0.8	
Forgery/counterfeit	8.1	44.9	23.6	11.8	13.4	5.9		
Extortion	3.4	60.0	20.0	20.0				
Bunco	5.1	50.9	32.1	5.7	7.5	3.8		

Source: Kansas City Case Assignment File, cases reported in May–November 1973.

[a]A case is defined to be suspended if 30 days passed without any activity by an investigator on the case.

9   How Crimes Are Solved

We have seen in Chapter 8 that the typical cleared crime entails only a small number of investigative man-hours prior to clearance and that, of the total working hours of an investigator, only a small proportion (7 percent in Kansas City) is devoted to activities that lead to clearing crimes. In addition, we know from our survey that most clearance rates of a police department are not correlated with the workload of investigators, when controlled for the workload of patrol officers; and from the work of Greenwood (1970) in New York City, that clearance rates of individual investigative units are not correlated with their workloads. These findings suggest the following hypotheses:

1. Many activities of investigators contribute little to the clearance of crimes.
2. Some characteristics of a crime itself, or of events surrounding the crime that are beyond the control of investigators, determine whether it will be cleared in most instances.

In this chapter we demonstrate the truth of the second hypothesis and, by implication, the truth of the first. Basically, we find that some crimes are easy to clear, with either no work by an investigator or with small amounts of routine administrative activity. The remaining crimes, which constitute the majority, are difficult, if not impossible, to solve, regardless of the efforts expended by the police. Some of these receive no attention by investigators, while others are pursued diligently. But the number of difficult crimes that are eventually cleared is so small, when they are compared to the number of cleared crimes that were easy to solve, that overall clearance statistics are little affected by the efforts devoted to them.

These findings lead to questions about the role of investigators and their contribution to achieving the goals of a police department that will be discussed at the end of the chapter.

For this analysis we selected samples of cleared crimes in six police departments and determined, by reading the case folders, how the crime was solved. In instances where the written documentation was inadequate for this determination, the investigator in charge of the case was interviewed. In all cases we accepted the department's determination of whether the crime was cleared or not. We defined the case to be "solved" at the point the police knew the identity of the perpetrator(s), even if additional work was needed to locate the perpetrators or to establish the facts needed to prove guilt in court.

At the start, we had no preconceived notions as to appropriate categories of answers to the question "How was this crime solved?" So we simply recorded all the facts, circumstances, actions, and evidence that had been used to solve the crime. At the same time, we did not know whether the organization of the department, the region of the country in which it was located, or the season of the year would be related to crime solution, so we began with a single type of crime, namely robbery, and collected data in four police departments: Berkeley, Los Angeles, Miami, and Washington, D.C. The months selected for study differed among departments. Within the selected months, crimes were listed according to the order in which they were reported to the police, and a systematic 50 percent sample of the cleared crimes was chosen for analysis.[1] The sample sizes are shown in table 9-1.

After reviewing these cases and concluding that there were no apparent geographical or temporal variations of relevance for this study, a sample of

Table 9-1
Data Sources by Crime Type

| | Departments | | | |
| | First Four[a] | Long Beach[b] | Kansas City[c] | |
Crime Type	Sample Size	Sample Size	Sample Size	Total Cases
Forgery/fraud	–	22	14	312
Auto theft	–	19	7	432
Theft	–	10	10	828
Commercial burglary	–	10	10	372
Residential burglary	–	20	14	686
Robbery	5	–	10	349
	22			
	8			
	28			
Felony morals	–	11	9	178
Aggravated assault	–	10	11	716
Homicide	–	7	7	46
Total	63	109	92	3919

[a]Robbery data are from Los Angeles, Ca. (cleared cases reported in the Wilshire Area in July 1974); Berkeley, Ca. (cleared cases reported May/June 1974); Washington, D.C. (cleared cases reported October 1974); and Miami, Fla. (cleared cases reported 1973-1974).

[b]For all crime types except residential burglary, these data are cleared cases reported October 1974; residential burglary, cleared cases reported July/August 1974.

[c]Cleared cases reported May/November 1973.

---

1. That is, every second cleared crime was chosen.

cleared crimes other than robbery was selected from a single police department: Long Beach, California. The crimes were categorized in accordance with the organization of investigative units in Long Beach: forgery/fraud, auto theft, theft, commercial burglary, residential burglary, robbery, felony morals, aggravated assault, and homicide. As in the case of the first four departments, we examined a systematic 50 percent sample of cleared cases reported during a given time period in Long Beach.

After analysis of these cases, it became apparent that many cleared cases fall into categories that can be identified from the Kansas City Case Assignment File[2] without reading the case folders. Thus, rather than continuing to sample from the totality of cleared crimes, we processed the Case Assignment File so as to identify the subset of cleared cases for which it was necessary to examine the case folders in order to determine how the crime was solved. A 10 percent random sample of this subset was selected, and the case folders were read as in the other five departments.

To permit comparisons between data from Kansas City and data from the other police departments, the crimes in Kansas City were organized into the same categories as used previously, even though they did not correspond to the organizational structure in Kansas City. Table H-5 in Appendix H shows the relationship between crime types as defined in Chapter 8 and the crime categories used in this chapter.

Data from First Five Departments

From the incident reports and earlier studies[3] it was obvious that for many crimes, the identity of the suspect was available at the time of the first report to the responding patrolmen—i.e., the case was solved without any detective involvement. Therefore, our first step was to divide the cases into two categories: initial identification and no initial identification. *Initial identification* occurs when there is an arrest at the scene of the crime or when the information required for clearance is present in the crime report, i.e., a victim or witness either furnishes the name and address of a suspect or some uniquely linking evidence. If only a name or only an address is given, the case was not placed in this category. To be considered "uniquely linking," the evidence had to correlate directly with the suspect's name and address (e.g., an automobile license or an employee badge number). *No initial identification* includes all other cleared cases.

The results from tabulating the data in this manner are shown in table 9-2. From stealing credit cards to murder, the majority of cleared cases in our sample had both quickly identifiable and locatable suspect(s). With the exception of

---

2. See Chapter 8 for a description of this file.

3. See, for example, Isaacs (1967), Conklin (1972), and Feeney et al. (1973).

Table 9–2
Suspect Identification in Cleared Cases by Level of Investigative Effort

Crime Type	Routine: Initial Identification %	Routine: Initial Identification N	Possibly Nonroutine: No Initial Identification %	Possibly Nonroutine: No Initial Identification N	Total %	Total N
Forgery/fraud	91	20	9	2	100	22
Auto theft	47	9	53	10	100	19
Theft	70	7	30	3	100	10
Commercial burglary	80	8	20	2	100	10
Residential burglary	80	16	20	4	100	20
Robbery	52	33	48	30	100	63
Felony morals	73	8	27	3	100 •	11
Aggravated assault	100	10	–	–	100	10
Homicide	43	3	57	4	100	7

Source: Review of case folders for sample cases from Berkeley, Long Beach, Los Angeles, Miami, and Washington, D.C.

two crime types (robbery and auto theft) less than one-third of all cleared cases had no suspect immediately identifiable.

Initial Identification

In cases with initial identification, *investigator involvement* in case clearance is minimal, and therefore we say that the solution is, at best, "routine." Either the suspect is already apprehended (e.g., by arrest at scene of crime) or some clerical effort on the part of the detective is needed for apprehension (e.g., issuing a "want" to patrol officers to pick up a suspect completely identified by a victim, or contacting another agency to find out the name and address matching a particular automobile license number).

Table 9-3 displays the circumstances in which an initial identification was obtained. The first two categories ("patrol capture" and "held at scene by citizen") involve an arrest at the scene of the crime, either through patrol action or citizen involvement. This method of solution occurs with particular frequency in cleared cases of commercial burglary. Typically, a patrol in the immediate vicinity of a just-activitated burglar alarm is able to respond quickly enough to catch the suspects.

Most solved cases of residential burglary, felony morals, and aggravated assault are solved because a victim or witness knows who and where the suspect is (see table 9-3). In residential burglaries, for example, an estranged husband removes property from his wife's home, or a roommate moves out and takes some of the other person's furniture. In aggravated assault and felony

Table 9-3
Initial Identification: Method of Solution

Crime Type	Patrol Capture %	Patrol Capture N	Held at Scene (by Citizen) %	Held at Scene (by Citizen) N	Complete ID by V/W %	Complete ID by V/W N	Uniquely Linking Evidence %	Uniquely Linking Evidence N	Total %	Total N
Forgery/fraud	5	1	14	3	9	2	64	14	91	20
Auto theft	26	5	–	–	16	3	5	1	47	9
Theft	30	3	–	–	20	2	20	2	70	7
Commercial burglary	70	7	–	–	10	1	–	–	80	8
Residential burglary	10	2	5	1	40	8	25	5	80	16
Robbery	13	8	5	3	21	13	14	9	52	33
Felony morals	9	1	–	–	55	6	9	1	73	8
Aggravated assault	40	4	–	–	50	5	10	1	100	10
Homicide	–	–	–	–	29	2	14	1	43	3

Source: Review of case folders for sample cases from Berkeley, Los Angeles, Long Beach, Miami, and Washington, D.C.
Note: Percentages may not add to total because of rounding error.

morals, the suspect and victim are usually acquainted—many times they are actually related or at least living together. In the former crime type, a father may beat his son, or vice versa. In the latter, a mother may report her husband or boyfriend for having sexual relations with her child.

Cleared forgery/fraud cases are most frequently solved by use of uniquely linking evidence, as shown in table 9-3. In such cases the suspect typically signs a personal check against either a closed account or insufficient funds. The uniquely linking evidence is the identification presented by the suspect when he cashes the check, corroborated when a handwriting expert matches the signature on the check to the signature on the suspect's driver's license.

No Initial Identification

We now look at the possibly nonroutine cases, i.e., those cases in which a suspect is not identified in the initial crime report and which may therefore require action by the investigator to solve. Several types of effort are involved in the solution to these cases. In some instances, the investigator has only to follow obvious leads to solve the crime. For example, the disgruntled wife of a burglar notifies the police that her husband committed this crime and that he and the stolen goods can be found at his girlfriend's house.[4] In yet other instances, what

---

4. We categorize the solution to this case as a tip. See the more detailed discussion that follows.

might be an inherently difficult if not impossible crime to solve is solved because of certain procedures that the department has adopted. For example, mug shot files are organized and maintained in such a way that the victim is able to make *cold hits*. Or, the department has computerized information about stolen cars, allowing a *spontaneous* solution to cases when a stolen car is spotted. Or, the department holds daily briefings and lineups concerning recent crimes, criminals, and their methods of operation (MO), allowing investigator recognition of MO on some cases without an initially identifiable suspect. In these types of cases, investigator action is characterized as "routine," even though the actions involved may be routine only to an investigator. The solution to all other cases involves "nonroutine" investigative effort.

Table 9–4 examines the principal method of solution for crimes in which there is no initial identification of the suspect. The categories of solution are discussed below. Keep in mind that the labels for the routine cases are not in and of themselves routine. That is, the use of fingerprints to solve a case does not mean that the case is routinely solved. What we considered was *how* the fingerprints were used. In the following discussion, this distinction should become clear.

Fingerprints. In one instance, the victim named the person he believed responsible for the crime, and gave reasons for his suspicion. Although the suspect could not be found, his fingerprints (on file because of a previous record) were matched with those found at the scene of the crime, and on this basis alone, the case was cleared. This case was classified as routine because only routine processing of the latent prints was necessary for case solution. Any instance where a fingerprint match is made from a cold search, for example, is classified as "special action," described below.

Tip. Although investigators often speak of "their informants" as being essential to their work in solving crimes, the case we examined did not bear this out.[5] It may very well be that for these classes of crimes, informers are not used at all, or are not used with any great frequency.

In the single robbery case from our sample that falls into the category of "tips," the informant was a citizen volunteering information about a crime he witnessed rather than a person "cultivated" as an informant (and perhaps paid) by robbery investigators. The homicide cases in our sample were closed on the basis of anonymous callers identifying the culprit. In one instance, three years after the murder, an informant called a newspaper that had a "citizen alert" program and revealed the murderer's identity. The other anonymous call was made unsolicited to the police station, the caller's motive possibly revenge.

---

5. However, the sample size is not large enough to assert that informants are not used.

Table 9-4
No Initial Identification: Method of Solution

Crime Type	Routine												Nonroutine				Total	
	Prints		Tip		Mug Shot/ Other Picture or Lineup		M.O. (only)		Spontaneous		Unrelated Interrogation		Special Action		Unknown[a]			
	%	N	%	N	%	N	%	N	%	N	%	N	%	N	%	N	%	N
Forgery/fraud	–	–	–	–	9	2	–	–	–	–	–	–	–	–	–	–	9	2
Auto theft	–	–	–	–	–	–	–	–	47	9	5	1	–	–	–	–	53	10
Theft	–	–	–	–	30	3	–	–	–	–	–	–	–	–	–	–	30	3
Commercial burglary	–	–	–	–	–	–	–	–	10	1	–	–	10	1	–	–	20	2
Residential burglary	5	1	–	–	–	–	–	–	15	3	–	–	–	–	–	–	20	4
Robbery	–	–	2	1	27	17	3	2	5	3	2	1	10	6	–	–	48	30
Felony morals	–	–	–	–	9	1	–	–	–	–	–	–	9	1	9	1	27	3
Aggravated assault	–	–	–	–	–	–	–	–	–	–	–	–	–	–	–	–	–	–
Homicide	–	–	12	2	6	1	–	–	–	–	6	1	–	–	–	–	23	4

Source: Review of case folders for sample cases from Berkeley, Los Angeles, Long Beach, Miami, and Washington, D.C.

Note: Percentages may not add to 100 because of rounding error.

[a]The case file omits information on how the case is solved.

Mug Shot/Lineup. For crimes that were cleared, this investigative method appeared to be the most significant in closing cases in such crime categories as theft and robbery. It involves several different kinds of actions, requiring differing degrees of investigative involvement.

In one-fourth of these cases, the investigator recognized a familiar MO, and on that basis, pulled mug shots that enabled positive identification of the suspect. Other cases were cleared because the suspect was arrested and on the basis of that arrest, his mug shots were shown to victims of similar crimes in the hopes of making multiple clearances. Sometimes a "hit" was made from random showing of mug shots, and at other times, a victim or witness knew the name of a suspect, and if the suspect had a previous record, mug shots could be pulled for identification.

Sometimes a picture other than a mug shot was used. For example, in one case the victim believed he had seen the suspects at the school where he worked. The investigator had the victim leaf through a school yearbook, from which the victim positively identified the culprits. In another robbery case, a taxi driver identified his robber by accident. While reading the newspaper, he saw her picture, which had been published concerning another case.

Modus Operandi (MO). Two robbery cases in the sample were cleared on the basis of matching MO. That is, an arrested suspect either admitted to other robberies or the case was cleared anyhow, because of similarities between the crime in the sample and the crime for which the suspect was arrested. It is certainly possible that the crime for which the suspect was originally arrested was solved through "special action" on the part of the investigator. However, we only looked at the crime that was part of the sample; in this case the solution was routine, regardless of how the original crime was solved.

Spontaneous Solution. In some of these cases, the property was located and *then* the case was cleared. Either the suspect was arrested on another charge, and subsequently found in possession of stolen goods, or an automobile was stopped because of a traffic violation and stolen property was found in the car. For the automobile theft cases in our sample, a suspect did not have to be found to clear the case; the case was sometimes cleared based on recovery of automobile.

Some instances involved the victim's locating the suspect (at some point after the commission of the crime) and notifying the police. Either the victim acted as his own investigator, carefully tracking down clues that led to the culprit, or the victim "accidentally" spotted his assailant and notified police.

Unrelated Interrogation. In these cases routine questioning of the suspect led to a confession. For example, in an auto theft case, a man took his damaged car to a repair shop and borrowed a loaner which he kept (having no money to retrieve his own car). Through an error, the loaner car was not on a hot list or in any information system, even though the owner reported it stolen. After being stopped for a traffic violation and asked for the vehicle registration, the suspect admitted that it was not his car.

Special Action. All cases requiring more than procedural investigative skill are classified as needing "special action" for solution. Even these cases fail to read like the classic detective stories of popular fiction because even when extraordinary effort or initiative is required, the case is usually solved in a short time. Persistence is to be found in only the more sensational homicides.

A store owner reports the theft of two guns valued at over $200. The guns were locked away in a special place in the store—and the owner suspects someone, Y, who had been to the store many times without buying anything, and who knew about the guns. Y's prints are lifted from a window broken to gain entry to the store. A check of the neighborhood points to a nearby gas station where Y is known to hang out. Here he conducts his "business," offering to sell certain goods (e.g., calculators) cheaply. The police set Y up by having an undercover man pretend to be interested in buying guns; Y offers to sell the hot guns. The goods are recovered, and Y arrested.

Other cases require less complex actions. For example, a robbery was committed in which the suspect had a very distinctive hairdo and facial features. The investigator put out a bulletin to patrol units with the suspect's description; several days later a patrol unit picked up the suspect within a few blocks of the crime. Although this case certainly illustrates the results of good interaction between investigator and patrol units, it is also an example of investigator initiative.

The data in table 9-4 suggests that when there is no initial identification of the suspect, most cases are solved either because the solution is obvious or because the department has developed procedures that have "routinized" methods of suspect identification.

Data from Kansas City

When we analyzed the Long Beach data for crimes other than robbery, we found no special action cases whatsoever in our sample for several crime categories. While this permitted us to conclude that special action cases are uncommon, the sample sizes in any single crime category were sufficiently small that no very precise estimates could be obtained of how often special action cases occur. For example, in the theft category there is a reasonable chance (better than 1 in 20) that over one-quarter of the Long Beach clearances could be special action despite the fact that none appeared in the sample.

To obtain better estimates, a larger sample would be required. In addition, if some special action cases appeared in a larger sample, we would then have some idea of their characteristics. However, the process of selecting a sample, retrieving the appropriate case folders, and reading the files (plus interviewing the investigator when necessary) was sufficiently time-consuming that we were unable to continue sampling from the totality of cases. Instead, we developed a method for processing the Kansas City Case Assignment File so as to separate out cleared cases that were extremely unlikely to involve any special action. Then we sampled cases from the remaining group, thereby enhancing the probability that cases of special action would be found in the sample. The sampling design is illustrated in figure 9-1.

Basically, three types of cases were assumed to fall into the routine category (i.e., *not* special action) based on the information in the computer file. Type 1 consisted of incidents that appeared in the file with a clearance credited to the patrol force on the first day the detective worked on the case. Many of these clearances were recorded on the same day that the crime was reported, and therefore were very likely to represent on-scene arrests by patrol officers.[6] In addition to these, the Type 1 cases include some later patrol arrests (based perhaps on pickups issued by a detective) that were assumed to be routine because the detective did not record any time spent on the case prior to the arrest.

Type 2 consisted of a small number of incidents cleared by patrol after a detective had worked on the case, suspended activity for 30 days or more, and did not work on the case again until the arrest was made. These were assumed to represent "spontaneous" solutions, which have been described above.

Type 3 consisted of incidents that were cleared by an investigator with little work. We defined the amount of work to be "little" if two hours or less were spent on all activities other than arrest processing, court and prosecutor time, and writing reports; this includes time spent after arrest as well as before arrest.

After these three types of cases were eliminated, 24.6 percent of the incidents remained as "possibly nonroutine." We selected a random 10 percent sample from this group and reviewed the case folders. The resulting sample sizes have already been displayed in table 9-1.[7]

After the sample was chosen, we found that some on-scene patrol arrests had been erroneously classified as "possibly nonroutine," based on incorrect entries in the data file. We therefore adjusted our estimates of the number of "possibly nonroutine" cases downward slightly, resulting in the figures shown

6. The file does not have a code for "on-scene arrest," but we assumed that clearances by patrol recorded on the date the crime was reported were on-scene arrests. To the extent that a few instances of fast investigative work, coupled with good interaction between the detective and a patrol officer, were erroneously included in this category, they are counterbalanced by on-scene arrests that happened not to be recorded until the next day and therefore failed to be categorized as on-scene arrests.

7. In a random 10 percent sample, each incident has one chance in 10 of being selected, but it will not necessarily happen that the sample size is exactly one-tenth of the number from which the sample is taken. In this case, 92 cases were selected out of 963.

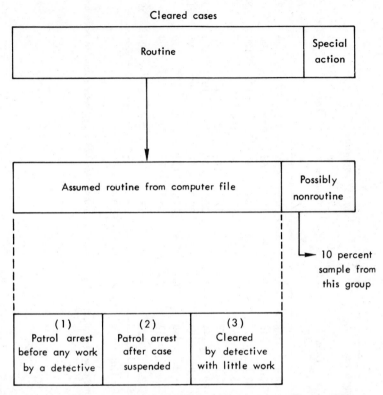

Cleared cases

| Routine | Special action |

| Assumed routine from computer file | Possibly nonroutine |

→ 10 percent sample from this group

| (1) Patrol arrest before any work by a detective | (2) Patrol arrest after case suspended | (3) Cleared by detective with little work |

Figure 9-1. Schematic representation of sampling design in Kansas City.

in table 9-5. In this table, Type 1 and Type 2 cases have been coalesced into a single column labeled "patrol clearances."

Table 9-5 not only summarizes the number of cases in the groups from which we sampled in Kansas City, but also indicates the extent to which patrol officers contribute to clearances in each crime category. Overall, 50.5 percent of clearances were produced by patrol officers, of which 9.5 percent (or 4.8 percent of all clearances) involved a half-hour or more of work by a detective that may have led to the patrol arrest.

After reading the case folders, two special action cases were found in the sampled robberies, two in the commercial burglaries, and one in the homicides; no special action cases were found in the other six categories. Thus, we did not succeed in finding examples of special action cases in crime categories where none were found in Long Beach. However, the sampling design in Kansas City did permit obtaining better statistical limits on the maximum fraction of cases that could be special action, as shown in table 9-6. Two estimates of the percentage of cleared cases that are special action are shown in the table: (a) the best

Table 9-5
Level of Investigator Effort: Kansas City

| | Assumed Routine from Computer File | | | | | | Possibly Nonroutine | | | | | | | |
| | Patrol Clearances | | Investigator Clearances | | Total | | Patrol Clearances | | Investigator Clearances | | Total | | Total | |
Crime Type	%	N	%	N	%	N	%	N	%	N	%	N	%	N
Forgery/fraud	42.0	131	27.9	87	69.9	218	9.3	29	20.8	65	30.1	94	100	312
Auto theft	48.6	210	31.5	136	80.1	346	4.6	20	15.3	66	19.9	86	100	432
Theft	54.5	452	33.1	274	87.7	726	3.3	27	9.1	75	12.3	102	100	828
Commercial burglary	33.6	125	41.9	156	75.5	281	4.6	17	19.9	74	24.4	91	100	372
Residential burglary	43.7	300[a]	37.6	258	81.3	558[a]	1.3	10[a]	17.2	118	18.5	127[a]	100	686
Robbery	40.7	142[a]	29.2	102	69.9	244[a]	4.0	14[a]	26.1	91	30.1	105[a]	100	349
Felony morals	30.3	54	18.5	33	48.8	87	11.2	20	39.9	71	51.1	91	100	178
Aggravated assault	50.7	363[a]	26.1	187	76.8	550[a]	6.1	43[a]	17.2	123	23.3	167[a]	100	716
Homicide	28.3	13	–	–	28.3	13	15.2	7	56.5	26	71.7	33	100	46
Total	45.7	1790[a]	31.5	1233	77.2	3023[a]	4.8	187[a]	18.1	709	22.9	896[a]	100	3919

Note: Numbers may not add to 100 because of rounding error. Crime types refer to mixtures defined in Appendix H.

[a]Estimated number. These numbers were adjusted after some cases sampled from the "possibly nonroutine" category were found to have been arrests by patrol at the scene of the crime.

Table 9-6
Special Action Cases
(Percent of all cleared cases)

Crime Type	First Five Departments[a] Sample Estimate	Maximum Estimate at 95% Confidence	Kansas City Sample Estimate	Maximum Estimate at 95% Confidence
Forgery/fraud	0	12.7	0	5.7
Auto theft	0	14.6	0	6.9
Theft	0	25.9	0	3.2
Commercial burglary	10	39.4	4.9	12.4
Residential burglary	0	13.9	0	3.5
Robbery	9.5	15.6	7.1	16.6
Felony morals	9.1	36.4	0	14.5
Aggravated assault	0	25.9	0	5.9
Homicide	0	34.8	10.2	37.3
All Types[b]			1.3	2.7

[a]Los Angeles and Berkeley, Ca.; Washington, D.C.; Miami, Fla.; Long Beach, Ca.

[b]This figure is shown for Kansas City only and reflects the relative numbers of cleared cases of each type in that city.

estimate based on the sample design,[8] and (b) the maximum estimate with 95 percent confidence.[9]

We see from table 9-6 that in Kansas City, at most 2.7 percent of cleared crimes are solved by special action. (The maximum estimate for the total is smaller than the maximum estimate for any one of the crime types, because the total sample size was comparatively large, namely 92.) Moreover, the estimates are now sharp enough for us to distinguish certain crime types as being substantially less likely than others to be solved by special action. These are forgery/fraud, automobile theft, theft, residential burglary, and aggravated assault, all of which have less than 7 percent solved by special action in Kansas City.

---

8. If a sample of size S is taken from the totality of all cases of a given crime type, and A special action cases are found, the sample estimate is simply $100 \times A/S$. (The number 100 converts a fraction to a percent.) In the design used in Kansas City, a sample S is taken from n "possibly nonroutine" cases out of a total of N, and the sample estimate is then $100 \times (A/S) \times (n/N)$.

9. Suppose no special action cases are found in a sample of size S taken from n cases. If p is the true fraction of special action cases, the probability of finding none of them in the sample is $(1 - p)^S$. Thus, p could be as large as $P = 1 - (0.05)^{1/S}$ and we would still have a 5 percent chance of finding none of them in the sample. The "maximum estimate with 95 percent confidence" is thus $100 \times P \times n/N$. (For the first five departments, $N = n$; for Kansas City, N is the total number of cleared incidents of the crime type in question.) A similar calculation can be performed if one special action case is found in the sample, etc.

Commercial burglaries, robberies, felony morals, and particularly homicides may be somewhat more amenable to solution by nonroutine actions. However, even in these categories the typical crime was solved routinely.

Table 9-6 also reveals a striking similarity in the findings for Kansas City as compared to the other five departments, despite the differences among cities and sample designs. Indeed, in every instance the sample estimate from the first five departments falls well within the maximum estimate for Kansas City, so there is no statistically significant difference between the two sets of estimates.

The sample design in Kansas City also permits us to obtain rough estimates of the fraction of cleared cases that were solved by initial identification in Kansas City. We have already indicated how the number of on-scene arrests can be estimated directly from the computer file. To estimate roughly the number of cases with complete identification by victim or witness and the number with uniquely linking evidence, we used the proportions of such cases found in the sample and applied them to the collection of all cases other than on-scene arrest or special action, as shown in figure 9-2. This method should produce conservative (i.e., low) estimates for the fraction of cases with initial identification, since we did not sample from cases cleared by investigators with little work.

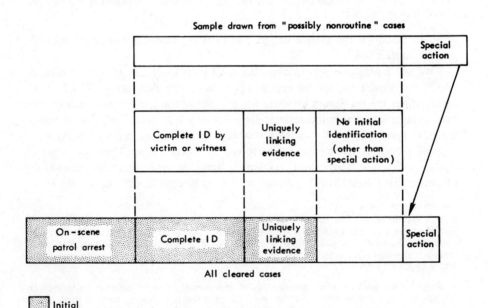

Figure 9-2. Schematic representation of method used to obtain conservative estimate of initial identification cases in Kansas City

Such cases are presumably more likely to involve an initial identification than the cases from which we did sample.

However, even these conservative estimates, shown in table 9-7, yield approximately the same fraction of cases solved by initial identification as was found in the other five departments.[10] By comparison with table 9-3, the explanation appears to be that more cases are cleared by on-scene patrol arrest in Kansas City than in the other cities. In any event, the Kansas City data again confirm that the great majority of cleared crimes are solved because the identity of the perpetrator is already known when the crime report reaches the investigator. The main job for the investigator in these cases is to locate and apprehend the perpetrator, and to assemble evidence adequate to charge him.

Typical Cases

We now discuss each of the crime types to give a clearer picture of routine and nonroutine cases. We begin with the crime types for which we were unable to find an example of a special action solution in any of our samples: forgery/fraud, automobile theft, theft, residential burglary, and aggravated assault.

Table 9-7
Method of Solution for Cleared Cases
(In percent)

Crime Type	Arrest at Scene	Complete ID by V/W	Uniquely Linking Evidence	Total Initial ID from Kansas City	Total Initial ID from Other Departments
Forgery/fraud	30.6	20.0	39.7	90.3	90.9
Auto theft	38.5	12.7	< 7.8	>51.2[a]	47.4
Theft	48.4	8.6	17.2	74.2	70.0
Commercial burglary	24.4	16.9	16.9	58.2	80.0
Residential burglary	26.7	42.7	< 6.2	>81.7[a]	80.0
Robbery	28.4	20.9	10.6	59.9	53.4
Felony morals	25.8	27.8	27.8	81.4	72.8
Aggravated assault	28.6	63.4	7.9	>94.1[a]	100.0
Homicide	28.3	34.8	10.9	74.0	42.9

Note: Numbers may not add to total because of rounding error.

[a]If no cases of uniquely linking evidence were found in the sample, or no cases other than initial identification, 95% confidence points are shown.

---

10. Using a chi-square test at the 0.05 level (wherever justified by the number of cases in a cell), there is no statistically significant difference between the percentage solved by initial identification in Kansas City and the percentage in the other cities.

Forgery/Fraud

Typical forgery/fraud cases did not require investigative action to identify the perpetrator. Most cases involved the writing of bad checks. Others involved hiring a cab without being able to pay the fare at the end of the ride, or eating in a restaurant without being able to pay the bill. In these instances and in some credit card frauds, the perpetrator was arrested at the scene of the crime.

Examples of those few cases that were solved without an initial identification include:

A furniture store owner lost over $400 because he accepted a check for which he provided goods and cash. The check later turned out to be stolen. The victim informed the police that he cashed the check because the perpetrator had been given an excellent credit reference from another furniture store. This credit reference was contacted and identified the perpetrator. Her mug shots were positively identified by the victim.

In a Jamaican Switch case, the only instance of bunco in our sample, the victim was convinced to give the suspects her money to hold, along with money of their own, so it would be safe. The bunco detective recognized the case as matching the MO in a quite similar case which was recently solved in a nearby jurisdiction. Mug shots were shown to the victim, who positively identified the suspects.[11]

In each of the above instances, no special investigative efforts were required to solve the crime, as would be required, for example, if the person forging a signature to the stolen check had given no credit reference, or if the bunco perpetrators had no previous record for the same crime in the same area.

Auto Theft

In auto theft cases solved through later identification, the culprit is usually identified when he is stopped in the stolen car by a patrol unit.

In one instance, the victim, George, reports his motorcycle stolen; he suspects X (and supplies his name and address), whom he previously refused the loan of his bike. X is in possession of missing bike. However, X claims that he did not steal the motorcycle, that he "rented" it from a third party, Y. X then shows the investigators a rental agreement drawn up between himself and Y, who is subsequently arrested.

It should be noted that although there are professional car thieves and lucrative auto theft rings, with one exception, these types of cases did not

---

11. This is an example in which the monitoring of arrests in another jurisdiction pays off with a clearance. However, since the suspects were experienced con artists with extensive records, it is unlikely that linking them to this second offense will affect their prosecution.

appear in our sample. The exception involved an automobile ring that was broken when a gang member gained revenge (and, incidentally, immunity) by unsolicitedly informing on a wrecking yard owner who specialized in stolen cars.

Theft

For most cases in our sample, the suspect was easily identified: a man vacates his apartment, taking several hundred dollars worth of the landlord's furniture. He leaves his forwarding address with the electric company; the suspect is an estranged spouse; the suspect is either caught in the act or is observed leaving and an automobile license number is recorded. In cases where no initial identification was possible, the detective recognized the MO of the suspect and was thus able to provide mug shots for identification.

Residential Burglary

These cases appear more than any other to be mostly cleared by luck: first the stolen property is found (because the suspect is arrested on another charge or is stopped for careless driving and stolen goods are found in the car), and *then* the suspect is linked to the crime. The investigation, in other words, proceeds after the suspect is in custody. In other cases, either the victim or witness knows the suspect. In many of the instances where the victim knows the suspect, the victim refuses to prosecute.

Aggravated Assault

In these cases, victim and suspect either know each other, or, in the case of the strangers, the commotion is so loud and the struggle so obvious that the police are able to make an arrest at the crime scene. The former instance includes such cases as the victim is beaten by his neighbor, a tenant assaults his landlady, a bail bond company man is severely beaten by a client he attempts to arrest, a husband beats his wife, and a suspect having a feud with the victim's family allegedly damages the victim's car. Among the latter cases: a woman is assaulted in her home and the neighbors hear screams and call the police; a husband beats his estranged wife and her boyfriend with a hammer; a brother shoots at his brother and sister-in-law; a man holds a knife to a victim's throat in a restaurant and threatens to kill her; a drunk man attempts to gouge out a policeman's eye.

For other crimes, we did find examples of investigator skill and initiative that led to case clearance. As table 9-6 shows, examples of these types of cases occurred infrequently. Even among those solved crimes characterized by relatively high (40 percent) later identification of the suspect (commercial burglary and robbery), *at the least,* half are routinely solved.[12] In homicide alone there is the *possibility* that investigator initiative solved the crime about 40 percent of the time.

What kinds of commercial burglary, robbery, felony morals, and homicide cases are cleared?

Commercial Burglary

Most cases are cleared because patrolmen are near a just-activitated burglar alarm. An example of later identification is: a patrol responds to an alarm but is unable to catch the burglars in the store. A witness points out the apartment of these men, where they are subsequently found with the stolen goods. The suspects, however, are not charged since there is no direct evidence linking them to the crime.

One example of a nonroutine solution to a commercial burglary was given earlier. In another example, a grocery store is broken into and the suspect drinks a soft drink in the store and leaves the bottle on the floor. Latent fingerprints are lifted and a "hit" is made during a search of the known offender fingerprint file.

Robbery

Within the robbery detail, there is a wide range of types of cleared cases—from simple pursesnatching to armed bank robbery, from cases where the victim suffers only momentary fear, to those where the victim is severely injured. Yet for the most part, clearance of these cases involves routine investigative procedures— either there is an initial identification, or the victim can describe the suspect well enough to identify him from mug shots. In many of the arrests at the scene of the crime, patrol units pick up the suspect from a broadcast description, or the suspect is pursued and trapped by the victim or witnesses until a patrol unit can arrive. In other self-solving cases, the victim either knows the perpetrator or has noted his automobile license number. Sometimes the perpetrator uses the victim's credit cards to buy gas and can thus be traced by the license number. In one instance a complainant, robbed by a suspect sitting in a parked car, gives police officers the license number and location of the car; the suspect is still sitting in the car when the officers arrive to make the arrest.

---

12. For some crimes classified as routinely solved, investigators invested sometimes up to hundreds of hours in attempting to solve the crime. However, if these efforts did not result in a case clearance, and the suspect was identified, for example, by a tip, the case was classified as being routinely solved.

Examples of robberies demanding more than routine action for solution include a robbery/kidnapping in which the FBI was called in, a robbery with a severely battered victim, and a series of bank robberies perpetrated by a man with no prior record. The solution of each case demanded a variety of investigative measures, no one of which could have solved the case alone. A description of one such case was given in Chapter 8.

Felony Morals

In the typical cleared felony morals crime, the victim is physically abused by a relative or friend: a mother in hysterics reports that her boyfriend has engaged in some kind of sex play with her 4-year-old daughter; a wife reports her husband for having intercourse with their 12-year-old daughter; a woman reports that she was raped by a man she has known for seven years. Other cases involve indecent exposure: officers on patrol arrest a nude man in the street; two high school girls complain about a man who was exposing himself and yelling obscenities from his car. An investigator remembers the same MO (location, words, car), and the man is positively identified by the girls from mug shots.

With the exception of the last mentioned case, which was solved when the officer remembered repetitive unusual behavior by a suspect previously booked for the same crime, the cases cited above are essentially self-solving. Certainly, the investigator typically engages in lengthy interrogation of witnesses and suspect (and the case file minutely details not only the type of offense committed, but also such subsidiary details as what clothes the victim was wearing and what the room looked like). However, the crime is, in effect, cleared before the investigator appears.

Homicide

Even with the thoroughness of investigative procedures described earlier, only one homicide case in our sample was cleared as a direct result of investigation into that particular crime. In their own way, each of the cases essentially solved itself—although some much sooner than others. In some instances, the murderer is identified to the police by knowledgeable informants shortly after the crime is committed; a girl confesses that she killed a man who raped her; a neighbor reports hearing a violent argument between a couple minutes before he responds to the calls of one, only to find him fatally stabbed; an escaped murderer kills his common-law wife (the mother of the victim reveals his past, and he is convicted of first-degree murder).

Other cases are solved by anonymous informants, often long after the case has been suspended because no further clues were available. In another, a juvenile arrested for robbery implicates a companion in a murder occurring several months earlier; and a man arrested for murder as a result of an independent investigation in one part of the state, confesses to an unsolved murder in the southern part of the state, from where we drew the sample.

Other Observations

"Self-solving" crimes by definition become cleared crimes. Are the uncleared crimes, then, the more complicated cases?—the ones requiring the detailed inductive work that television has made so familiar? Although unsolved crimes are not within the province of this chapter, two cleared cases in our sample (which for years were unsolved) are suggestive both of what types of cases remain unsolved and how "non-self-solving" crimes are finally cleared. In one case, citizen involvement becomes the necessary factor to case solution; in the other, investigator initiative.

The Case of the Persistent Parents

A similar rape a year ago remained unsolved: a man in an orange sports car offers a ride to a 16-year-old waiting at a bus stop, asks her to ride in the back since the front seat is broken, soon threatens her with a carving knife, ties her hands and covers her head with a towel, takes her to his house and rapes her, then drives her around before releasing her. The police cruise the neighborhood with the victim in an attempt to find the house, but no luck.

Then, in the more recent case, the felony morals people recognize the MO but have no more success in locating the house where the rape occurred than in the previous case. In this instance, however, the parents of the victim are determined to catch the culprit. They persistently drive their daughter around the neighborhood, until she tentatively identifies the house. After locating the scene of the crime, the police are notified, inside the house find many clues described by the victim, and make an arrest. Mug shots are positively identified by both victims, and the man confesses. Thanks to the concerned parents, the case is closed.

The Case of the Smelly Rapist

For over two years, the "smelly rapist" had been victimizing women on the north side of town. With his now familiar MO, the felony morals detail knew when he was responsible for a rape, but they had thus far been unable to find him.

One evening, two investigators were dispatched to the scene of a burglary that had just occurred. One went to the apartment of the victim, while the other searched the vicinity for the suspect; he found a blue International pickup truck, similar to the vehicle described in numerous burglaries and rapes; the radiator was still warm. After a short time, his partner returned to report that the victim had been attacked by a large man with a knife, who fled when she resisted the attempted rape. Both men then checked out the cab of the truck and noticed a strong personal odor, symptomatic of the "smelly rapist."

With these clues, the detectives decided to lift prints from the truck and from the apartment of the victim, and to stake out the vehicle until its owner returned. When the owner of the truck returned, the denouement of the 3-year-old case was swift: a knife found on the suspect matched that described by the victim, as did a mole on the back of his neck. Latents from the truck and apartment matched those of the suspect.

Both a state and an FBI check revealed the suspect had a long record of burglaries and rapes, with the MO always the same. During a lineup, the suspect was positively identified by several of his victims; upon interrogation even his wife implicated him.

We can only speculate as to whether more careful investigative work (e.g., fingerprinting) would have cracked the case sooner. Certainly, without the alertness of the officer and the stakeout that followed, this case might still be among the unsolvable.

Concluding Remarks

As these data have shown:

- In more than half of the cleared cases, the identification of the offender is available at the time of reporting.
- Most remaining cases that are eventually cleared are cleared through simple routine actions.

Given these findings, it is easy to see that clearance rates cannot be expected to vary substantially according to the organization of investigative units, the training and selection of investigators, whether they specialize by crime type or not, their workload, and other variables that were explored in our survey. With the possible exception of homicide, if investigators only performed the obvious and routine tasks needed to clear the "easy" cases, they would solve the vast majority of crimes that now get cleared. All their efforts in relation to other cases have a very marginal effect on the number of crimes cleared.

It is therefore not appropriate to view the investigator's role as that of solving crimes. Investigators do not spend much time on activities that lead to clearances, and most of their work in this connection could be performed by clerical personnel. Any justification for the work of investigators must lie in areas other than crime solution. Perhaps they perform a useful public service function. Perhaps their activities help to deter crime. Perhaps the care they exercise in recording evidence, processing prisoners, taking statements, and the like are vital for successful prosecution. These possibilities will be explored in later chapters.

Our findings also highlight the importance of patrol officers in producing clearances. A substantial fraction of clearances are produced by patrol arrests at the scene of crimes. In other cases, it is the patrol officer who records the information that we labeled as "initial identification." The efforts that many departments are currently making to structure their crime reports so that this information is properly recorded appear to be highly desirable. Such information creates a routine case out of one that would otherwise be difficult.

Technology has also converted many previously difficult investigative tasks into routine ones. The ability of patrol officers to check rapidly whether a car is stolen, or the driver is wanted, made possible many of the spontaneous clearances that we classified as routine. Well-organized and -maintained mug shot or modus operandi files also helped produce routine clearances that either would never have occurred or would have been nonroutine in the absence of such files.

Finally, our review of these case folders persuaded us that actions by members of the public can strongly influence the outcome of cases. Sometimes private citizens, by ruse or restraint, hold the perpetrator at the scene of the crime. Sometimes they recognize the suspect or stolen property at a later time and call the investigator.[13] In other cases, of which we have given some examples, the victim or his relatives conducted a full-scale investigation on their own and eventually presented the investigator with a spontaneous solution. Collectively, these types of citizen involvement constitute a sizable fraction of cleared cases. We feel that many more cases would be solved if the public were made aware that they cannot depend on the police to solve cases magically but rather must provide the police with as much information as possible.

---

13. Conversely, fear of retaliation or reluctance to prosecute neighbors causes some victims to offer almost no help to the police beyond their first call for help.

10   Collection and Processing of Physical Evidence

Data analyzed in the previous two chapters have shown that activities pursued by traditional investigators, such as diligent and painstaking follow-up investigation, contribute little to the clearance of crimes. Further, investigative personnel do not even spend the majority of their day engaged in activities designed to identify a given perpetrator; rather, almost half of an investigator's routine day is spent performing administrative duties, serving the public, and doing other work not related to pursuing a case solution.

The overall objectives of this study were much broader than simply analyzing the role personnel assigned to investigative units (traditionally referred to as detectives or investigators) play in crime solving; our charter also included assessing the contributions made by various support personnel who assist the investigative division in identifying and/or apprehending perpetrators.

This chapter describes and analyzes the role of physical evidence collection and processing. Chapter 13 will evaluate contributions made by special strike force units.

Data presented here on the contribution of physical evidence to case solution are entirely consistent with findings from the work discussed in previous chapters. Basically, we found that the most important factor in clearance is the victim's or witness's identification of the suspect, even in the case of burglary, where the victim and perpetrator rarely see each other. Our analysis of evidence technicians and their activities also suggests that organizational differences in response time, percentage of reported crimes processed, and type of personnel responsible for processing (police or civilian) has no discernible effect on the number of perpetrators identified as a result of retrieved physical evidence.

When department statistics reflecting all crime types combined were compared, the percentage of latents that were matched with a suspect's prints was similar across departments, even though the systems employed and the manpower allocated were markedly different.

However, this analysis did help us identify activities that are valuable in the process of suspect identification in individual departments, and recommendations for changes in the processing of physical evidence are suggested to departments for implementation on an experimental basis. This chapter describes these various activities in select police departments and examines case samples and departmental statistics in an analysis of the role physical evidence contributes to the primary purpose of police investigation—suspect identification.

143

Introduction

The ability of a police agency to properly collect and process the physical evidence retrieved from crime scenes is thought to be important to the process of successful police investigation. Development of more sophisticated laboratory equipment and criminalistic techniques has heightened interest in the possible expanded role physical evidence may play in future apprehension and prosecutions efforts. It was thought that Supreme Court rulings such as *Escobedo* (1963) and *Miranda* (1966), which imposed additional restrictions on the police and limited the police practice of interrogation, would encourage investigators to rely more heavily on the scientific analysis of physical evidence and less on confessions and other forms of evidence which may later be judged as an infraction of the accused's lawful rights. But, as the President's Crime Commission pointed out in 1967, physical evidence and other forensic science mechanisms were not being used frequently in the investigation and adjudication of criminal offenses. The logic offered by the Commission was that police departments were handicapped by the lack of training programs to develop sophisticated evidence processing skills (President's Commission on Law Enforcement and Administration of Justice 1967, p. 18).

As incentives for more thorough collection of physical evidence at the crime scene have increased, many police departments have added specially trained evidence technicians, or Crime Scene Search Officers (CSSOs) to their police force. Evidence technician units have been growing steadily over the past decade. In a 1971 study of 106 police departments throughout the United States, 76 percent of the agencies reported that they had specialized evidence technician units available for crime scene processing (Ward 1971, p. 128). In responding to our 1974 survey, most departments (88 percent) stated that they had specialized evidence technicians who were available to be dispatched to crime scenes. The Rand survey reported that, on the average, police departments allocated 2.4 percent of their total police manpower to collecting physical evidence from crime scenes. In addition to increasing the manpower, departments have begun to purchase mobile evidence vans and update and expand their criminalistic equipment.

Notwithstanding the increased allocation of police manpower to physical evidence collection, and the expanded technical capabilities of the department, current crime scene search efforts continue to fall below what might be considered adequate. A recent study concluded that law enforcement agencies more frequently than not make no attempt to process crime scenes for physical evidence; and when they do process crime scenes, the searches are often incomplete or unsystematic (Peterson 1974).

Police administrators, recognizing this deficiency, have begun to experiment with a variety of organizational changes designed to increase the number of crime sites processed for physical evidence. Several departments have adopted a policy that evidence technicians be dispatched to all felony crime scenes. Other departments are experimenting with the use of patrol or investigative officers to collect physical evidence at specified crime scenes. Some departments have purchased costly mobile vans containing evidence laboratories, which usually cruise in a specific sector until dispatched directly to a crime scene. These policy decisions are based on the assumption that there is a positive correlation between the amount of physical evidence retrieved and the number of suspects identified from such evidence.

The research reported here was undertaken to see whether or not such a relationship exists. Our primary purpose was to conduct a comparative analysis of the physical evidence collection and processing efforts in six police departments[1] selected on the basis of their contrasting evidence collection and processing efforts. In each of the six police departments we visited, data were collected from the evidence gathering unit so that the role of physical evidence could be assessed under different methods of operation. The following research questions were addressed:

- What is the role of physical evidence, and particularly latent prints, in case clearances?

- Are more perpetrators identified as a result of retrieved physical evidence when evidence technicians are more frequently dispatched to crime scenes?

- Does lifting prints at a higher percentage of searched crime scenes lead to higher suspect identification?

- Is there any discernible effect of processing the crime scene immediately following the report of the incident?

Our research was both qualitative and quantitative in nature. The activities of each department were observed, case samples drawn, and knowledgeable individuals interviewed. As a result, this chapter describes the physical-evidence related activities of each department and attempts to assess their productivity. However, we focus mainly on latent fingerprint collection and processing, since we have indicated that other types of physical evidence are less important in most cases.

Nature and Role of the Evidence Technician

As documented in Chapter 6, the majority of police departments report that they rely for the most part on evidence technicians to collect the physical

---

1. Long Beach, Berkeley, Los Angeles, and Richmond, California; Washington, D.C.; and Miami, Florida.

evidence, although some departments allocate the responsibility for some types of crime scenes (usually minor) to the investigator or to the patrol force. Evidence technicians are customarily given the responsibility for deciding what evidence at the scene will be preserved, collected, and submitted to the laboratory for scientific analysis. To make these decisions in a competent manner demands specialized training, an understanding of basic procedures, and close attention to detail in carrying them out. The technician must be acutely aware of the types of evidence he is looking for and the most likely places in which they are to be found. At most crime scenes, the scientific evidence is often there, but it has to be discovered and properly processed.

The value of physical evidence is determined by how useful it is in verifying that a crime has been committed, in identifying the person or persons who did it, and in exonerating all other persons who may be under suspicion. To this end, the evidence technician searches for the following types of evidence:

1. Evidence to prove crime was committed (broken door locks, ripped safe, bodily injury to complainant, torn clothing).
2. Evidence to prove suspect was at the scene of the crime (glass fragments from broken door in suspect's clothing, safe insulation on suspect's clothing, suspect's footwear impressions in insulation dust, injury to suspect's fist where he beat victim, scratches on suspect caused by victim, body fluids, hair, fibers, footprints, finger and palm latents found at scene).
3. Evidence to prove complainant was at the scene of the crime and/or came into contact with the suspect (same as suspect, since it is often just as important to place the complainant on the scene as it is the suspect).[2]

These requirements obviously constitute a large order for the evidence technician. In reality, evidence technicians concentrate the largest amount of their time and efforts on trying to prove that the suspect was at the scene of the crime; this is usually done by lifting latent prints. However, they may also take a picture of the crime scene in order to aid in proving that a crime was in fact committed.

It has been estimated that a thorough crime scene search could take days; however, rapidly rising crime rates in most cities, combined with relatively stable police budgets, imply that the evidence technician has little time at the crime scene for any single crime—rarely more than a half-hour. Since many police departments mandate that a larger percentage of reported crimes be processed for physical evidence than were formerly, the workload of the average evidence technician has been increased. Technicians we spoke with frequently complained that they were having to sacrifice the quality of search so that more crime scenes could be processed.

---

2. *Washington, D.C., Manual for Crime Scene Search*, 1973.

Several factors affect the amount of time evidence technicians spend processing a particular crime scene. They mentioned the following most frequently:

- Seriousness of crime
  - Whether violence involved
  - Amount of property loss
- Backlog of crime scene searches pending
- Physical condition of crime scene (outdoor, indoor)
- Responding patrolman's estimate of physical evidence potentiality

A two-day sample of the reports filed in Miami for each crime scene processed (which list the time the technician reached the scene and the time he departed) was examined so that an estimate of the time spent per crime scene, by crime type, could be made. The results are given in table 10-1.

The evidence technician does not devote his time entirely to searching crime scenes; he is also responsible for testifying in court concerning retrieved evidence, writing evidence reports, etc. Evidence technicians in Washington, D.C., and Miami were asked to estimate the amount of time they spend involved in these complementary activities (see table 10-2).

Presence of Physical Evidence at Crime Scenes

Past research has documented the high potential for retrieving physical evidence at the majority of crime scenes. Moreover, studies have shown that a

Table 10-1
Time Spent Per Crime Scene by Evidence Technicians,
Miami Police Department

Type of Crime	Amount of Time Spent Processing (minutes)	Number of Cases
Homicide	55.0	2
Residential burglary	44.1	32
Rape	45.0	3
Business burglary	32.2	14
Robbery	22.6	8
Assault	16.0	4
B&E of automobile	22.0	4
Auto Theft	18.6	6
Total	–	73
All felonies (weighted average)	36.3	–

Table 10–2
How Evidence Technicians Spend Their Time

Activity	Washington, D.C. (%)	Miami (%)
Crime scene searches	35–50	55–65
Court appearances	15–20	30–35
Writing reports, bringing evidence to lab, training, other	30–35	15–20
Cruising in mobile crime lab waiting for assignment	15–20	–

conscientious effort is seldom made to retrieve any physical evidence from the crime scene, much less all that is available. In many police departments a request for an evidence technician to process the scene is seldom made. In those instances where a technician is requested, he retrieves only a small portion of the available evidence (Parker and Peterson 1972).

In 1966, the President's Commission on Crime in the District of Columbia reported that in Washington, D.C. less than 10 percent of Part 1 crime sites were investigated by technicians, dusted for fingerprints, or photographed (President's Commission, Washington, 1966, p. 202).

A three-month study of the Berkeley Police Department examined the level of crime scene physical material suitable for, and capable of, laboratory testing (Parker and Peterson 1972). The researchers accompanied evidence technicians to the crime scene and compared the evidence retrieved from the scene with their independent assessment of what could have been retrieved. It was hypothesized that law enforcement officers often screen out physical materials present at the scene but judged not worthy of, or not capable of, laboratory attention. The researchers defined 23 categories of physical evidence, including tool marks, fingerprints and palm prints, clothing, blood, etc. It was determined that the evidence technician seldom makes an attempt to search for evidence in several of these categories, and most often retrieves evidence from only a single physical evidence category (usually fingerprints, although tool marks are very often present). Of the 749 cases investigated, 88 percent were assessed by the researchers as showing physical evidence in three distinct categories. Nevertheless, a laboratory examination of physical evidence was made in only 4 of the 3,303 cases encompassing all burglaries, auto thefts, robberies, thefts, rapes, assaults with battery, and murders committed during the study period. After the researchers eliminated thefts of under $50 and minor assaults (over 1,900 cases), they found that over 1,300 cases might have been subjected to laboratory review. Of the 489 cases analyzed by the laboratory during that study period, 452 cases (92 percent) involved drugs and narcotics, but only 4 (1 percent), as noted above, were from the most serious crime categories. The crime laboratory received only one item of evidence on a robbery case during the period studied, and none for burglary, even though the police department handled 875 burglaries and 101 robberies during this period. The researchers observed that, despite this small proportion of available evidence submitted to the criminalistics laboratory, the latter was barely able to keep pace. In fact, such limitations on laboratory capabilities may be a major cause of the low rate of evidence submission in Berkeley and elsewhere (Peterson 1974, p. 8).

The 1967 Science and Technology Task Force Report described a case study of 626 burglaries, of which 307 had "indications of evidence at the scene of the crime," but fingerprint evidence was booked in only 28 cases, representing 5 percent of the total burglaries and 10 percent of the cases where evidence was thought to be present (Institute for Defense Analyses 1967, p. 99).

Dispatching Evidence Collection Units

Operational assignment of evidence-gathering units in the six departments covered by our survey occurs in three ways:

- The responding patrol officer has the responsibility of deciding whether or not to request an evidence technician. Patrolmen in these departments are expected to request an evidence technician when they suspect the crime scene may contain retrievable physical evidence, or when they feel that a photograph of the crime scene would be beneficial.

- Evidence technicians are dispatched to crime scenes similar to the manner in which patrolmen are dispatched. Frequently, the evidence technicians are cruising the streets in patrol cars or in mobile evidence vans, awaiting an assignment. When a crime of a specific type (designated by the department) occurs, then the dispatcher will automatically notify an evidence technician to report to the crime scene.

- The patrolman or investigator requests that a specific site be searched, and this request is sent to the evidence technician unit where it may be placed in a waiting line of crime scenes to be searched. Evidence technicians then take the cases in sequence.

Each police department visited organizes its evidence collection efforts according to one of the above methods. Data were gathered from each unit so that the productivity of the technicians, organized according to these various procedures, could be compared. The organization and rate of deployment of evidence collection in the sampled police departments may be distinguished as follows:

Berkeley, California

The Berkeley Police Department has three civilian evidence technicians. The responding patrolman requests technicians at particularly complicated crime scenes; however, the patrolman-investigator has the equipment and training to take photographs of the crime scene and lift prints. Whether or not technicians are dispatched depends on the patrolman's judgment concerning the likelihood of obtaining evidence from the technicians' activities.

Long Beach, California

The Long Beach Police Department employs eight civilian evidence technicians, or one technician for every 2982 felonies reported in 1973.[3] The evidence technician, by department policy, is to be requested by the responding patrolman in all felony crime scenes. However, the patrolman may refrain from calling an evidence technician when he is certain that there is no retrievable physical evidence; but the technician *must* be called to all crime scenes where it appears that the perpetrator entered the scene through a window, or the loss is more than $2,000.

The evidence technician unit has two newly purchased mobile evidence vans. The technicians search crimes singly, and they average four to five crime scene searches per day.

Los Angeles, California

In August 1974, the Los Angeles Police Department adopted a new procedure for lifting latent prints from crime scenes, designed to ensure that a higher percentage of reported crimes are processed for latent prints. Patrolmen now have the responsibility of lifting latent prints at nonviolent crime scenes (primarily burglary and auto theft). Each car assigned to a police team is equipped with a fingerprint kit, and when a team responds to a nonviolent crime scene, one of the members is expected to search for and lift all available prints. However, when the crime is clearly of a violent or serious nature, the patrolman requests that a Headquarters Latent Print Specialist be dispatched.

There are 37 civilian personnel assigned to the Latent Section of the Scientific Investigation Division. These persons are responsible for processing crime scenes *for latent prints only*. If there are blood traces, footprints, etc., the patrolman requests that another group of specialized technicians be dispatched to the scene.

---

3. Based on 1973 FBI-UCR data.

During the months after this procedure for lifting latents was first instituted, the department estimated that patrol officers in the field lifted approximately 37 percent of the total prints sent to the Latent Identification Section, with Headquarters Unit lifting the remainder.

Miami, Florida

The Miami Police Department employs 18 Crime Scene Search Officers (CSSOs), a ratio of one CSSO for every 10.5 investigators, or one CSSO for every 1,600 felonies reported in 1973.[4] All of the CSSOs are civilians under a civil service classification. The department does not intend to employ sworn officers in this capacity because they feel that the sworn officer is very likely to return to the "field" at some point in his career, and when he does, the training he received as a CSSO is not taken advantage of, whereas a civilian technician is likely to remain a CSSO indefinitely.

A CSSO must pass a basic civil service test to qualify for the position; the test is not based on prior crime search experience. Once employed, the technician attends approximately six FBI-sponsored classes on the techniques of searching a crime scene. After completing the classes and serving a probationary period of about two months in the Identifications Section, the technician begins accompanying an experienced CSSO to crime scenes. This apprenticeship lasts for about one month; then the CSSO begins searching crime scenes alone.

The general procedure for dispatching a CSSO to the crime scene is as follows: The patrol unit responding to the crime conducts a preliminary investigation and subsequently may request an identification technician. The general practice is to call a CSSO to all felony offenses, except in instances of burglary and robbery where the responding officer is certain no physical evidence can be gathered.

Usually, when a patrolman requests a CSSO—unless it is a particularly serious crime—the request will be placed in the one- to two-day backlog of cases. When the CSSO arrives at Headquarters Unit for his shift, he picks up several of those requests and begins making his rounds. Very seldom does the CSSO wait for a crime scene search assignment. Evidence technicians frequently complain about operating with a backlog, saying that they often feel rushed.

Richmond, California

The Richmond Police Department places heavy emphasis on obtaining physical evidence at crime scenes, and on making identifications through fingerprints.

---

4. Based on 1973 FBI-UCR data.

Four percent (eight men) of the police force are in the Crime Scene Search Unit. There was one CSSO for every 900 felonies reported in 1973.[5] The evidence technicians operate in a manner similar to the patrol units, in that they cruise the streets until they are dispatched to a crime scene. As a matter of departmental policy, evidence technicians are automatically dispatched to the scene of all felonies, and detailed accounts of their activities routinely accompany the crime reports. However, if the crime is not obviously a felony, the patrolman responding to the scene will make the decision about whether or not an evidence technician should be requested. The evidence technicians unit uses four sedans (with the back seat removed) equipped with such items as photographic equipment, fingerprint kit, tiretrack and casting equipment, and portable light. Technicians on patrol and on call respond immediately to the crime scene. Although the evidence technicians most frequently lift latent prints, the technicians claim they often check for tool marks, shoeprints, and tire marks.

Washington, D.C.

The Washington, D.C., Metropolitan CSSO Unit has 90 sworn police officers, divided among the seven police districts and a Headquarters Unit. This is a ratio of one CSSO to every 54 investigators, or one CSSO for every 567 felonies reported in1973.[6] There are approximately 10 Crime Scene Search Officers in each district and 19 officers in the Headquarters Unit.

The separation of jurisdiction between the districts and the Headquarters Unit is covered by a general order. Primarily, the Headquarters Unit is responsible for processing the scenes of the more serious crimes such as

- Deaths of a violent or suspicious nature of unidentified persons.

- Rapes and all serious sex offenses.

- Critical injury assaults (particularly on a police officer).

- Armed robberies.

- Burglaries when there is physical evidence or loss of property in excess of $500.

- Other major offenses (particularly bombings, arson, and kidnappings).

If, at the time the crime is reported, the dispatcher recognizes that it is one of the designated crime types that require a Headquarters CSSO, he may

5. Based on 1973 FBI-UCR data.

6. Based on 1973 FBI-UCR data.

automatically call Headquarters Unit. This call will be made first to one of three Headquarters Mobile Crime Vans which cruise the streets with two CSSOs awaiting dispatch to the scene. If the Mobile Crime Van is not available, the dispatcher will call Headquarters Unit directly, and they in turn will dispatch a technician. If a Headquarters Crime Scene Officer is not able to respond, the Headquarters Coordinator has the authorization to dispatch a District CSSO to handle the case.

If the crime reported is not clearly of a nature to which Headquarters Unit would respond, the dispatcher will not automatically call a District Crime Scene Officer. Instead, the patrolman who responds will immediately notify an official of his assigned district and request the services of an investigator operating out of one of the specialty units such as Homicide, Sex, Robbery, etc. Once the investigator arrives on the scene and determines exactly what type of crime has been committed, a decision is made whether or not to call a District or Headquarters Crime Scene Search Officer. In any case, although the dispatcher may take the initiative of notifying a CSSO, it is always the responsibility of the responding patrolman to make certain that search personnel are called if there is any potential for recovering physical evidence.

The responding officer is not permitted to exercise discretion in those crimes that have been designated as requiring a Headquarters CSSO to process the scene. It is the policy that the Headquarters Unit will be automatically activated in all of these specified crime categories.

Fingerprint Lifting and Suspect Identification

We took a sample of cleared and uncleared cases to get an overall indication of the frequency with which a technician responds to residential burglaries, how frequently he lifts prints, and how frequently the prints result in an identification. This sample, consisting of 200 residential burglary cases per department in three cities,[7] indicated that in only about 1 percent of the cases in each department did an identification result from a latent print. Table 10-3 shows that in Richmond, where evidence technicians are dispatched to nearly 90 percent of the reported burglaries, and recover prints from 70 percent of the scenes they process, their "hit rate" (or percentage of all cases where an identification resulted) is the same as in Long Beach and Berkeley where evidence technicians are dispatched to the scene less frequently and lift prints less often.

From these data, we infer that a heavier investment in evidence technicians and a policy of routinely dispatching technicians to all felony crime scenes produce a higher print recovery rate; however, they appear not to affect the rate at which fingerprint identifications serve to clear burglary cases. In addition,

---

7. See Chapter 9 for a description of the sampling method.

Table 10–3
Productivity of Crime Scene Processing for Fingerprints, Residential Burglary Sample[a]

Item	Long Beach	Berkeley	Richmond
Percentage of cases in which technicians were requested	58.0	76.6	87.6
Percentage of technician-requested cases in which print recovery was made	50.8	42.0	69.1
Cases in which print recovery was made, as percentage of total cases	29.4	32.2	60.5
Cases in which perpetrator was identified as a result of lifted prints, as percentage of total cases	1.5	1.1	1.2

[a]200 randomly selected residential burglary cases from each of three departments (cleared or uncleared).

the data suggest a higher print recovery rate in Richmond where the crime site is processed immediately following the report of the incident. We suggest that this is because there is a payoff gained by processing the crime scene immediately following the report of the incident when the CSSO arrives at the same time as other police personnel. In that case, he often hears the victim's initial statement in which the victim often points out areas where possible contact was made by the perpetrator. The CSSO will likely dust for prints in all of those areas. If the CSSO processes the crime scene some time after the actual incident has occurred and is not able to take full advantage of the victim's knowledge, he may dust fewer areas for prints.

Another advantage of processing the site immediately is that the prints are uncontaminated. If the site is not processed immediately, latent prints left by the suspect may subsequently become smudged, even though the CSSO has attempted to protect the scene.

There are several plausible explanations as to why lifting more prints does not actually result in a higher rate of burglary suspect identifications. It is possible that the prints lifted are not of sufficiently high quality. However, this is unlikely, since all of the departments said that approximately the same percentage (approximately 60 percent) of retrieved prints were considered to be of readable quality. The most reasonable explanation appears to involve the fingerprint file searching capabilities of the individual department. That is, a high proportion of recovered latents are never used to search fingerprint files in an attempt to make identifications from comparisons.

No matter how competent the evidence technician is at performing his job, the gathering of physical evidence at a crime scene will be futile unless such evidence can be properly processed and analyzed. Since fingerprints are by far the most frequently retrieved physical evidence, making the procedures for analyzing such prints more effective should contribute the most toward greater success in identifying criminal offenders through the use of physical evidence.

We made a careful comparison of the effectiveness of the fingerprint identification sections in four of the six police departments. These departments—Washington, Los Angeles, Miami, and Richmond—differ significiantly in terms of size, fingerprint files maintained, and types of fingerprint services performed. We used the identification success rates of the fingerprint sections as a measure of their effectiveness. Such sections contain fingerprint specialists who are responsible for classifying, preserving, and attempting to identify the latent prints lifted by the evidence technician from the crime scene. Secondarily, the latter's duties might also include processing pieces of clothing for possible latents, identifying decreased persons through their fingerprints, fingerprinting arrestees, and testifying in court.

As a preliminary to describing our comparison of the four departments' identification sections, we shall first review the processing operation.

The General Process of Suspect Identification by Fingerprints

A fingerprint identification section first evaluates the prints, judging them to be of "value" or "no value," depending on their quality. Those that are of value (i.e., distinguishable enough so that an identification would be possible) are then compared with the "elimination prints"—prints of persons known to have legally come in contact with the crime scene and who possibly could have left the latents (e.g., the victim, relatives, police). These sets of ten fingerprints are referred to as elimination prints, since they may eliminate the possibility that the latent prints were left by the perpetrator. Prints not screened out in this manner are then classified and categorized so that a variety of searches, which attempt to match the latents with the offender, can subsequently be performed.

Request Searches

The most frequent type of search performed by fingerprint specialists is referred to as a *request search*. In this case, the investigator has suggested one or more possible suspects for the crime, and has submitted their names to the fingerprint unit so that a search of the latents against their fingerprints can be made.

Several factors may lead an investigator to request a specific latent search. First, the victim may actually know the perpetrator, either by name, nickname, or description. Second, a name of the suspect may be suggested when an arrest is made of an individual in the process of committing the crime. Identifications of latent fingerprints of these suspects would form valuable corroborating evidence during trial proceedings.

Third, the named suspect may come out of the experience of the investigator. It has been observed that after an investigator has worked in one area for a period of time, he becomes well acquainted with the criminal element of that area. Therefore, when a crime is committed, he can draw up a list of possible suspects based on his knowledge of the habits and MO of the criminal elements in his area. In this instance, a latent print sent to the identification section would be accompanied by a list of suggested suspects. The productivity of this approach may be less in a large city, with its shifting population, than in a less populated area. The analysis that follows suggests that request searches are responsible for a majority of suspect identifications.

Latent Print File Searches

When suspects are not named by the investigating officer, the identifications bureau may perform one of two types of independent searches on the latent prints. The first, and most common type, is a *latent print file search*. The prints of an arrested suspect are automatically searched for a match in the latent prints, usually the crime type and area in which he was arrested. In addition, the fingerprint specialist may choose to search a specialized "repeat offender" file that many departments maintain.

Cold Searches

Some fingerprint identification sections, usually those located in smaller police departments, also conduct *cold searches*. In a cold search, the specialist takes a latent print and manually searches the entire fingerprint file, or a section of the file, in an attempt to match the print with one of the fingerprint cards. This is an extremely laborious process, and nearly impossible in large police departments where the fingerprint file may contain more than 300,000 sets of prints.

Our research indicates that the vast majority of latent prints are never used in such searches, and consequently do not lead to the identification of a criminal offender. The prints are simply stored on the chance that they may be used in the future.

Why a Print May Not Be Identified

Even when a search is performed, the resulting identifications are few. A latent print may not be identified during a search for a number of reasons, primarily because the fingerprints of the person who left the latent print are not in the file of known fingerprints. The majority of fingerprint files contain only the prints of persons arrested within that particular jurisdiction, and the perpetrator may never have been fingerprinted there. The latent print also may belong to a perpetrator who is a juvenile under fingerprintable age by law or who may never have been arrested before.

Even if the correct set of fingerprints is in the fingerprint file, it still may not be found, for the following reasons:

- The main file fingerprints may be coded or classified incorrectly with respect to the print corresponding to the latent print.

- The latent print may be incorrectly coded or classified.

- Distortion in the latent print may alter its classification sufficiently to cause the file print to be missed during the search.[8]

A Comparison of Fingerprint Identification Sections

Although the data in our samples show that the fingerprint identification sections in various departments identified approximately the same proportion of burglary suspects through latent prints, a closer examination of their productivity reveals disparities. But first, we describe and contrast how the fingerprint specialist units operate in each of the departments.

Descriptions of the Washington, D.C., Miami, and Richmond identification sections that follow include the size and descriptions of the maintained fingerprint files, the types of searches performed, and identification success rates (i.e., *hit rate*).[9]

Washington, D.C.

The Identification Section of the Washington, D.C., Police Department is divided into two distinct operational units: the Classifications of Arrestees Section and the Fingerprint Examination Section. The Classification Unit, not of interest to this study, is responsible for photographing and taking the fingerprints of all adult criminal offenders arrested with felonies or serious misdemeanors in the District of Columbia.

The Fingerprint Examination Section is responsible for providing the department with fingerprint identification services, the most important of which (according to the unit's supervisor) is identification of criminal offenders by the

8. See Kingston and Madrazo (1970) for complete discussion.

9. Although statistics are presented for the Los Angeles Fingerprint Identification Section, no description of that section is included.

latent print evidence recovered from crime scenes, and subsequently furnishing "expert testimony" in the prosecution of criminal cases.

The section is comprised of 21 fingerprint specialists, four of whom are police officers, and the remainder are civilians with previous FBI fingerprint identification experience. This is a ratio of one fingerprint specialist for every 4.2 CSSOs.

The D.C. Fingerprint Examiner, more so than the specialists in Miami or Richmond, is involved with several fingerprint-related activities, in addition to matching latents. The supervisor of the D.C. Identification Unit estimated that the average fingerprint examiner apportions his time among the various activities roughly as follows:

- File searches (no request): 30-40 percent

- Comparing latent prints with those on file by request: 35-50 percent

- Classifying, rating, and indexing prints: 15-20 percent

- Chemical processing of evidence for latent prints: 5-10 percent

- Outside the police department: 10-15 percent
  - Providing "expert testimony" in court, attending lectures, giving instruction

- Establishing the identity of unknown deceased: 5 percent

- Preparing exhibits for court presentation: 5 percent

The Washington, D.C. Fingerprint Examination Section maintains three active criminal files:

1. *Known Offender File.* This is the master criminal file which contains fingerprints of all known criminal offenders who have been arrested for serious misdemeanors or felony offenses in the Washington district. When a suspect is arrested, the Classifications Section takes a full set of fingerprints (all ten fingers) which are classified, searched, and filed by the Henry Classification System.[10] This file currently consists of the fingerprints of approximately 300,000 known criminal offenders.

2. *Five-Finger File.* This file contains the fingerprints of approximately 30,000 career offenders who have been selected for inclusion in this special file because of their repeated criminal activities in the area. It is divided by crime type and nature of the print (i.e., right- and left-hand fingerprints, and right- and left-hand palm prints). This file is the one used by fingerprint specialists when they conduct independent cold searches.

---

10. For a description of this system, see footnote 12 below.

3. *Latent Fingerprint File.* This file contains all of the latent fingerprints lifted at the crime scene by a District or Headquarters Crime Scene Search Officer. Statistics show that in 1973 the section evaluated approximately 150,000 individual latent prints recovered from 14,191 crime scenes (10 prints per crime scene on the average). If the prints are of value, they are filed by crime type and the district of the city in which they were lifted. Within the file, all of the prints lifted at the crime scene are kept in a single jacket. If the prints are judged to be of no value, they are filed in a separate cabinet in numerical order. On the jacket containing the prints, the specialist records the date, the name of the Crime Scene Search Officer who lifted the prints, location of crime scene, location of exact place in dwelling where prints were lifted, and the crime category.

The Fingerprint Examination Section evaluates all latent prints recovered from crime scenes, and in 1973 judged approximately 65 percent of the recovered prints to be of value. A majority of the fingerprint specialist's time is spent comparing, by request from investigators, latents with prints from the master criminal file. There were 9,780 request searches conducted in 1973, resulting in 465 positive identifications,[11] or a hit rate of 0.047 (76 percent of all IDs made in 1973).

The section also conducts a number of independent searches, the most common of which is a latent file print search. For example, if a suspect is arrested on a Burglary II charge in District 3, the fingerprint specialist may choose to independently search the latent prints lifted in that district for that crime type in the hopes of matching the arrestee's prints with several latents. At a later time, if that suspect is rearrested and processed again by the ID branch, the specialist may independently decide to expand his search of the latent print file to other districts or crime types.

The second type of search conducted is a cold search through the Five-Finger File (Career Offender File). This process consists of taking latent fingerprints or palm prints and trying to match them with the prints of one of 30,000 persons in this specialized file. To search this entire file takes approximately six to eight hours. Whether this type of cold search is conducted depends on the workload of the specialist, and, as such, is almost never performed. In the District of Columbia this type of search receives very low priority, since it is assumed there is very little payoff for the considerable amount of time invested.

Miami, Florida

The Miami Latent Fingerprint Examination Section consists of four civilian fingerprint specialists, a ratio of one fingerprint specialist for every 4.5 CSSOs.

---

11. This department counts only one identification per individual identified, even if several identifications are made of one individual in one case. Identifications of deceased individuals (either from latents or elimination latents) are not included in this figure.

Two specialists compare latent prints obtained from crime scenes with finger-prints on file, and testify in court when fingerprints are submitted as evidence. The other two specialists are responsible for coding all incoming fingerprints (both criminal and civilian) according to the Henry Classification System[12] and entering the prints into the appropriate file.

The Miami Fingerprint Examination Section maintains three fingerprint files: the Single Digit Criminal File, the Master File, and the Latent Print File.

1. *Single Digit Criminal File.* A computerized searching system became operational in April 1974, and in the following eight months assisted in 143 identifications. The data bank of this system consists of the ten-digit prints of 3,600 persons (3,200 juveniles and 400 select hard-core offenders). All ten digits of each juvenile arrested in Miami are entered into the data bank of this searching system, as are selected repeat adult offenders. When a good single-digit latent print is lifted from the crime scene, it is automatically searched in the Single Digit File for a match. The system produces a listing of all those persons to whom this latent might belong. Once the listing has been produced, the master file must be searched manually to compare the latent with the actual print for a match. This sytem is limited by the size of the data bank it can accommodate. If the data bank increases past its current capacity, the listing it produces will be too extensive to manually search through the master file.

2. *Master File.* This file contains the ten digits of approximately 285,000 civilian and criminal persons. The fingerprints of all arrested adult offenders are entered into this file, as are the fingerprints of all civilian persons who make application for a Miami identification card. The current master file contains approximately 200,000 civilian prints, and 85,000 criminal prints.

Prints in this file are categorized by the Henry Classification System. As such, the master file cannot be cold-searched unless the latents can also be given a Henry code. The master file is also used for retrieving all prints used in conducting

---

12. The Miami Police Department, along with a majority of police forces in the United States, employs the "Henry" Fingerprint Classification System, which uses the prints of all ten fingers in arriving at a descriptor consisting of numerals and letters. The classification takes notes of the different patterns (arch, loop, whorl) and subpatterns such as ulnar loops, radial loops, tented arches, etc.; it also depends on the ridge counts between the core and delta of loops. The Henry Classification System does not provide a unique descriptor for each set of fingerprints, and, as a matter of fact, in some of the more common codes there are thousands of fingerprint cards with the same Henry Classification. The system has an obvious shortcoming because it is not able to match a latent print with prints in the file unless a Henry code can be assigned to the latent prints, and no definite code can be assigned without the presence of all digits. However, if there are at least three or four excellent fingerprints, and the sequence of the prints as well as the fact that they all belong to one person can be established, then the possible categories to which the prints might belong can be defined. *Very* seldom can this information be confirmed, and even with this information (since it is based on only three or four prints), the categories have only been narrowed. Should the latents be of a common type, there may be hundreds of fingerprint cards within each of the possible categories. Therefore, a file like Miami's coded entirely by the Henry Classification System, is basically inoperable for searching latent prints with no known clues as to possible suspects.

request searches, and all searches resulting from the fingerprint specialist's own initiative.

3. *Latent Fingerprint File.* This file contains all latent fingerprints and palm prints lifted at the crime scene by a CSSO. If they are of value, they are filed in chronological order by crime type and district where lifted. The prints lifted at a single crime scene are all contained in a single jacket. If the prints are judged to be of "no value," they are filed in a separate cabinet, chronologically by crime type and district.

In Miami, when a Crime Scene Search Officer turns in a latent print to the Fingerprint Examination Section, it is first rated "value" or "no value"; in 1973, approximately 80 percent of the prints were judged to be of value.[13] The valuable prints are then automatically searched through the computerized Single Digit File. If this search results in no match, the prints are turned over to one of the two fingerprint ID specialists. The fingerprint specialist will perform all request searches listed on the crime report. If no request searches are asked for by detectives, the latent specialist will act on his own initiative in attempting to make an ID, in which case he takes the prints of several persons he knows to be active in the area with similar MOs and tries to match their prints with the latent. In addition, he maintains contact with the Arrestees Section, and when a person is arrested with a similar MO, the ID specialist will take his prints and search them with all of the latents in that geographical area.

The unusual aspect of Miami fingerprint specialists is their close coordination with the department detectives, patrolmen, and Criminal Information Center. Rather than depend totally on the investigator to suggest names of possible suspects, the specialists attempt to follow closely the criminal activities in their area (e.g., by reading the crime reports, talking with investigators and patrolmen, reading the daily bulletins on wanted suspects) so that when several crimes of a similar nature are committed, the fingerprint technician may independently choose to compare the latents. In Miami, the fingerprint technician is not isolated from the rest of the investigation, and in some sense he acts as his own detective.

The latent fingerprint specialists distinguished the IDs resulting from request searches versus independent searches during 1973, and concluded that 48.2 percent (183) of the IDs made were a result of a request search, and 46.4 percent (176) resulted because of "own initiative" searches. Compared to Washington, D.C., this is a very high percentage of IDs resulting from independent searches.

Richmond, California

The Richmond Identification Section basically consists of one fingerprint specialist (a sworn officer), who has been serving in this capacity for six years.

---

13. This is high compared to 65 percent of the prints being of value in Washington, D.C.

This is a ratio of one fingerprint specialist for the eight evidence technicians. He estimates he uses his time as follows:

- Cold searches: 35 percent
- Request searches: 35 percent
- Rating and classifying latent prints: 15 percent
- Testifying in court: 15 percent

This officer maintains his own special file of 3,500–4,000 fingerprints of active criminals, and a smaller file of palm prints. He checks the file every couple of years to remove prints of deceased persons or persons in prison. The file, consisting mostly of repeat offenders, is used for cold searches and request searches. In addition to these specialized files, there are latent fingerprint and palm print files, and the department master file consisting of the prints of all arrested persons.

A unique aspect of the Richmond Identification Unit is that true cold searches have been quite successful in identfying suspects. The Richmond experience suggests that cold searches, and latent searches in general, can be quite productive of suspect identification if a dedicated and experienced specialist performs them on a file of manageable size using latent prints collected by well-trained evidence technicians.

Some Findings on the Productivity of Fingerprint Specialists

In table 10-4 we compare the productivity of fingerprint identification operations in the four cities we examined. Using the measures shown, it is clear that:

- Miami, Richmond, and Los Angeles make approximately the same percentage of identifications from retrieved latent prints—approximately 9 percent of the prints retrieved are subsequently used to identify a suspect. In Washington, D.C., only about 4 percent of the retrieved prints are matched with those of a suspect.

- In Washington, D.C., a majority of identifications result from *request searches*. Miami specialists produce nearly half of their identifications from *own initiative* searches; Richmond is able to make nearly 20 percent of their identifications from *cold searches*.

- When the manpower devoted to identification efforts is considered, it is clear that the productivity levels of the different fingerprint units differ significantly. A fingerprint specialist in Washington, D.C., averages 42 suspect identifications per year (assuming 70 percent of his time is spent searching prints); whereas Richmond averages 397. In terms of cost, an identification in Washington, D.C. entails 140 hours of man-power at a cost of $875. In the other three cities the cost for each identification is less than $100.

Plausible explanations that account for *some* of the very wide differences observed in the productivity levels of these four fingerprint identification sections include the following:

- The Washington, D.C., specialist is responsible for several fingerprint-related activities, more so than in the other three cities. And it is likely that the average Washington, D.C., technician does not spend 70 per-cent of his time searching prints, but in fact, spends much less. (How-ever, even if he spends only half, i.e., 35 percent, of the time searching prints, there is still a factor of five difference in suspect identifications per specialist between Richmond and Washington.)

These additional activities may prevent the D.C. specialist from becoming as thoroughly familiar with latent fingerprints and the various files maintained as someone who is involved solely in this activity.

The Richmond Identifications Specialist explained that his large number of suspect identifications made per year were due to the fact that evidence tech-nicians were well trained, that he works closely with the detectives, and that he spends a considerable amount of time (over one-third) on cold searches. Also, he has become familiar with the prints of many of the repeat offenders, and when a good latent is lifted, he can often make an initial identification of its owner without having to consult the fingerprint files. Of course, final identification is made by consulting the files.

- In all of the four departments, the majority of suspect identifications result from a request made by an investigator to have the fingerprint specialist compare a certain latent print with those of a named suspect. This implies that the productivity of the fingerprint specialist depends primarily on the quantity and quality of the leads or requests made by the investigator.

Does identification productivity depend on the number of requests made by investigators? A Washington investigator averaged two requests for searches per year; in Richmond, we estimate that on the average an investigator requests fifteen searches per year. So, such dependence may be significant.

- The absolute number of prints maintained in the different fingerprint files certainly affects the productivity of the specialist. In Richmond

Table 10–4
Productivity of Fingerprint Identification Sections

Item	Washington, D.C.[a]	Miami, Fla.[a]	Richmond, Ca.[b]	Los Angeles, Ca.[a]
1. Approximate number of crime scenes processed per year	33,783	8,700	4,000	28,000
2. Number of Crime Search Officers (tech/total police employ.)	90 (0.018)	18 (0.020)	8 (0.042)	37 specialists plus patrolmen
3. Number of crime scenes processed per Evidence Technicians per year	375	483	500	NA
4. Approximate number of crime scenes where prints were lifted	14,191 (42%)	4,166 (47.8%)	2,800 (70%)	14,000 (50%)
5. Total number of identifications[c]	612	379	278	1,277
a. Request searches	465 (76%)	183 (48.2%)	224 (80.5%)	NA
b. Own initiative	147 (24%)	176 (46.4%)	54 (19.5%)	NA
c. Cold searches	0	20 (5.2%)		NA
6. Percentage of identifications from latent prints (hit rate)	4.3	9.0	9.9	9.1
7. Number of fingerprint ID specialists	21	4	1	11
8. Number of equivalent specialists (assuming 70% of time is search time)	14.7	2.8	0.7	7.7
9. IDs per equivalent fingerprint specialist per year	42	135	397	165
10. Hours/cost[d] per ID	140 hours/$875	15.3 hours/$95.6	5.2 hours/$32	8.8 hours/$55

[a]Based on Department Records, 1973 (includes all crime types).

[b]Based on Department Records, 1972 (includes all crime types).

[c]Suspects identified, not cases cleared.

[d]Cost based on $13,000 salary per fingerprint specialist.

and Miami the specialized criminal file (usually repeat offenders) contains the prints of 4,000 persons; in the District of Columbia a similar file contains the prints of over 30,000 career offenders. In practical terms, the D.C. career file cannot be cold-searched.

This limitation makes the D.C. technician dependent on his own initiative or on request searches.

- Miami fingerprint specialists, maintaining close contact with the rest of the police department, are able to associate several crime scenes based on similar MO, and then proceed on their own initiative to search latents. So in Miami, their own "detective" work has proved most profitable in leading to suspect identifications.

The current organization of the Washington Fingerprint Examination Section makes a situation similar to Miami's impossible. The D.C. section receives latents from eight police districts, and with the large volume of criminal activity in each of these districts, it is doubtful that any specialists could follow the criminal activities in all of them. Therefore, *own initiative* searches in the District of Columbia are limited primarily to situations where a suspect has been arrested and the specialist chooses to search the latents retrieved from the area in which he was arrested.

Concluding Remarks

Police departments across the country are emphasizing collection of physical evidence by allocating more personnel to it, buying new equipment, and processing a larger percentage of crime scenes for physical evidence. These measures are being taken in the belief that the greater the amount of physical evidence retrieved, the greater will be the number of suspect identifications from such evidence. Our study fails to confirm so simple a relationship. For example, our sample of burglary cases reveals that within the range of variation exhibited in the departments we studied, collecting fingerprints at a higher percentage of crime scenes does not necessarily lead to more suspect identifications. We are led rather to the inference that an improved fingerprint identification capability is more productive of identifications than a more intensive print collection effort. Departments expanding their physical evidence collection activity should correspondingly increase their physical evidence processing capabilities.

But simply increasing resources devoted to fingerprint identification activities does not necessarily assure that more identifications will be produced. Fingerprint files may become inoperable because of excessive size. The print identification process in larger police departments should be facilitated by keeping the print files by geographical area, with a fingerprint specialist assigned to each area. (Career offender files should be particularly amenable to this sort of decentralization.) To make cold searches more practical, the area subfiles should contain the prints of no more than several thousand, say 4,000 to 5,000, persons.

Request searches, which imply cooperative effort between investigator and fingerprint specialist, clearly appear to be the most productive type. An information system should be devised to link investigators and fingerprint specialists in an efficient manner. This should help motivate and facilitate the reciprocal exchange of information.

11 The Relationship Between Thoroughness of Investigation and Case Disposition

Police investigation, whether or not it can be regarded as contributing significantly to the *identification* of perpetrators, is a necessary police function because it is the principal means by which all relevant evidence is gathered and presented to the court so that criminal prosecution can be initiated. As demonstrated by data in Chapter 8, the majority of an investigator's time is spent gathering evidence for purposes of prosecution, *after* the suspect has been identified. A police investigator is responsible for gathering all available evidence, and appearing and testifying as to its legality; subsequent court disposition of the case often depends on how efficiently the investigator has carried out these tasks.

The police, the court system, and the correction systems have all received widespread criticism, but the heaviest appears to be directed at the courts. Public consciousness of shortcomings in the prosecutorial process has been heightened by vocally critical police, who frequently complain that a patently guilty suspect has been released because the prosecutor is unwilling to file criminal charges; or that defendants receive unduly lenient sentences as the result of excessive plea bargaining. Police feelings of frustration seem to arise, at least in part, because the police sometimes do not acknowledge the difference between strong suspicion and proof beyond a reasonable doubt. The police themselves, when they fail to perform a timely, thorough investigation of a crime and to provide adequate reports of their findings, may be largely responsible for lack of legal proof of guilt. Prosecutors frequently find that they have insufficient evidence on which to proceed. Without investigatory resources of their own, prosecutors may then be compelled to reject cases, to suffer dismissals, or to make heavy concessions to defendants for a plea of guilty or else go to trial at a serious disadvantage. The police can help prevent the outcomes that so dissatisfy them by being more knowledgeable about the type and amount of information that a prosecutor requires to establish guilt for each type of offense and by better allocating their investigative efforts to provide this information.

The research reported here was undertaken to illuminate two facets of the controversy between police and prosecutor about responsibility for prosecutorial failures. The specific questions that we addressed were the following:

- What was the investigative completeness (i.e., the "thoroughness") in robbery cases presented by the police to the prosecutor for filing in two local jurisdictions during the first four months of 1974?

167

That is, how fully were the evidentiary requirements of the prosecutor met by the efforts of the reporting patrolmen and investigators?

- What seemed to be the effect of the degree of completeness of the police-provided information on the disposition of the defendant?
  Are these cases consistent with a claim that a lack of thorough police investigation and reporting is responsible for filed charges being dismissed, for pleas being heavily bargained, and for sentences being light?

One useful by-product of our study is the instrument that we designed to analyze the information content of police reports (see fig. 11-1). This data form, which contains 39 questions that a prosecutor might want the police to address in conducting a robbery investigation, was developed on the basis of discussions with prosecutors, detectives, and police supervisors. Of course, some individual cases may require less investigative information than is covered by this form; others may require more. Nonetheless, it is sufficiently comprehensive to be useful for investigator training; to be applied as a checklist in conducting an investigation; to serve as a performance measure for the needs of investigator supervisors; and to aid the prosecutor's office in making decisions on complaint filing. The form should be readily modifiable to crimes other than robbery.

Assessing the Thoroughness of Police Investigations

The two California prosecutors' offices that were selected for this study were chosen to reflect contrasting prosecutorial practices concerning felony case screening. We took from each office a sample of robbery cases presented to them by the police during the first four months of 1974. The information from these sampled cases has enabled us to draw inferences about the *thoroughness*[1] of police investigation underlying them. They also serve as a basis for our assessment of how the disposition of defendants appears to depend on the quality of investigation.

One of the offices (denoted A) tends to be extremely strict[2] in screening cases for filing. The standard it follows is that of filing only those charges it believes can be proved to a jury. If basic elements are missing from the police reports, or the facts of the case are not convincing, the case is not filed. On the other hand, once a case has been filed, Office A is highly resistant to accepting

---

1. The term *thoroughness* is used here to designate investigative completeness, i.e., how much of the information that the prosecutor deems desirable is provided in written documentation given him by the police.

2. Greenwood et al. (1973) led us to expect significant differences in police investigative effort and prosecutorial posture between the two selected jurisdictions.

a plea bargain to a lesser charge. The police are aware of this policy, and although individual officers are often resentful of the prosecutor's stand, they make a conscientious attempt to comply with his demands.

The other office (denoted B) appears to operate with significantly greater accommodation to routine police procedures, accepting their practice of presenting minimal information to substantiate the filing of a case.

Twenty-one cases from A and 22 from B comprise our two samples. At least one count of the complaint issued in each case was a robbery offense. To assess the completeness of investigation in each sampled case, we examined the documents presented to the prosecutor by the police. At the time of screening, a case file would include such police-provided items as a crime report and an arrest report, sometimes augmented by reports of stolen property and of physical evidence and perhaps a criminal history record and a follow-up investigation report. With these documents and later-added items we looked for every indication of police efforts to collect information that prosecutors might feel necessary to assure successful prosecution. For this purpose, we developed an information form (see fig. 11-1) divided into subject areas pertaining respectively to the offense, the suspect, the victim or witnesses, and the arrest. Within each area are listed questions that experienced prosecutors informed us should be addressed by a police investigation to facilitate prosecution of the case. In applying the instrument to a specific case, we would simply enter a checkmark where a question could be answered from information in the police-provided documents. One may observe that the form shown in figure 11-1 distinguishes from whom (victim, witness, or suspect) the information came and indicates the time and place of its acquisition (at the crime scene, at the place of arrest, or by follow-up investigation).

Merely categorizing the police-provided information, as in figure 11-1, helps to answer such relevant questions as the following: What types of information does the responding patrolman usually collect or fail to collect at the crime scene? What evidentiary matters are often not addressed in the course of an investigation? Whom does the investigator typically interview for follow-up information on what subjects?

Before we present the results of the research, we must acknowledge the methodological limitations inherent in conducting research of this type. Such limitations necessarily constrain, but do not negate, the inferences we are able to draw from the data.

First, although the two jurisdictions and their companion police departments are both branch offices of a single district, they cannot be considered truly matched samples. The written polices governing the prosecutor and police practices are similar, but the nature of the "working" policies of the prosecutor and the police, the composite of the criminal population, and other components of the court (e.g., judges, public defenders' office) may be dissimilar.

Defendant Identification _____
Case Identification_____
Date Presented for Filing _____

Case Information Desirable for Prosecution	Interviews Conducted						Other Sources
	V_{AI}	S_{AI}	W_{AI}	V_{FU}	S_{FU}	W_{FU}	
1. What INTERVIEWS were conducted?							
Offense							
2. Is there a verbatim report of the instant OFFENSE?							
3. Is there a verbatim report of the FORCE USED?							
4. What was the PHYSICAL HARM to the victim?							
5. Is there a detailed description of the PROPERTY taken?							
6. What was the method of S(uspect)'s ESCAPE?							
7. What type of VEHICLE was used by S?							
8. What type of WEAPON was used by S?							
9. If a gun was used, was it LOADED?							
10. If a gun was used, when was it ACQUIRED?							
11. Where is the LOCATION of the weapon now?							
Suspect							
12. Was S UNDER THE INFLUENCE of alcohol or drugs?							
13. What are the details of S's DEFENSE?							
14. What is S's ECONOMIC STATUS?							
15. Was S advised of CONSTITUTIONAL RIGHTS?							
16. If multiple suspects, what is their RELATIONSHIP?							
17. Is there evidence of PRIOR OFFENSES by S?							
18. Is there evidence of S's MOTIVES?							
19. Is there evidence of past PSYCHIATRIC TREATMENT of S?							
20. What is S's PAROLE OR PROBATION status?							
21. Does S have an alcohol or drug ABUSE HISTORY?							
22. Where is S EMPLOYED?							
Victim/Witnesses							
23. What is the RELATIONSHIP between S and V(ictim)?							
24. What is the CREDIBILITY of the W(itnesses)?							
25. Can the W make a CONTRIBUTION to the case prosecution?							
26. Were MUG SHOTS shown to V or W?							
27. If shown, are the PROCEDURES and RESULTS adequately described?							
28. Was a LINE-UP conducted?							
29. If conducted, are the PROCEDURES and RESULTS adequately described?							
30. Was an effort made to LIFT FINGERPRINTS at the scene?							
31. If made, were USABLE FINGERPRINTS OBTAINED?							
32. Were PHOTOS TAKEN at the crime scene?							
33. Is the EXACT LOCATION from where the photos and prints were taken given?							
34. Did V VERIFY his statements in the crime report?							
35. Did V have IMPROPER MOTIVES in reporting the offense?							
Arrest							
36. What was the legal BASIS FOR SEARCH AND SEIZURE?							
37. How was the LOCATION OF EVIDENCE learned?							
38. How was the LOCATION OF S learned?							
39. How was the ARREST OF S made?							

Key to Figure 11-1

V_{AI}, S_{AI}, W_{AI} — Refers to interview conducted with the victim (V), suspect (S), or witness (W) at the time of the incident or arrest report.

V_{FU}, S_{FU}, W_{FU} — Refers to interview conducted with the victim (V), suspect (S), or witness (W) in the course of a followup investigation.

Other Sources — Reflects either the patrolman's or investigator's comments, information provided by other agencies (such as criminal records), or other information from police reports (such as physical evidence reports).

Question

1 — Applied to any conversation or interview concerning the case between party and police.

2 — Must include exact words used by the V, S, or W to describe the offense; also must include description of S's movements before, during, and after the offense.

3 — Must include exact words S used in the commission of the offense.

4 — A statement indicating what physical injury V incurred as a result of the offense; if no injury, a statement of that fact.

5 — Must include an itemized account of the stolen property; if money involved, must include a listing of the denominations.

17 — Could include any information on S's prior criminal offenses, either information secured from S, the officer, or official criminal history records.

27,29 — "Adequate descriptions must specify the number of persons or photos shown and the instructions given by the police to the viewer; also must record the verbatim reaction of the viewer to the line-up or mug shot showing.

Figure 11-1. Investigation Information Form

In addition, it must be remembered that the offense type, rather than the characteristics of the defendant, served as the control factor in matching the samples. No one would attempt to argue that the defendant's social characteristics, employment history, parole and probation experiences, drug and alcohol history, etc., do not have an effect on several aspects of the police and court processing. Although the effects of each of these variables have never been quantifiably measured and as such cannot be adequately controlled in research of this type, it is important that their implications not be forgotten. Therefore, in our research, where we have simply controlled for the offense characteristics and attempted to draw inferences concerning dismissals, plea bargaining, and sentencing, it must be remembered that extraneous variables, which cannot be estimated, have possibly intervened and confounded the results.

Our findings concerning thoroughness are based on *written* reports filed by the police. We recognize that these forms are surrogates for the actual information obtained, and that investigators in both jurisdictions may collect more information than is presented to the prosecutor. As such, it might be argued that we have measured the quality of *reporting,* rather than the *thoroughness* of the investigation. In fact, our research is designed to measure the written information conveyed to the prosecutor, since this is the information that will be used to dispose of the case in both of the sample jurisdictions. It is irrelevant for our purposes to know if more information was gathered than is presented in written form. It is the policy in each of these offices that the case will be handled by several different prosecutorial and defense personnel. If some information is verbally conveyed at the filing stage, it is likely to be lost as valuable information throughout the remainder of the case processing. We feel confident that the written information is representative of the quality of the investigation, and is the only clear measure by which an investigation can currently be evaluated.

These methodological constraints, once acknowledged, need not limit the research conducted under these conditions. Our analysis does much to suggest a means by which investigators can be evaluated, draws preliminary inferences on the relationship between thoroughness and case disposition, and suggests areas for further research.

Research Results

General Comparison of Police-Provided Reports

The reports provided by the police to the prosecutor in our two samples of robbery cases imply, as anticipated, that the thoroughness of police investigation in Jurisdiction A was perceptibly better than in Jurisdiction B. In A, the reports to the prosecutor were typewritten, painstaking in detail, and documented each investigative activity in chronological order. The police reports provided to the B prosecutor were generally handwritten, were difficult to read and understand,

and generally contained only the major facts of the case, so that a reader could not readily determine whether or not any follow-up investigation had been conducted and, if one had, what information was obtained.[3]

The information provided to the A prosecutor at the time of screening would always include a crime report, an arrest report, and at least one follow-up investigation report. The crime report is prepared (in both A and B) by a patrol officer, usually the one who initially responds to the crime scene. It purports to recapitulate all events relating to the crime incident. In A, the crime report would usually include a verbatim account of the incident from the victim and from each witness. Although these several accounts were often redundant, all were reported so that inconsistencies among the statements would be noted. Further, the crime report provided in A would include a detailed description of the property taken in the robbery (and if it was money, the denominations of the bills); a description of the physical injury, if any, sustained by the victim; and a description of the physical evidence retrieved from the crime scene, including latent fingerprints. An example of a crime report as prepared in Jurisdiction A is included in Appendix I.

The arrest report is also usually prepared by a patrolman, but in some instances the arresting officer may be an investigator. It recounts the circumstances of the arrest at a minimum. As prepared in A, this report would often include information about the way in which the police learned of the suspect's location, what resistance he may have offered, whether or not the suspect was advised of his constitutional rights at that time, whether or not the officers conducted a search and, if so, what was searched with what justification and what was seized. Further, if the arresting officer had attempted to interrogate the suspect, then the A arrest report would contain a verbatim account (including the *Miranda* warnings as given and the suspect's response).[4] Finally, the A arrest report would state the specific jail to which the suspect was taken and whether or not he was then booked. An example of an arrest report as prepared in Jurisdiction A is shown in Appendix I.

One conspicuous difference between A and B is that the A prosecutor invariably was given a follow-up investigation report and (within our sample of cases) the B prosecutor invariably was not. This report, made by the investigator

---

3. One rationale advanced in some police quarters for minimizing the factual content of formal investigative reports is that these reports are subject to discovery by defense counsel and thereby facilitate the impeachment of prosecution witnesses, frequently policemen. Hence, the results of detailed investigations, when made, are better communicated orally to the prosecutor's office. The results of this research would tend to refute the argument that negative consequences are likely to result if all information is presented in written form. Jurisdiction A, where this procedure is followed, no such negative consequences could be noted.

4. Police policy in A was that an arresting officer would not question a suspect unless personally familiar with the case.

assigned to the case, purports to relate all facets of his investigation. The names and addresses of all persons whom he interviewed or attempted to reach are stated, along with the important points of the interviews. If the investigator showed mug shots or conducted a lineup, the report would describe his procedures meticulously; give the identity, by police number, of persons or pictures used; describe the location (hospital, home, police station) of the event; and recite the verbatim instructions given by the police to the viewers. Such information is often crucial to a successful prosecution, for defense counsel is quick to allege coercive or unduly suggestive police tactics. Even more crucial may be the precise nature of the viewer's identification statement, which the A investigation report would quote verbatim. For example, it might be, "I am positive that Number 3 is the guy who robbed me," or "Number 2 looks like him but I can't be 100 percent sure." This difference in confidence of identification may be determinative of the decision to file and, if the complaint is filed, of the case outcome.

Another type of information sometimes available in an A investigation report is that obtained from an interview of the suspect in jail. The investigator may have elicited information as to the suspect's motives, his prior criminal record, his account of the offense (especially as to weapons involved and his state of intoxication), and his relationship to the victim. Finally, the A investigation report would serve as a vehicle for the investigator to characterize the evidence that had been gathered. For example, he might assess the credibility of the victim or of witnesses, or he might underscore inconsistencies in specific facts reported. Such comments undoubtedly aid the prosecutor in evaluating the strength of a case. An investigation follow-up report as prepared in Jurisdiction A is shown in Appendix I.

In our sample of robbery cases from the B prosecutor's office we found that a crime report and an arrest report were given to the prosecutor but no separate report of a follow-up investigation (even though the transcript of the preliminary hearing might indicate that some investigative activity of this nature had been conducted). The B crime report typically contained the identity of the victim and the witnesses, together with the victim's account of the crime, but seldom more than this single account of the event, which the responding patrolman would record as volunteered. Consequently, B crime reports tended to be not only short, but also fragmentary as to details. To illustrate, the description of a crime incident might resemble the following:

Officer Jones and I responded to 4665 Tamarack Blvd. in the Downtown District after receiving a radio call that a robbery had just occurred at that location.

The victim, Mrs. Martha Smith, is the manager of the motel whose office was robbed. She told us that two MN (male Negroes) entered the lobby at about 10:30 p.m. One of them pointed a gun at her and demanded that she give him the money in the cash register. She handed over approximately $75 in a bank bag, and they fled. Mrs. Smith immediately called the police and reported the robbery.

The victim said that the two perpetrators were wearing denim jackets and seemed to be about 6 feet tall. She said that she was too nervous to look at the suspects closely and doubted that she could identify them from photographs.

—Officer B. Conally

Because of their brevity, such crime reports in B often lack the detailed information that a prosecutor needs to prove his case. For example, the verbatim words used by the robber are often helpful in establishing the threat of force in the commission of the offense. The prosecutor may be able to develop this evidence at the preliminary hearing, but there is the risk that the victim's memory has faltered in the interim. In the above illustration, for example, the officer failed to report whether or not the victim observed the vehicle used by the robbers, heard any conversation between them, believed them to be under the influence, could identify the type of weapon, etc. A further common weakness in the B crime reports we examined was their failure to indicate any attempt to collect physical evidence at the crime scene, particularly whether or not latent fingerprints were lifted or photos taken.

Our sample of arrest reports prepared in B contained only limited information about the events of the robbery arrest. Typically, there would be statements about how the arresting officers learned of the suspect's location, whether a search of the premises, car, or person occurred, and whether the suspect was advised of his rights at the time of the arrest. If the suspect confessed to the crime when arrested, his statement (usually not verbatim) was recorded. The B arrest report generally contained no indication that the arresting officer had interrogated the suspect about other matters of concern to the prosecutor. To illustrate, a typical narrative might resemble the following:

Officer Conroy and I responded to 85 Green Ave., having received a radio call that a robbery was in progress at the liquor store at that address.

When we arrived, we observed an adult male Caucasian running from the store, holding a bag and what appeared to be a knife. We observed a man in the liquor store pointing toward the party who had run from the store, so we began to chase the suspect.

The suspect was captured, handcuffed, and read his constitutional rights from the standard form. The knife, with a 5-inch blade, was confiscated as evidence, as was the bag containing money and miscellaneous checks.

The suspect acknowledged that he heard and understood his rights. He then confessed that he had robbed the store because he had been laid off work, needed money, and was getting desperate. He was transported and booked as charged.

—Officer H. Simmons

We found, on the other hand, that when a search was conducted and property seized, the B arrest reports did contain statements that purported to justify the search and seizure.

As noted earlier, no documentation of follow-up investigation was found in our sample of robbery cases in B. The arrest report might refer at times to investigative work, for example, stating that "John Doe was the suspect because his mug shot had been identified by the victim in a showup. His picture was thereafter circulated in the department." But such arrest reports would not contain a description of showups or lineups if conducted. Judging, therefore, from the cases of our sample, the prosecutor in B was provided little, if any, information on follow-up investigations by means of formal written police reports. Lacking information on follow-up interviews with victim, witnesses, or suspect, the prosecutor would make his decision to charge, we infer, solely on the basis of the reports by the responding patrolmen and arresting officers—reports commonly sparse in detail.[5]

Statistical Comparison of Police-Provided Reports

Our statistical results on the comparison of the quality of robbery investigation as reported in A and B are conveniently displayed by means of the research form shown earlier as figure 11-1. Tables 11-1 and 11-2 give the percentage of cases within the samples (the total number of cases being 21 in A and 22 in B) that provided the indicated item of information to the prosecutor at the time of screening. On its face, these summary tabulations seem to support the prosecutor's view that his needs for information are not fully and consistently met by law enforcement agencies. The data underlying the tables show that each of the 39 questions was on the average covered in 45 percent of the cases in our A sample; 26 percent of the cases in our B sample. (However, there was considerable variation in percentage coverage among the individual questions.) One may observe directly from tables 11-1 and 11-2 that there were significant differences between A and B in the frequency with which specific items of information were corroborated in our samples by several accounts of the same events.

The first line in table 11-1 confirms our earlier assertion that follow-up interviews were often conducted in A. In nearly one-half of our sample of A robbery cases, the victim had a follow-up contact by the investigator; in over 70 percent, the suspect was interviewed.

We next briefly comment on the results for the four subject area sections of tables 11-1 and 11-2.

---

5. In some instances, the case may be presented to the prosecutor for filing by the arresting or investigation officer, and the charging deputy and the officer are able to discuss details not included in the reports. However, in many instances the officer presenting the case will not have participated in the investigation and will not be able to supplement the facts in the reports.

Table 11-1
Presence of Information in Police Reports, Jurisdiction A[a]
(In percent)

Case Information Desirable for Prosecution	Interviews Conducted						Other Sources	Information From at Least One Source[b]
	V_{AI}	S_{AI}	W_{AI}	V_{FU}	S_{FU}	W_{FU}		
1. What INTERVIEWS were conducted?	81.0	43.0	57.0	47.6	71.4	9.5		100.0
Offense								
2. Is there a verbatim report of the instant OFFENSE?	76.0	23.8	23.8	23.8	57.1			90.4
3. Is there a verbatim report of the FORCE USED?	66.6	9.5	9.5	14.2	43.0	4.7		95.2
4. What was the PHYSICAL HARM to the victim?	47.6	4.7		14.2	14.2			47.6
5. Is there a detailed description of the PROPERTY taken?	52.3	9.5	4.7	28.5	19.0			90.4
6. What was the method of S(uspect)'s ESCAPE?	38.0		28.5	14.2	14.2			71.4
7. What type of VEHICLE was used by S?	14.2	9.5	19.0	4.7	9.5			38.0
8. What type of WEAPON was used by S?	52.3	14.2	14.2	9.5	52.3			85.7
9. If a gun was used, was it LOADED?		9.5			9.5			19.0
10. If a gun was used, when was it ACQUIRED?		9.5			9.5			28.4
11. Where is the LOCATION of the weapon now?		9.5		4.7	14.2			9.5
Suspect								
12. Was S UNDER THE INFLUENCE of alcohol or drugs?	9.5	19.0		4.7	23.8		9.5	42.8
13. What are the details of S's DEFENSE?		4.7			14.2			18.9
14. What is S's ECONOMIC STATUS?		4.7			14.2			14.2
15. Was S advised of CONSTITUTIONAL RIGHTS?		33.3			52.3		9.5	100.0
16. If multiple suspects, what is their RELATIONSHIP?		14.2		4.7	23.8		4.7	42.7
17. Is there evidence of PRIOR OFFENSES by S?		4.7			23.8		38.1	66.6
18. Is there evidence of S's MOTIVES?		23.8		4.7	28.5			47.6
19. Is there evidence of past PSYCHIATRIC TREATMENT of S?								9.5
20. What is S's PAROLE OR PROBATION status?			4.7	4.7	9.5		4.7	37.8
21. Does S have an alcohol or drug ABUSE HISTORY?					23.8		23.8	23.8
22. Where is S EMPLOYED?		4.7			23.8		9.5	28.5
Victim/Witnesses								
23. What is the RELATIONSHIP between S and V(victim)?	4.7							4.7
24. What is the CREDIBILITY of the W(itnesses)?							9.5	9.5
25. Can the W make a CONTRIBUTION to the case prosecution?				29.0		8.5	23.8	23.8
26. Were MUG SHOTS shown to V or W?							14.2	51.7

Offense items 2–11: 57.5%

Suspect items 12–22: 39.3%

27.	If shown, are the PROCEDURES and RESULTS adequately described?		30.0	30.0
28.	Was a LINE-UP conducted?		53.0	53.0
29.	If conducted, are the PROCEDURES and RESULTS adequately described?		40.0	40.0
30.	Was an effort made to LIFT FINGERPRINTS at the scene?		41.0	41.0
31.	If made, were USABLE FINGERPRINTS OBTAINED?		59.0	59.0
32.	Were PHOTOS TAKEN at the crime scene?		35.0	35.0
33.	Is the EXACT LOCATION from where the photos and prints were taken given?	18.0	29.0	29.0
34.	Did V VERIFY his statements in the crime report?		6.0	24.0
35.	Did V have IMPROPER MOTIVES in reporting the offense?		4.7	4.7 } 31.1%
	Arrest			
36.	What was the legal BASIS FOR SEARCH AND SEIZURE?		23.8	23.8
37.	How was the LOCATION OF EVIDENCE learned?		33.3	33.3
38.	How was the LOCATION OF S learned?		66.6	66.6
39.	How was the ARREST OF S made?		85.7	85.7 } 52.3%

Overall 45.0%

Note: The percentages within the matrix refer only to the presence of information the police chose to record; they may not represent a complete picture of the information gathered by the police in the course of the investigation. It is possible that certain police officers record only "positive" information and assume that an omission of information automatically implies that the information is either not applicable or inappropriate in a specific case.

[a] 21 cases in sample.

[b] Percentage of cases that presented this information from at least one source.

Table 11-2
Presence of Information in Police Reports, Jurisdiction B[a]
(In percent)

Case Information Desirable for Prosecution	Interviews Conducted						Other Sources	Information From at Least One Source[b]
	V_{AI}	S_{AI}	W_{AI}	V_{FU}	S_{FU}	W_{FU}		
1. What INTERVIEWS were conducted?	100.0	63.0	45.0					100.0
Offense								
2. Is there a verbatim report of the instant OFFENSE?	91.0	4.0	9.0					95.2
3. Is there a verbatim report of the FORCE USED?	32.0		4.5					36.5
4. What was the PHYSICAL HARM to the victim?	13.6		4.5					18.5
5. Is there a detailed description of the PROPERTY taken?	27.2							27.2
6. What was the method of S(uspect)'s ESCAPE?	41.0		13.6					45.4
7. What type of VEHICLE was used by S?	41.0		13.6					45.4 36.2%
8. What type of WEAPON was used by S?	54.0	9.0	4.5				4.5	63.6
9. If a gun was used, was it LOADED?		9.0					4.5	13.5
10. If a gun was used, when was it ACQUIRED?		9.0						.0
11. Where is the LOCATION of the weapon now?		9.0					9.0	18.1
Suspect								
12. Was S UNDER THE INFLUENCE of alcohol or drugs?	4.0	9.0					9.0	22.7
13. What are the details of S's DEFENSE?								.0
14. What is S's ECONOMIC STATUS?		4.5						4.5
15. Was S advised of CONSTITUTIONAL RIGHTS?		63.0					4.5	63.6
16. If multiple suspects, what is their RELATIONSHIP?								.0
17. Is there evidence of PRIOR OFFENSES by S?							9.0	9.0
18. Is there evidence of S's MOTIVES?		18.1						18.1
19. Is there evidence of past PSYCHIATRIC TREATMENT of S?		4.5						4.5 14.0%
20. What is S's PAROLE OR PROBATION status?		9.0					9.0	18.1
21. Does S have an alcohol or drug ABUSE HISTORY?							9.0	9.0
22. Where is S EMPLOYED?		4.5						4.5
Victim/Witnesses								
23. What is the RELATIONSHIP between S and V(ictim)?	9.0							9.0
24. What is the CREDIBILITY of the W(itnesses)?								.0
25. Can the W make a CONTRIBUTION to the case prosecution?			4.5				9.0	13.5
26. Were MUG SHOTS shown to V or W?	4.5							4.5

27. If shown, are the PROCEDURES and RESULTS adequately described?		.0 } 3.4%
28. Was a LINE-UP conducted?		.0
29. If conducted, are the PROCEDURES and RESULTS adequately described?		.0
30. Was an effort made to LIFT FINGERPRINTS at the scene?	4.5	4.5
31. If made, were USABLE FINGERPRINTS OBTAINED?	9.0	9.0
32. Were PHOTOS TAKEN at the crime scene?	4.5	4.5
33. Is the EXACT LOCATION from where the photos and prints were taken given?		.0
34. Did V VERIFY his statements in the crime report?		.0
35. Did V have IMPROPER MOTIVES in reporting the offense?		.0
Arrest		
36. What was the legal BASIS FOR SEARCH AND SEIZURE?	36.3	36.3 } 52.2%
37. How was the LOCATION OF EVIDENCE learned?	32.0	32.0
38. How was the LOCATION OF S learned?	68.1	68.1
39. How was the ARREST OF S made?	72.7	72.7
		Overall 26.4%

Note: The percentages within the matrix refer only to the presence of information the police chose to record; they may not represent a complete picture of the information gathered by the police in the course of the investigation. It is possible that certain police officers record only "positive" information and assume that an omission of information automatically implies that the information is either not applicable or inappropriate in a specific case.

[a]22 cases in sample.

[b]Percentage of cases that presented this information from at least one source.

Information Reported on the Offense

It is clear from tables 11–1 and 11–2 that the details of the offense itself appear to dominate the information reporting in both A and B. The underlying data inform us that each of the offense items of information was covered on the average in 57 percent of the cases in our A sample, by 36 percent of the cases in our B sample. The tables confirm that corroborative accounts of the offense were commonly reported in A, infrequently in B. The A investigators often (71 percent of the cases) conducted a follow-up interview with the suspect and recorded his verbatim account of the offense in 57 percent of the cases and his account of the force used in the robbery in 43 percent of the cases.

The tables also reveal the more frequent investigative reporting in A than in B concerning the force used, the victim's injuries, and the nature of the property taken. Both A and B reports often contain information on the type of weapon used, but seldom answer more detailed questions.

Information Reported on the Suspect

Differences between A and B in information reported about the suspect are marked, especially because of the follow-up interview frequently conducted in A. Each question in this area, the underlying data show, was covered on the average of 39.3 percent of the cases in the A sample, but only 14.0 percent of the cases in the B sample.

The arresting officers in B, although they conducted an interview with the suspect in 63 percent of the cases, rarely recorded information listed here as desired by the prosecutor. Since B police reported no follow-up interviews with the suspect, the case files of our sample usually contained no information at time of screening about the suspect's drug and alcohol use history, about his relationship to the victim and other defendants, about his motives, etc. Police in A did not necessarily provide the prosecutor with full coverage of information items about the suspect, but he was sometimes better informed at time of screening than his counterpart in B, especially because of the follow-up interview.

Information Reported on the Victim or Witnesses

Police reports, particularly those of patrolmen, tend to neglect the detailed knowledge of the victim and witnesses, if we are to judge from our samples. This information can be important to the prosecutor, and unless he succeeds in bringing out unreported facts at the preliminary hearing, the subsequent prosecution of the case may suffer. Typically missing is information about a relationship between the victim and the suspect and about possible improper motives that the victim might have in reporting the alleged offense. Table 11-1 shows that police reporting in B was sparse in this subject area. As noted earlier and con-firmed by tables 11-1 and 11-2 there is a conspicuous difference between A and B in the reporting of the results of showups and lineups, as well as of the procedures for conducting them.

Information Reported on the Arrest

Items 38 and 39 of tables 11-1 and 11-2 suggest that information on the arrest itself was reported by the police to the prosecutor with roughly the same fre-quency in A and B. The explanation of the smaller and more disparate entries in items 36 and 37 may be in the irregularity with which search and seizures for evidence occur in concert with arrest.

In summary, these are the major findings in this section:

- The strictness of prosecutorial filing practices[6] does appear to have a significant effect on the thoroughness of investigations conducted by local police departments. However, even where policies are strict, our samples indicate that the police collect only about half of the informa-tion desired by the prosecutor.

- The police reports filed in Jurisdiction B were handwritten, difficult to follow, and usually contained no more than minimal information concerning the case. There were no references to any follow-up in-vestigative work. In contrast, the reports in Jurisdiction A were type-written, easy to follow, and contained the most minute details of the case. In addition, separate reports documented the activities of the follow-up investigation in A.

- In Jurisdiction A, where follow-up investigations were always con-ducted in our sample cases, the following additional information was provided to the prosecutor:
  - Verbatim accounts from more than one person concerning the details of the offense and the extent of force used by the perpetrator.
  - Detailed accounts of lineups and mug shot showings.
  - Inclusion of information concerning retrieved physical evidence.
  - Investigator summaries of the case, often commenting on the quality of a given witness, the credibility of a victim, or pointing out incon-sistencies in the uncovered facts.

---

6. In both jurisdictions we examined a small sample of cases that were rejected for filing by the prosecutor in that jurisdiction. These intrajurisdictional, rather than interjurisdic-tional, comparisons indicated that the investigative thoroughness in rejected cases was not substantially different from that in the filed cases in either location.

— Information from the suspect about himself and his relationship to the case.

In Jurisdiction B, where our samples contained no instances of follow-up investigations, we infer that this information was almost never presented to the prosecutor.

Relationship Between Thoroughness of Investigation and Case Disposition

The second phase of this study, seeking to relate case disposition to the thoroughness of police investigation and reporting, required us to trace the judicial processing of each sampled case. This was accomplished by examining the court files. The documents generally presented in a court file included the Complaint, the Transcript of the Preliminary Hearing, the Information, Minute Orders, Motions, Transcript of Hearing on Plea Bargaining (in A only),[7] Bail and Own Recognizance Applications, Transcript of the Probation and Sentencing Hearing, and Final Sentencing Orders. Our comparisons between A and B concerning the rate of dismissals, the heaviness of plea bargaining, and the type of sentences imposed are based on an examination of these materials.

Robbery cases may differ not only in the degree of the crime, but also as to the filing (or threat of filing) of special allegations. The circumstances of the case may present the prosecutor with various options to allege prior convictions, possession and use of guns or deadly weapons, and infliction of great bodily injury on the victim. Such special allegations, if admitted or proved, may significantly enhance a state prison sentence if one is imposed.

To obtain comparability between our two samples of cases, it was necessary to classify each case by the special allegations appearing in the Information.[8] Because the two samples had not initially been matched by these allegations, the classification produced an uneven representation—some combinations of charges are in the A sample but not in the B sample, and vice versa. Nevertheless, as shown in table 11-3, some combinations are common to both A and B samples and enable us to draw limited inferences about the relationship between the presence of the additional information and the case disposition.[9]

Table 11-3 presents the details of the dispositional data, by eleven categories which have been matched according to the exact charge as specified in the

7. A separate transcript of the plea bargaining hearing was not compiled in Jurisdiction B.

8. We realize that the threat of amending the complaint by available special allegations may be as instrumental (say, in affecting plea bargaining) as the actual filing would be. Our samples of cases were too small to deal with this effect.

9. The sample for the second phase of research consists of 18 cases from A and 22 cases from B. Court records were unavailable for a few of the cases in the original sample.

Information. The X's in the first six columns indicate which special allegations were added to the robbery charge. Within each row, the percentage indicates the number of cases in the sample that possessed those special characteristics. In the sections below, we base our inferences on summary computations derived from results shown in this table; however, it is also worthwhile to study individual rows, where enough cases appear in a category to warrant examination. In category 5 (robbery with no special allegations), for example, the data support the argument that cases from Jurisdiction A were plea bargained less, and that defendants received more severe sentences. However, in category 3, the opposite appears true, in that cases from Jurisdiction B were treated more severely. Because of the inconsistent results, no definitive inferences can be drawn, regardless of the fact that in the category where the largest percentage of cases appear, the data show less plea bargaining and more severe sentencing in Jurisdiction A.

The Stability of the Original Charges

The stability of the charges in our sample cases between the complaint and the information may be perceived by means of table 11-4. Of course, the preliminary hearing is the principal intervening event. Table 11-4 indicates a greater stability of original charges in A, where the quality of investigative reporting was significantly more thorough. A possible explanation might include a higher quality of detective work in A, where investigators gather evidence sufficient to support the arrest charges.

Case Dismissal Rate

No cases in our A sample were dismissed. Nearly 23 percent (5/22) of the cases in our B sample were dismissed, the reasons being given as follows:[10]

Number of Cases Dismissed	Reason
1	Absence of indispensable party
1	995 PC (lack of probable cause)
1	Prosecution not ready
2	1538.5 PC (wrongful search and seizure)

---

10. To determine whether or not the large differences in dismissal rates between the two jurisdictions (none in A versus 23 percent in B) held constant in a large sample, another 50 cases were randomly selected from each jurisdiction to look at dismissal rates only. In this larger sample, 24 percent of the cases in B were subsequently dismissed, whereas none were dismissed in A. Therefore, we can conclude that indeed there is a significant difference in the number of cases that are subsequently dismissed in the two jurisdictions.

Table 11-3
Disposition of Cases, Jurisdictions A and B

	Description of Offense as Specified in Information						Jurisdiction A[a]			Jurisdiction B[b]		
	664/211[c]	211[d]	Prior Alleg.[e]	Armed Alleg.[f]	Use Alleg.[g]	Injury to V[h]	% of Sample	Disposition[i]	Sentence	% of Sample	Disposition[i]	Sentence
1.	x	x	x	x			0			9.0%	P/G as charged[j] Allegations stricken (100%) P/G of lesser offense P/G of lesser degree 211 Case dismissed	{ State prison (50%), Prob. and cnty. jail (50%), Probation, CYA }
2.	x	x		x			5.5%	P/G as charged Allegations stricken (100%) P/G of lesser offense P/G of lesser degree 211 Case dismissed	{ State prison, Prob. and cnty jail, Probation, CYA (100%)[l] }	13.6%	P/G as charged (100%) Allegation stricken P/G of lesser offense P/G of lesser degree 211 Case dismissed	{ State prison (66%)[k], Prob. and cnty. jail (33%), Probation, CYA }
3.	x			x	x		16.6%	P/G as charged Allegations stricken (100%) P/G of lesser offense P/G of lesser degree 211 Case dismissed	{ State prison, Prob. and cnty. jail, Probation (100%)[m], CYA }	18.1%	P/G as charged (50%) Allegations stricken (50%) P/G of lesser offense P/G of lesser degree 211 Case dismissed	{ State prison (100%), Prob. and cnty. jail, Probation, CYA } { State prison (50%), Prob. and cnty. jail, Probation, CYA (50.0%) }
4.	x		x				0			4.5%	P/G as charged Allegations stricken P/G to lesser offense P/G to lesser degree (100%) Case dismissed	{ State prison, Prob. and cnty. jail (100%), Probation, CYA }
5.	x						66.6%	P/G as charged (91.6%) Allegations stricken P/G to lesser offense P/G to lesser degree (8.3%) Case dismissed	{ State prison (45%), Prob. and cnty. jail (45%), Probation, CYA (10%) } { State prison, Prob. and cnty. jail, Probation, CYA (100%) }	31.8%	P/G as charged (14.2%) Allegations stricken P/G to lesser offense P/G to lesser degree (28.5%) Case dismissed (57.3)	{ State prison, Prob. and cnty. jail (100%), Probation, CYA } { State prison, Prob. and cnty. jail (50%), Probation (50%), CYA }

#							%	Disposition	%	Disposition	Outcome
6.				x		x	5.5	P/G as charged / Allegations stricken (100%) / P/G to lesser offense / P/G to lesser degree / Case dismissed — { State prison / Prob. and cnty. jail / Probation / CYA (100%) }	4.5	P/G as charged (100%) / Allegations stricken / P/G to lesser offense / P/G to lesser degree / Case dismissed	{ State prison (100%)[n] / Prob. and cnty. jail / Probation / CYA }
7.				x	x		0		4.5	P/G as charged / Allegations stricken / P/G to lesser offense / P/G to lesser degree (100%) / Case dismissed	{ State prison / Prob. and cnty. jail / Probation / CYA (100%) }
8.			x	x			0		4.5	P/G as charged / Allegations stricken (100%) / P/G to lesser offense / P/G to lesser degree / Case dismissed	{ State prison (100%) / Prob. and cnty. jail / Probation / CYA }
9.	x						0		4.5	P/G as charged / Allegations stricken / P/G to lesser offense / P/G to lesser degree / Case dismissed (100%)	
10.	x		x				0		4.5	P/G as charged / Allegations stricken / P/G to lesser offense / P/G to lesser degree (100%)–CJ only / Case dismissed	
11.	x	x	x				5.5%	P/G as charged / Allegations stricken / P/G to lesser offense (100%) / P/G to lesser degree / Case dismissed — { State prison / Prob. and cnty. jail / Probation (100%)[m] / CYA }	0		

[a] This sample contains 18 cases.
[b] This sample contains 22 cases.
[c] Attempted robbery.
[d] Robbery alone, no special allegations.
[e] Prior offenses alleged.
[f] Armed with firearm in the commission of the offense allegation.
[g] Use of firearm in the commission of the offense allegation.
[h] Injury to victim allegation.
[i] Except where specified, all of the cases were disposed of, a not guilty plea being changed to a guilty plea by the defendant.
[j] P/G is an abbreviation for plead guilty.
[k] Jury trial.
[l] CYA is an abbreviation for the California Youth Authority.
[m] State prison suspended, probation granted.
[n] Court trial.

Table 11-4

Comparison of Jurisdictions A and B in Charge Changes Between the Complaint and the Information

	Percentage in A Sample	Percentage in B Sample
Charges unchanged	88.8	63.6
Charges added (usually a lesser included offense)	5.5	13.6
Special allegations added	5.5	13.6
Some charges dismissed	–	–
Case dismissed prior to filing of Information	–	9.0

It is not clear that any of these dismissals could have been avoided by better police investigation and reporting in B. Yet, if the investigation had been more thorough in B, the charges might not have been filed, and valuable court resources not wasted.

Handling of Special Allegations

As indicated in table 11-5 our samples showed that special allegations were added to the basic robbery charge (211 PC) twice as frequently in B as in A. The table also shows that these special allegations were frequently stricken as a result of plea bargaining in B, while invariably stricken in A.

Our samples suggest that special allegations serve as prosecutorial leverage in inducing the defendant to plead guilty to the underlying offense. Prosecutors are encouraged to file special allegations when applicable,[11] but the consequences

Table 11-5

Comparison of the Disposition of Special Allegations in A and B

Special Allegation	A		B	
	Percentage in which Allegation Present	Percentage in which Allegation Stricken	Percentage in which Allegation Present	Percentage in which Allegation Stricken
None added (211 PC only)	66.6	–	33.3	–
Prior offense	5.5	5.5	20.0	20.0
Armed allegation	29.0	29.0	47.0	24.0
Use allegation	16.6	16.6	33.0	24.0
Great bodily injury	–	–	4.5	–

11. *Uniform Crime Charging Standards*, California District Attorneys Association, II. C.I.

of proving them appear to be so unduly drastic in many individual cases, that the allegations are readily stricken in return for defendant cooperation. In other words, the quality of police investigation does not appear to be a determining factor in how special allegations are handled.

Case Dispositions

None of the 18 cases in the A sample went to trial, i.e., all dispositions involved a change of plea from not guilty to one of guilty either to the original or to modified charges. And we have already noted that no cases in the A sample were dismissed. By contrast, the 22 cases of the B sample produced 5 dismissals, 1 court trial, and 2 jury trials, with the remaining cases being disposed of by a change of plea from not guilty to guilty.

A comparison between A and B of the heaviness of plea bargaining is shown in table 11-6. Although plea bargaining appears lighter in A than in B, this may simply reflect that the gravity of criminal conduct in the A cases was less than in the B cases, i.e., special allegations were considerably more frequent to begin with in B. One cannot conclude that only the quality of police investigation accounted for the difference.

Type of Final Sentence

Table 11-7 compares the frequencies with which various types of final sentences were imposed in the nondismissed cases of our samples from A and B. The outcomes summarized can be better understood by reference to table 11-3, where we observe that the final sentence results in A were dominated by the 5th category of cases (robbery with no special allegations), which contained two-thirds of the A sample. Almost all of these defendants pled guilty as charged,

Table 11-6
Comparison Between A and B of Dispositions by Pleas of Guilty

Disposition	Percentage in A Sample	Percentage in B Sample
Plea of guilty to original charges	61.1	31.8
Plea of guilty to original charges but with special allegations stricken or not considered	27.7	22.7
Plea of guilty to 2nd degree robbery reduced from 1st degree robbery	5.5	18.1
Plea of guilty to other lesser offense	5.5	4.5
Cases dismissed	–	22.7

with about one-half receiving state prison sentences and about one-half being granted probation. Again, by examining table 11–3, we find that the substantial number of state prison sentences imposed in B derived from several categories of cases (1st, 2nd, 3rd, and 6th) that all involved special allegations. It thus appears that the outcomes in table 11–7 reflect to a greater extent the "non-comparability" of our samples than the effects of differences in the quality of police investigation.

In summary, the major findings of this phase of the research are as follows:

- In Jurisdiction A, where police investigative reports were found to be more thorough, none of the sample cases were dismissed; whereas in Jurisdiction B, where the investigations were judged less complete, 23 percent of the sample cases were dismissed.

- The charges on which the defendant was bound over to the Superior Court were more frequently identical to the arrest charges in Jurisdiction A than in Jurisdiction B. Jurisdiction B more frequently added special allegations to the original charge than did A, but in both jurisdictions the special allegations were consistently stricken as part of the plea bargain.

- In Jurisdiction A, 61.1 percent of the defendants pled guilty to the crime as charged in the Information, with no apparent plea bargaining concessions; whereas in Jurisdiction B, 31.8 percent of the defendants pled guilty as charged. The remainder of the cases were either dismissed or plea bargained in some manner.

- All of the cases in Jurisdiction A were disposed of when the defendant entered a guilty plea to the charge; whereas in Jurisdiction B, 15 percent (3) of the cases ended in either a court or jury trial.[12]

- Overall, the average sentence in Jurisdiction B was more severe than that in Jurisdiction A.

- When the two samples are categorized according to the various special allegations, the data point to no consistent conclusions regarding case

Table 11–7
Comparison Between A and B of the Type of Final Sentence Imposed

Type of Final Sentence	Percentage in A Sample	Percentage in B Sample
State Prison	27.7	36.3
Probation plus County Jail	16.6	22.7
County Jail	.0	4.5
Probation	38.8	9.0
California Youth Authority (CYA)	16.6	4.5

---

12. All of the defendants in these cases were found guilty.

disposition or final sentences. In one category within the jurisdiction, it appears that the jurisdiction plea bargains less frequently and imposes more severe sentences, whereas in another category of the same jurisdiction the opposite appears to be true. However, in the largest category (211 PC only), the data show more severe sentencing in Jurisdiction A.

Concluding Remarks

Our observations make it obvious that a lack of coordination between police investigators and prosecutorial personnel causes significant problems for both. When we interpret the findings from this chapter, which suggest that the prosecutor is not given all of the information that he desires, with previous data which suggest that investigators spend the majority of their time gathering evidence on suspects in custody rather than on identifying suspects, we see no obvious reason why these investigative efforts should not be more closely coordinated with the prosecutor's function.

The objective data from this brief analysis are not as striking as one might at first suspect, although as an exploratory piece of research, we feel the analysis has merit. We did demonstrate a significant difference in the thoroughness of police investigation and reporting in two selected jurisdictions that had contrasting filing policies. Strict filing standards apparently resulted in more thorough investigation.

We expected to observe the impact of these differences in investigative thoroughness in all aspects of case disposition. Our hypothesis was that more thorough investigations would result in fewer dismissals, less plea bargaining, and more convictions.

In fact our sample did disclose a lower dismissal rate in the jurisdiction with more thorough investigation. As for case dispositions, the results were much less conclusive. In only one category of cases, albeit the largest, did the sentences in Jurisdiction A consistently exceed those imposed in Jurisdiction B. No cases in A went to trial, and all of those that did in B resulted in convictions.

Possibly a larger sample might disclose more significant patterns of differences between jurisdictions in the disposition of their cases. But the comparison would still entail the difficult task of weighting the different sentence alternatives and the methodological difficulties of controlling for all of the variables that affect court processing and disposition.

We believe that the differences in dismissal rates disclosed in this study are important. For this reason, among others, criminal justice officials should be mindful of the level of investigative thoroughness maintained in their jurisdiction. In addition, this research could be used to support a policy of presenting all available information to the prosecutor in written form, since no negative disposition effects were witnessed in a jurisdiction where such a policy was in effect. The information form devised in this research is also useful as a tool for evaluating investigative thoroughness.

12

Information Feedback to Crime Victims: A Survey of Burglary and Robbery Victims

Many investigators, as well as top-ranking police officials, have defended the investigative function, not because it contributes significantly to the identification of perpetrators, but because it is one of the principal contacts the police maintain with the victims of serious crimes. But although the police verbally espouse the public service function as an important part of the investigative role, most police merely respond initially to the crime scene and file a cursory report; subsequent police contacts with the victims concerning the progress of the case are rare.

If the public's confidence in their local police department is to be strengthened, it seems reasonable that when the perpetrator has been identified, the victim should be notified. However, a policy of routinely providing case information feedback to crime victims poses some risk of being self-defeating. For example, if a victim is informed that the perpetrator of his crime has been apprehended but not charged with his offense and is being prosecuted on another, the victim, rather than feeling more confident in the police or the criminal justice system, may in fact be disillusioned by such information. A resentful victim also could become highly vocal about his dissatisfactions and cause other citizens to be negative about police performance.

How much information to give the victim and when it is appropriate to convey it were the questions behind the research reported in this chapter. Our study is regarded as exploratory; the survey was conducted simply as an initial attempt to explore how victims feel about receiving information feedback regarding their specific case, and which types of information they feel are most important. The survey results are preliminary and will not support overall policy changes without further research.

An Illustrative Case

An actual case will depict the area of our concern. Mr V(ictim), retired and residing with his wife in a quiet, middle-class neighborhood for many years, returned home to find that a burglary had occurred. The entry appeared to have been made through a rear window which had been forced open. Missing was a portable color TV set. Mr. V called the police.

Two patrol officers soon responded. They queried Mr. V and examined the premises. They recorded details about Mr. V, the nature of the entry, and the

191

missing item of property. After completing the crime incident report as fully as they could, the officers departed. This case then became the responsibility of a detective. But Mr. V was never again directly in contact with the police.

Later in the day, neighborhood youngsters, learning of the burglary, informed Mr. V that they had seen an unfamiliar car parked nearby in the alley while he and his wife were away. These young witnesses said that, although a strange car parked in that location seemed suspicious, they spoke to no one about it at the time. Later, after learning about the burglary, the youths noticed what appeared to be the same car elsewhere in the neighborhood. They spoke of this incident to their parents who immediately telephoned the police and relayed the license number of the car and the location of the second observation. The police expressed their gratitude. But neither these informants nor Mr. V were later told of any action that resulted from this information.

In due course of events, Mr. V's case was marked in police files as "cleared by arrest." The suspect, Mr. B(urglar), had eventually been apprehended in the act of burglarizing another residence. His modus operandi in the later crime was again one of forcing a rear window of a home while the occupants were away. And he was carrying away a portable TV set when caught.

The initial intensive police questioning of Mr. B (which was not strictly necessary to convict him of the offense leading to his arrest) produced no admissions of other burglaries. Then the police promised Mr. B that he would be charged only with his latest crime even if he admitted prior burglaries; they encouraged him to "clear his slate" without suffering additional punishment. And they further promised that the receivers of the stolen property would not be prosecuted if they cooperated in returning it to the victims. These assurances persuaded Mr.B to confess. Unfortunately, he couldn't accurately recall all of the many burglaries he had committed, even after being driven to the locations of recent and unsolved burglaries in police files, including the one of Mr. V. Mr. B felt that he had probably been responsible for the burglary of Mr. V's house, but he wasn't certain; furthermore, he had no specific recollection of how he had disposed of Mr. V's television set if indeed he had stolen it. On the basis of Mr. B's statement, Mr. V's case was then deemed by the police investigators to have been cleared and its file was so marked. Mr. B was not charged with this offense, and the investigators did not inform Mr. V of this development.

Issues of Information Feedback to Victims

The foregoing experience has been presented as a suggestive context in which to place police dilemmas about giving case information to crime victims such as Mr. V. Should he have been told by the police that his case had been cleared by an arrest? Told that the suspect would be prosecuted for another crime but not for the one against him? And told that the information given by the suspect indicated that the stolen television set would probably not be recovered?

One approach to these questions would emphasize that crime victims may be regarded as clients of the police. Police investigative efforts are, at least in part, on the specific behalf of the victims. Given this relationship, shouldn't the police be obligated to communicate reports of case developments to their client-victims?

Another approach would underscore the duty of the police to provide a sense of security to the public and to individual citizens, who look to police to shield them from lawbreakers. In Mr. V's case, would his (and his neighbors') sense of security have been enhanced and would he have been more satisfied with police performance had he been informed that a suspect apparently responsible for his burglary among others had been arrested and would be prosecuted? And had been later informed that the suspect was convicted and sentenced?

Whatever the approach to these questions of information feedback to victims, the police may reasonably feel that decisive answers are lacking. The police do not dispute their broad duty to provide public service. But is information feedback to crime victims itself a distinguishable service that the public expects to be performed by the police?

Rand conducted a limited telephone survey of victim opinion about matters of information feedback. Below we describe the survey method and the sample of victims involved, the survey responses (which help to illuminate issues that have been set forth above), and some inferences that are suggested by these survey responses and that might have validity beyond the limited confines of the survey universe.

The Survey Method and the Victim Sample

The Survey Method

Our survey was conducted in a California jurisdiction whose population is roughly 100,000. A list of 72 victims of crime during the year ending April 1975 was drawn from the case files of the police department. Of this list, half were victims of burglary and half of robbery. The relative incidence of these two crimes in this jurisdiction in 1974 was approximately five burglaries for each robbery. Our list of victims thus did not purport to be representative of the true incidence of the two selected offenses. Rather, we sought a balance between victims who had personal contact with the offender (and may have been threatened by him) and victims who lacked this personal relationship.

A further characteristic of our sample list was that the cases of two-thirds of the victims had been marked cleared by the police; the cases for the remaining one-third were uncleared. These proportions are to be contrasted with actual clearance rates achieved by this police department in a recent period, namely, 13 percent for burglary and 31 percent for robbery. Again, our list of victims does not purport to be representative but is biased toward cases in which clearance occurred. Given that the focus of our survey is information feedback, we felt that more would be learned by interviewing victims in cleared cases, for feedback was more likely to be present in those circumstances.

Each of the 72 selected victims was sent a letter signed by the chief of police, informing him as follows:

- He would receive a phone call from a Rand employee with the purpose of interviewing him about his experience as a crime victim.

- His decision about whether or not to submit to an interview would not be reported to the police department.

- If interviewed, his responses would be anonymous.

Further, these victims were assured that the police department did not know the identity of the persons Rand had selected for the telephone survey.

Thirty-six of the seventy-two victims agreed to be interviewed. The preliminary letter signed by the chief of police appeared to be instrumental in eliciting their cooperation. Of the remaining thirty-six, only three directly refused to be interviewed. We were unable to reach the others after repeated attempts, some having moved away after the events of the case in which they were the victims.

The Sample of Respondents

The sample of 36 responding victims can be characterized in several ways. First, table 12-1 gives the composition of the sample in terms of whether the respondent was a victim of burglary or of robbery and whether the case was cleared or remained uncleared; and, if cleared, whether the clearance was based on an arrest only for the offense against this respondent or based otherwise.

Table 12–1
Classification of Victim Respondents by Crime Type and by Clearance in Their Cases

Clearance in Respondent's Case	Crime Type		
	Burglary	Robbery	Total
Uncleared	8 (22%)	6 (17%)	14 (39%)
Cleared	12 (33%)	10 (28%)	22 (61%)
By arrest in respondent's case only	5	5	10
Otherwise	7	5	12
Total	20 (55%)	16 (45%)	36 (100%)

Had our sample of victims been a representative one with respect to crime type and presence of clearance, the percentages for the main entries would have been as shown in the table below. Thus, in generalizing our sample of responses to the burglary and robbery victims in this jurisdiction, we should strongly weight the responses of the burglary victims in uncleared cases.

	Burglary	Robbery	Total
Uncleared	.72%	12%	84%
Cleared	.11%	5%	16%
	83%	17%	100%

Next, we characterize the sample of responding victims in terms of their receiving information feedback from the police department.[1] Table 12-2, which quantifies this aspect, suggests that feedback of information tended not to occur in the largest (72 percent) segment of the underlying population of burglary and robbery victims in the jurisdiction. For some purposes, then, we must be careful not to overemphasize the opinions of responding victims from cleared cases, who almost always (19/22) received feedback.

The results shown in table 12-2 should be considered in the light of the police policy in this jurisdiction concerning information feedback to victims. As expressed to us, this policy was to communicate with a victim at least once after the initial report of the crime had been made; moreover, if the crime were subsequently cleared, the policy mandated a further communication with the victim to explain the circumstances of the clearance. Table 12-2 indicates that if the department attempted to implement its policy during the period covered by our sample, then it was sometimes unable to reach the victim. In addition, table 12-2 suggests that a greater effort was made to communicate with the victim in a case that was cleared. The existence here of an affirmative police policy toward information feedback to victims does, of course, restrict the applicability of our findings to jurisdictions lacking such a policy.

Table 12-2
Proportion of Victim Respondents Receiving Feedback

Clearance in Respondent's Case	Crime Type		Total
	Burglary	Robbery	
Uncleared	1/8	3/6	4/14
Cleared	10/12	9/10	19/22
Total	11/20	12/16	23/36

1. The category "receiving feedback" was devised by asking the victim whether or not he received feedback information—not from any notations in the police case folder.

Finally, we characterize the survey respondents by the extent of knowledge they profess to have acquired about the outcome of their case as the result of police feedback. Table 12-3 presents this classification.

We do not attempt to deal here with issues of how well the victims who received feedback understood the information given. Rather, we simply observe from table 12-3 that feedback, when it was provided to our sample of victims, tended to inform of police progress rather than lack of progress; further, information about later events in a criminal prosecution, about which police investigators are themselves often not knowledgeable, was infrequently communicated.

Survey Responses

The questions we asked victims in our telephone survey were designed to reveal the advantages and disadvantages of information feedback. This section will be devoted to the substantive nature of the responses to these queries.

We attempted, first of all, to find out the nature of the information that a victim might want to be given about the status of his case. Table 12-4 summarizes the responses, which were so preponderantly affirmative that we need not be concerned about distinctions between robbery and burglary victims and between cleared and uncleared cases.

On its face, table 12-4 suggests several hypotheses about the "demand" for information feedback to victims from the police:

Table 12-3
Number of Respondents Having Specified Knowledge from Feedback[a]

Item of Case Information About Which Victim Was Asked	Number of Victims Replying			
	Yes (by feedback)	No (by feedback)	No Knowledge	Other Response
Did the police solve your crime?	17	5	14	—
Did the police make an arrest in your case?	18	2	13	3
Was the person arrested tried in court?	13	3	15	5
Was the person arrested given a sentence?	6	5	19	6
Has the person arrested for your crime been released from custody?	5	3	19	9

[a]Total respondents = 36; respondents with feedback = 23.

- Most victims desire very strongly to learn officially whether or not the police have "solved" their case.

- Most victims desire very strongly to be told when a suspect on their case has been arrested.

- Most victims desire, although less consistently and intensely, to be told about progress in the prosecution and adjudication of the defendant who the police believe was responsible for the offense against them.

- Victims are divided as to their wish to be informed when the person believed responsible for their victimization is released from custody.

Some light is cast on the possible strength of these hypotheses by examining the nature of the contrary responses in table 12-4. For example, the one individual who responded that he did not want to know when the police believed that they had solved his crime qualified his answer by adding that he did want to know if his case was closed by a conviction. Similar explanations apply to the negative responses to the question of desiring to know when a suspect had been arrested. The five contrary victims seemed to feel that a mere arrest was not conclusive enough of guilt to satisfy them. The explanation offered most frequently for not desiring to be told when the defendant had been released from custody was that such information would revive anxieties at a time when consciousness of the case had subsided. By contrast, victims who desired to know when the defendant was released seemed to manifest a "forewarned is forearmed" attitude, i.e., they wanted to be alerted against possible retaliation. These explanatory details tend to confirm the validity of the above hypotheses drawn from table 12-4, beyond the severely restrictive conditions of our survey.

Another hypothesis, one not obvious on the face of table 12-4, is that the greater the personal involvement of the victim in his case, the more likely is his

Table 12-4
Type of Information Desired by Victims

Survey Question: As a Victim, Did You Want the Police to Inform You?	Yes	No	Indif- ferent	If Your Answer Was "Yes" How Important Was It to You to Be Informed?	
				Very	Somewhat
If your case was solved?	32 (89%)	1 (3%)	3 (8%)	26	6
If a suspect was arrested?	30 (83%)	5 (14%)	1 (3%)	22	8
If a defendant was tried?	27 (75%)	4 (11%)	5 (14%)	15	12
If a defendant was sentenced?	27 (75%)	4 (11%)	5 (14%)	16	11
What sentence was imposed?	27 (75%)	4 (11%)	5 (14%)	16	11
If the defendant was released from custody?	18 (50%)	11 (31%)	7 (19%)	11	7

desire to be informed about events in the later stages of the criminal prosecution. One victim in our sample fits this hypothesis very closely, namely the employee-operator of a beachside hamburger stand who had been robbed. This victim wanted information on the progress of the case to help justify to his employer his repeated absences to make court appearances (which were generally frustrated by continuances). Another victim supporting this hypothesis was a woman who had devoted much time to examining mug shots and who felt, in view of her investment of effort, that the police owed her continuing reports on her case.

The inquiry summarized by table 12-4 was accompanied by two pairs of questions, with the first question of each pair addressing the victim's desire to have feedback on a specific matter and the second eliciting his probable reaction if the feedback occurred. Table 12-5 displays the responses on whether or not the victim desired to be told of a police decision to suspend or drop investigative effort on his case if such a decision were made. These suggest a consistent preference for knowledge about this police decision, but with an observable tendency in cleared robbery cases (a relatively small segment of the underlying population) to the contrary.

Table 12-6 exhibits the responses that the victims made when asked what their reactions would be if they had been told that no further investigation was intended on their cases. We note that approximately one-third of our sample would react negatively to unfavorable feedback (and the proportion would be higher if the disproportionate representation of robbery cases were eliminated). We may infer that even in a sample of victims substantially satisfied with police performance in their cases (see table 12-11), unfavorable feedback information would create an undesirable attitude toward the police in a minority of victims.

Next table 12-7 summarizes responses to the question of whether these victims would want to be told when police had cause to believe that a suspect arrested for a crime other than theirs was also responsible for their crimes. Table 12-7 suggests, particularly after allowance has been made for the overrepresentation of robbery victims and of cleared cases, that a sizable segment of the victim population makes no affirmative demand to be told of the

Table 12-5
Victim's Desire to Be Told of Police Decision to Suspend Investigation of His Case

Victim's Response	Burglary			Robbery			Total
	Cleared	Uncleared	Total	Cleared	Uncleared	Total	
Yes	10	6	16	5	5	10	26 (72%)
No	2	1	3	3	1	4	7 (19%)
Indifferent or no answer	–	1	1	2	–	2	3 (8%)
Total	12	8	20	10	6	16	36 (100%)

Table 12–6

Victim's Predicted Reactions to Information that Police Investigation of His Case Would Be Suspended

Victim's Prediction of His Reaction	Burglary	Robbery	Total
Appreciative of being told and agreeable to police decision	3	1	4 (12%)
Understanding and resigned	11	7	18 (53%)
Disturbed and resistant	4	1	5 (15%)
Angry and resentful	2	5	7 (21%)
			34[a] (100%)

[a]Two victims were omitted: the response to one was not applicable and the other declined to answer. Three of the 34 respondents gave especially perceptive answers, explaining that they understood the police did not necessarily work on every individual case, but sometimes focused their efforts on suspects, who might turn out to be responsible for many reported and unreported crimes. Thus, these three victims felt that suspending investigative efforts on their cases would not eliminate the possibility that a suspect might later be identified.

case development. But, on the same evidence, one may also infer that half or more of the victims do have a desire to be told.

Table 12–8 gives the distribution of the predicted reactions of victims to being told that the police had charged a suspect believed to be responsible for their crime, not with their crime but with another—perhaps because it was more serious, more recent, or provided stronger evidence of guilt. The victim population from which our sample is drawn evidences no propensity to second-guess the police and the prosecutor on prosecutorial tactics.

Our survey included an inquiry about what reactions would occur were victims to be told by the police that expectations of recovering their stolen

Table 12–7

Victim's Desire to Be Told When a Suspect Has Been Arrested for Another Crime but Believed to Be Responsible for Victim's Crime

Victim's Response	Burglary			Robbery			Total
	Cleared	Uncleared	Total	Cleared	Uncleared	Total	
Yes	8	4	12	3	4	7	19 (53%)
No	3	4	7	3	2	5	12 (33%)
Indifferent	1	–	1	4	–	4	5 (14%)
Total	12	8	20	10	6	16	36 (100%)

Table 12–8

Victim's Predicted Reactions to Information that a Suspect Has Been Charged on Another Case Rather than on His

Victim's Prediction of His Reaction	Burglary	Robbery	Total
Would prefer police prosecute the stronger case	2	4	6 (17%)
Indifferent or not opposed	14	9	23 (64%)
Mildly perturbed	3	1	4 (11%)
Angrily neglected	1	2	3 (8%)
Total	20	16	36 (100%)

property were poor (perhaps because the investigation and prosecution of a suspect were being concentrated on a crime other than theirs). Table 12–9 summarizes the responses. Here again we obtain a statistical indication that a sizable segment of the victim population (possibly between one-quarter and one-half) may allow their appreciation for being given information on their case to be submerged by the unfavorable nature of the information. The difference in the pattern of responses for burglary and robbery victims shown by table 12–9 may be accounted for by the fact that robbery victims have a threatening physical confrontation with the offender. Relief over being spared serious injury or death may make recovery of their property less important than it is to burglary victims.

Table 12–9

Victim's Predicted Reactions to Information that Police Regarded Recovery of His Stolen Property as Improbable

Victim's Prediction of His Reaction	Burglary	Robbery	Total
Indifferent	6	9	15 (45%)
Mildly upset	6	2	8 (24%)
Exceedingly upset	7	–	7 (21%)
Uncertain	1	2	3 (9%)
Total	20	13	33[a] (100%)

[a]Three responses excluded since the offenses against these victims did not involve loss of their own property.

Our survey attempted to ascertain what might be the nature of the actions that victims would take if they were sufficiently distressed by the negative quality of feedback information from the police. We learned, in particular, given dissatisfaction with being told that investigative effort on their cases was being suspended, only three of 36 victims predicted that they would complain to some official, possibly by letter. The remainder would make no express complaint, although three said that such notice would prompt them to be alert on their own for a possible suspect or for sight of the stolen property. We learned further that, given dissatisfaction with being told that a suspect was being charged on a case other than theirs, only two of the 36 victims felt that they would demand an explanation or otherwise complain. Two said that they might ask to see a photo of the suspect to confirm that he was the offender in their case, too. But the remainder would not act on their feelings. Finally, we learned that, given dissatisfaction with being told that the recovery of their property was unlikely, the propensity of victims to act was predicted to be as summarized in table 12-10.

Table 12-10 may merely reflect a broad public tendency to avoid abrasive contacts with the police department even when some grievance is held. We observe again, as in table 12-9, an indication that robbery victims are less concerned about property recovery than are burglary victims.

Finally, we report our survey findings on a question related to the resource cost of providing information feedback to victims. We understand that police departments generally feel that communicating information to victims by mail is cheaper, more convenient, and generally more reliable than trying to reach them by telephone. Does the mode of communication make a significant difference

Table 12-10
Victim's Predicted Reactions if Dissatisfied with Information that Recovery of His Property Was Improbable

Victim's Prediction of the Action that He Would Take	Burglary	Robbery	Total
Do nothing	12	12	24 (73%)
Complain and ask for increased recovery efforts	4	0	4 (12%)
Uncertain whether he would take action and what the action would be	4	1	5 (15%)
Total	20	13	33[a] (100%)

[a]Three responses excluded since the offenses against these victims did not involve loss of their own property.

to victims? The responses to our inquiry are shown in the table below. But generally the victims felt that police convenience should be the controlling factor.

Indifferent	.21	(58%)
Preferred telephone contact (mainly because questions could be conveniently asked)	.4	(11%)
Preferred mail contact (mainly to have a written record)	.11	(30%)

Concluding Remarks

Inferences from our telephone survey of victims may also be regarded as hypotheses about attitudes of victims in a universe much wider and more diverse than that of our sample. But before summarizing these inferences, we review the limitations of our survey as they affect the validity of our findings.

The sample of victims who were surveyed was small (36) and involved only two crime types, although common ones. The crimes occurred within a single jurisdiction and within a recent one-year period. The police department purported to exercise a policy of providing information feedback to victims, but our statistical evidence indicates that the implementation of the policy was uneven. The victim sample was, by design, not a representative one. Robbery victims and victims whose cases had been cleared were present in our sample to a far greater degree than they are in the population of burglary and robbery victims in this and other jurisdictions. Furthermore, about two-thirds of the responding victims in our survey had received information feedback from the police. And the sample, as a whole, expressed a highly affirmative feeling about the way this police department handled their cases, as table 12-11 shows.

Table 12–11
Degree of Victim Satisfaction with Police Performance

Question: How Did You Feel About the Police Handling of Your Case	Burglary		Robbery		Total
	Cleared	Uncleared	Cleared	Uncleared	
Very satisfied	8	2	5	2	17 (47%)
Satisfied	3	4	2	3	12 (33%)
Neutral		1	1		2 (6%)
Dissatisfied		2	1	1	4 (11%)
Very dissatisfied			1		1 (3%)

The principal inferences that are suggested by our survey data include the following:

- Most victims desire very strongly to learn officially whether or not the police have "solved" their case.

- Most victims desire very strongly to be told when a suspect on their case has been arrested.

- Most victims desire, although less consistently and intensely, to be told about progress in the prosecution and adjudication of the defendant who the police believe was responsible for the offense against them.

- Victims are divided as to their wish to be informed when the person believed responsible for their victimization is released from custody.

- The more the involvement of a victim in the prosecution of the suspect in his case, the greater his desire to be informed about events in the later stages of the proceeding.

- Most victims prefer to be informed when the police decide to suspend investigation in their case.

- Victims are divided in wanting to know when a suspect is arrested for a crime other than theirs but is believed to be responsible for the offense against them.

- A sizable minority of victims react unfavorably to the police when told of negative developments in their case, e.g., that investigation would be suspended or that their stolen property was unlikely to be recovered (although robbery victims tend to be less troubled about this prospect than do burglary victims).

- Most victims tend to respect or accept the exercise of professional judgment by the police or prosecutor's office.

- Even though distressed by the nature of the information feedback from the police, few victims would act to redress their grievance.

- The means of information feedback is only of incidental concern to victims.

To the extent that our survey results may reach beyond the confines of our small and special sample, they broadly underscore the belief that there exists a strong market for information feedback to victims from the police. But they also tend to confirm the view that giving unfavorable information to victims creates undesirable reactions in attitude toward the police in some of these victims. (We have no evidence of how widely the feelings of resentful victims might be propagated among the general public.) Finally, our results suggest that other repercussions from information feedback, of which the police are sometimes apprehensive, are of slight significance. Few victims, no matter how much distressed by information coming to them from the police would act inimicably to police interests. Reduced to its most rudimentary elements, this is how the balance between advantages and disadvantages of information feedback to victims is seen in our survey.

13 The Investigative Strike Force

In previous chapters we have examined the investigative function in the reactive mode, i.e., how investigators respond to reported crime. We have seen that solving crimes is not a significant part of the investigator's job. However, some departments organize part of their investigative force to respond proactively to crime, i.e., to be present when the crime occurs. This chapter initially describes, without critical comment, the operations of three different units which represent variations in the strike force concept. The operations of an additional two such units, Miami—STOP and Long Beach—SOB, are described and analyzed in further detail in the later sections of this chapter.

Variations in the Strike Force Concept

Police administrators are frequently frustrated by their inability to deploy police personnel for maximum effect against particularly acute problems as they are identified. Limited personnel, already overburdened with the responsibilities of traditional police routines, are seldom available to be deployed where there is a need for increased enforcement pressure. Recognizing the need for a flexible, compact, mobile task force, many police departments have developed tactical units or mobile striking forces to supplement routine operations.

Initially, these tactical units were used primarily to assist patrol forces in emergency situations requiring additional police manpower, such as riots, mob situations, or strikes. However, in the early 1970s police departments began to expand the concept of the tactical force, and now many police departments maintain small tactical strike units on a permanent basis. The majority of these tactical units are designed to assist the investigative divisions specifically in controlling the crimes of robbery and burglary. Comprised of police officers who are freed from the more routine duties of police work, these strike teams operate as compact flexible units with the capabilities for applying selective enforcement pressures.

The robbery and burglary strike force, usually funded in part by Law Enforcement Assistance Administration (LEAA) grants, often works closely with, and in a manner similar to, the regular robbery or burglary investigator. The purported advantage of these strike forces is that rather than being responsible for investigating reported crimes, its members are encouraged to proceed on their own initiative to develop cases against serious offenders.

Strike teams use intelligence gathered from informants or exploit the leads gathered by traditional investigators. Instead of responding in a traditional "reactive" sense, the strike force officer is encouraged to be aggressive; to find information that will assist him in anticipating the targets of criminal activities so that he can take action *prior* to an offense or can intercept the criminal in the act of committing the crime. This latter is seen as a good tactic for the criminal justice system because it means that the arresting team has a solid case—one that will be easy for the district attorney to prosecute and that has a high probability of being disposed of without going to trial. Once information is received, the strike team will usually stake out the anticipated target, or put a "tail" on the suspect.

Another tactic that has been used for the generation of self-initiated arrests involves strike force members' operating their own fencing operation to buy stolen property. Such operations can recover large quantities of stolen goods and provide excellent evidence for burglary or possession of stolen property charges.

The robbery or burglary strike force is normally a small force carefully selected from the police department's own personnel. Usually young and self-motivated, they are often recruited from patrol divisions and from those investigative divisions where their background and experience will help them develop informants and work undercover. The units generally operate in an informal manner; frequently there are no uniforms, vans are often used in place of police cars, members have long hair and beards, and there are no duty schedules. The unit's personnel may vary from a few men on a small force to twenty in larger departments. Depending on the department, the strike teams may cooperate closely with traditional investigators, or they may operate independently from other divisions on the police force.

Although the strike force officer has considerable flexibility with regard to the way he wishes to proceed on a particular case, he is usually more closely supervised in his day-to-day operations than the officers in traditional investigation divisions. Supervisors claim that this extra attention is necessary because these units are relatively new, and as such, there is no established routine to be followed. In addition, since strike force officers are not responsible for a caseload, they have much more free time, and the supervisor tries to make certain they are using that time to follow up potentially profitable leads.

Denver—SCAT

Since strike teams are frequently the only compact flexible units in the department, they are often deployed to saturate troublesome areas with anticrime activities. Although almost all strike forces rely on saturation techniques to some degree, an example of a strike force that relies heavily on saturation patrol is the Special Crime Attack Team (SCAT) in Denver, Colorado.

SCAT is a combined team of 1 lieutenant, 2 sergeants, 22 patrolmen, 8 detectives, and 3 evidence technicians. They are organized within the patrol division, and the unit commander is directly responsible to the Division Chief of Patrol Operations. Funded for one year's operation in 1972 with an LEAA Impact City grant, SCAT was to use saturation techniques, combined with prevention activities, to convince potential crime perpetrators that the burglary risk factor had increased.

The commander in charge of SCAT is provided with a daily computer update of crime information in a temporal, spatial, and geographical context. He then makes the logical allocations of his resources to cope with the problem. Although the team concentrates primarily on antiburglary activities, they are also deployed to areas experiencing other types of crime problems. The idea is to saturate the identified area with antiburglary activities, and then leave before the effect of those activities wears off. The team relocates approximately each month.

SCAT employs both covert and overt saturation techniques. When the commander feels that a deterrent in the form of additional officer presence is needed, then SCAT is employed in uniform and in marked vehicles. Overt saturation is thought not only to deter potential criminals, but also to restore a sense of security to the local community. On the other hand, SCAT is frequently deployed covertly to situations where the team is trying to locate the source of increased criminal activity.

Once deployed to an area, SCAT members engage in a variety of activities designed to prevent burglaries and apprehend burglary suspects. The team covers all burglaries reported in their area on their tour of duty. On each call, members of the patrol force respond to conduct the preliminary investigation and make the report. At the same time, the evidence technician responds to conduct the crime scene search. In addition, the detectives also respond with additional patrolmen and begin to canvass the neighborhood, looking for evidence and witnesses.

Besides acting as a comprehensive burglary investigation team, members of SCAT are involved in activities designed to educate the community about crime prevention measures and to elicit its support. SCAT canvasses the homes and businesses in the area and inspects their security systems. They also provide residents with educational handout material to inform them about improving their security systems.

SCAT is an example of a tactical strike force that has combined overt and covert saturation, thorough burglary investigations, crime scene searches, and prevention measures in an attempt to combat the burglary problem. Although several of SCAT's activities, such as security checks and citizen contacts, cannot be evaluated quantitatively, SCAT did gather statistics showing that the burglary rate decreased significantly in several of its target areas.

Berkeley, California—Crime-Specific Bureau

A few police departments have chosen to reorganize portions of their investigation details so that some of the activities usually performed by tactical teams could be incorporated into traditional investigative divisions. The Berkeley Police Department established a Crime-Specific Bureau in 1973 as the product of an LEAA grant titled "A Systems Approach to Control Burglary." The Special Investigations Bureau (responsible for investigating violations of narcotics, prostitution, gambling, and liquor laws), the Burglary Detail, and that portion of the Theft Detail that coordinates receiving and/or possession of stolen property investigations were combined in order to provide a coordinated effort toward the control of these closely associated crime problems. The new unit employed a "systems approach" to the burglary problem, considering the total environment of the crime, the suspect, and the target. The unit attempted to integrate resources in prevention, detection, and apprehension efforts, blending traditional police methods with some of the innovative approaches developed by tactical strike forces.

Besides combining the two details, additional resources made it possible to expand the manpower previously dedicated to suppressing burglary activities. The additional manpower reduced the caseload each investigator was responsible for, thus giving him more time to devote to single cases. The investigators were encouraged to develop informants, tail suspects, and survey locations in efforts to make cases against serious burglary offenders. In addition, the combined unit was assigned several crime scene search officers, specifically trained to retrieve evidence from burglary scenes. As the program developed, public awareness and home security activities also became points of major emphasis for the unit.

The crime statistics used by the Berkeley Police Department to evaluate the new unit showed that during their first year in operation the unit failed to reduce the number of burglaries. The number of reported burglaries during 1973 was higher than in 1972, despite the fact that the number of burglary arrests increased significantly. Because of these discouraging results, the unit was not re-funded for a second year of operation.

As the proponents of the unit had expected, the full effect of the department's unique burglary control activities was not felt until the following calendar year. During 1974, burglary rates dropped while the arrest, clearance, and conviction rates increased. However, before these encouraging statistics were available, the unit had been disbanded because of its apparent lack of effectiveness.

New York City—Operation Fence

For the past two years, New York City detectives have been operating undercover fencing operations in which they set up phony business covers to buy stolen property. Their typical operation involves a one- or two-man cleaning business or trucking operation. Several such operations may be going at any one time.

They seek out a location in a racially transitional neighborhood so that both blacks and whites will feel comfortable coming to the premises. They completely refurbish the building to suit their own special needs for surveillance, communications, and safety. The operation requires five or six officers to man it—two in the store and several others in a surveillance position across the street—usually in an apartment. One officer inside deals with the clients. The other, hidden from view, operates taping or surveillance equipment and provides immediate backup to the first officer in case of an emergency.

During the operation of their first location, two holdup men executed one of the officers before his partner had time to respond.[1] Since that time, a number of additional precautions have been taken to protect officers on the premises. The entry of clients is controlled by a buzzer-latch system.[2] The officer on duty is completely separated from clients by a chest-high counter that is completely armor-plated, both top and sides. The backup man is positioned so that he has a clear field of fire at any would-be robbers, and the field of fire is so confined that there is no danger to pedestrians passing the store.

Most operations remain active for about four to six months. No arrests are made until the operation is shut down.[3] Several techniques are used to ensure accurate identification of their clientele.

- The premises are located in areas away from public transportation so that clients will be likely to drive. They also pick a place where there is nearby parking. In that way the surveillance team can often get a license plate number.

- Each transaction is recorded on videotape.

- Frequently touched surfaces on the premises are dusted for fingerprints and cleaned after each transaction.

- Transactions are handled in such a way that clients are often required to leave a phone number where they can be reached.

Conversations with clients sometimes lead to the identification of other receivers, or stolen property can sometimes be traced back to a particular offense. Leads such as these are turned over to other investigators for follow-up

---

1. The backup officer and the surveillance team were aware that the robbery was going on, but since the robbers both had guns drawn, the other officers felt that the safest alternative, for their fellow officer, was to let the robbers begin their escape. The execution occurred so suddenly it was too late to help.

2. This security procedure apparently is not suspicious to clients in a high crime neighborhood.

3. One of these operations received considerable press coverage when the detectives held a party for their clients, to make the arrests. The clients were driven, in twos and threes, by cab to what they thought was a "secure mob-sponsored party site." As soon as they entered they were handcuffed and led out the back door for booking.

and arrest without disclosing the source of the information. Very few men in the department are aware of the location of these fencing operations.

General Evaluative Approach

The principal difficulty in evaluating strike force performance lies in identifying their unique contribution to overall department performance. Given that some of the department's brightest and most aggressive investigators are assigned to a special unit, relieved of caseloads, and provided with special resources such as informant funds, special cars, or radios—there is no doubt that such a unit will make arrests. The critical question is: How many of these arrests would not have been made if the investigators had not been operating as a special unit? In some instances the strike force is routinely given credit for an arrest that could just as easily have been made by the patrol force—simply because the strike force got to the suspect first or were the only ones given the assignment. For their own evaluative purposes, police departments have assembled various data to determine the strike force's impact. Crime rates, clearance rates, and total arrests are the data most frequently cited.

A primary objective in establishing these strike forces is to reduce the incidence of a particular type of crime—usually robbery or burglary. This reduction is supposed to result from the containment of frequent offenders by arrest and prosecution and through the deterrent effect which the unit's activities, dramatically publicized by the press, are expected to have. Therefore crime trends—especially when they show a decrease—are usually cited as an indication of the strike force's success.

The problem with this approch is that many other dynamic factors also affect crime rates in some unknown way: employment, social attitudes, population shifts, changes in the commercial characteristics of the area, sentencing practice, other police programs, etc. Even if all of these other factors are measured, we still have no models that allow us to sort out their differential impacts, nor sufficient data points to do it statistically. Even when a dramatic shift in crime trends follows the introduction of such a strike force, there is cause to suspect the result. During the first year, the impact of the program is usually quite low because procedures need to be developed and personnel selected. Also, containing offenders will have had little time to take effect. Where dramatic reversals in reported crime rates follow the introduction of a new unit, the most likely explanation of the shift is some change in reporting practices, changes in other areas of police operations, or a temporary deterrent effect caused by the offender's uncertainty concerning the novel policing techniques introduced.

Clearance rates and arrests suffer from the disadvantage that they reflect the activities of the entire department and not just the strike force. An increase in clearances may reflect improved apprehension efforts, changes in crime trends, or increased attention devoted to clearing up old cases as a result of current arrests by other units.

Even when arrests are made by the strike force, it cannot be assumed that they would not have been made by some other unit. The regular patrol force or investigation units often use strike force members as a special resource that can be tapped for making arrests, simply because they are readily available. A more accurate picture of the strike force contribution to overall apprehension efforts can only be obtained by examining each arrest they make and distinguishing those cases in which their special attributes[4] were actually used from those in which they were simply functioning as a special arrest detail for another unit.

The following discussion presents a detailed description and performance evaluation of two such units, the Strategic Oriented Project (STOP) Robbery Unit in Miami, Florida, and the Suppression of Burglary (SOB) Unit in Long Beach, California. In addition to examining evaluation data prepared by these units, we examined a sample of cases from each one in order to determine the unique role played by strike force officers.

Miami—STOP Robbery Unit

In 1971 the Miami Police Department received LEAA funding to expand its Criminal Investigation Section. The funds were earmarked for a crime specific robbery control project, and portions of the money were subsequently used to form a tactical robbery strike force, the STOP Robbery Unit. The initial results of the unit were encouraging, so that a STOP Burglary Unit was soon developed. The goals of the Miami units are similar to those of other strike forces; that is, to use the additional manpower to engage in activities designed to prevent and suppress robbery and burglary.

These two units have a combined authorized strength of one captain, 2 lieutenants, 4 sergeants, and 25 detectives. The project director was given authority to select any officers from the department. Selection criteria were based on past performances indicating investigative ability, knowledge of robbery and burglary offenses, initiative and desire, minimal use of force, and ability to work with a minimum of supervision.

To orient and familiarize the officers about robbery and burglary procedures, the goals of the unit, and how to use the various criminal information files within the Department, they attended two seminars, one conducted by a local college and the other by the Miami Police Department. Additional in-house training was provided in flash recognition procedures to assist in spotting wanted and known felons.

---

4. Informant tip, surveillance, background investigation, etc.

The tactical units work for neither the patrol nor the robbery and burglary details. The squad officers do not exercise operational supervision over field patrol officers at crime scenes (as traditional investigators do). The STOP Units are not assigned a caseload, but are available to robbery investigators for assistance in investigations without normal chain-of-command approval.

These two units, although they operate in a manner similar to other strike units in their use of surveillance, undercover, and stake-out tactics, work much more closely with the regular robbery and burglary investigators than is evident with some other strike forces. The STOP Units operate less on information received from informants and undercover operations and more on the leads developed by the traditional investigators. Frquently, once the investigator has identified the suspect and a warrant has been issued for his arrest, the STOP Unit will dedicate its additional manpower resources to locating the suspect and serving the warrant.

The following case typifies the coordination and working relationship that exists between the STOP Robbery Unit and the traditional robbery investigators.

A black, female cashier at a loan company reports a robbery of $400 cash and $1600 in checks. A robbery investigator responds to the crime scene and speaks with the victim. The victim's statement is very vague and at times inconsistent. She states that two black males approached her, pulled a gun and demanded all the money. There were no witnesses to the crime, and the victim said she was too shaken to notice any of the physical features of the perpetrators.

The robbery investigator interrogates the victim further and is suspicious about the circumstances of the robbery. He asks the woman to take a polygraph test, which she submits to and fails. The victim subsequently confesses to the robbery investigator that the robbery was not real, but alleged, and that she had conspired with two of the men she was living with to falsify the report. The victim does not know where the two men are now, but she gives the robbery investigator their description.

The robbery investigator gives all of the information to the STOP Robbery Unit. The STOP Unit conducts a stakeout at the victim's apartment for a week, at the end of which the two perpetrators appear, and are arrested by the STOP Robbery Unit at the scene.

Trying to locate an identified suspect often requires that the strike team use the department's well-developed Criminal Information Center, which maintains a variety of files designed to let the officer retrieve as much information on individual offenders as possible, including physical characteristics, MO, past records, nicknames, friends, etc. With this information, the strike team may then put a "tail" on the suspect or friends of the suspect, or possibly conduct stakeouts at locations he is known to frequent.

The purported advantage of the Miami strike teams is that since they are not responsible for a caseload, they are available to "work the streets," locating identified suspects. Most often, the strike teams have served as manpower extensions for the regular investigative divisions, making it possible for the department's investigative effort to include not only identifying suspects, but becoming more actively involved in their apprehension. For example, one of the first activities of the STOP Robbery Unit was to serve outstanding warrants. When they began operation, they found over 760 outstanding robbery warrants had not been served, 120 of which had been issued by the Miami Police Department. The 120 warrants were divided among the STOP officers. Each officer compiled a dossier on the wanted suspects (photographs, criminal history data, defense attorney, name of bail bondsman, etc.) and then proceeded to arrest 85 of the 120 suspects.

Apprehending identified suspects is one of the most crucial functions of the STOP Units. Very frequently, traditional investigators, overburdened with growing caseloads, are not able to make more than a cursory attempt at apprehension. With the STOP Units, the department is now able to make a concerted effort to apprehend identified robbery and burglary suspects. It is hoped that an immediate arrest of suspects will cause a reduction in recidivist offenses.

With extra resources and funds available, strike teams are frequently able to purchase special crime control equipment. The equipment needed and purchased by these various units differs, depending on the functions of the tactical force, but very often includes sophisticated surveillance gear, unmarked cars, and special photographic lenses. Miami's STOP Robbery Unit has experimented with several pieces of experimental equipment since the operation began. One of the most unusual was their Bait-Pack experiment. They placed 50 bait-money packs in commercial establishments which were selected by the computer as repeated robbery targets. The Bait-Pack is a pyrotechnic device which is disguised as a pack of money in a cash register until lifted from its metal plate, which triggers a timing device. Four minutes after activation the device explodes, dispersing red smoke which distracts and upsets the thief, calls public attention to his actions, and stains the money and clothing. This system is not particularly sophisticated, but it has attention-getting potential from the media and the general public. The STOP Unit thought the publicity generated made the item psychologically effective in preventing robberies and appeared to provide merchants with peace of mind, as well as aiding apprehension of robbery offenders. In addition, an unexpected result was the deterrent effects the packs had on employees who were in the habit of stealing the company's money and claiming a robbery.

In this analysis we are primarily concerned with the six-man tactical robbery squad that continued to operate as a hybrid plaincothes patrol/investigative unit for the first 27 months of the project—from October 1, 1971, to December 31, 1973.

During STOP's first 27 months, its operations allegedly produced a number of positive benefits for the department. Because STOP was responsive to all robbery calls, one of the first benefits derived was improved quality in reports by the first uniformed officer on the scene. Another benefit was the atmosphere of cooperation between uniformed and detective bureau personnel which transcended the traditional division between these two sections.

It had been anticipated that this squad, being a group of well-dressed (suits and ties) officers driving new rental cars, without a case load or subject to routine calls, would create an aura of elitism and would evoke jealousy. Allegedly however,[5] the squad officers went to great lengths to voluntarily respond immediately to all types of calls to assist field officers and performed in other ways as assistants to the robbery investigators. The result was that the STOP Squad soon gained the respect of both field officers and detectives.

Also, assignment to the robbery office presented an opportunity for squad members to free up information flows between themselves and robbery investigators. Informant solicitation, ordinarily a very difficult task, began to flow rather readily. Many persons with whom squad members had had contact prior to being assigned to the squad regarded their new position as one of trust and responsibility and soon began to offer leads.

Concentration on areas that were most apt to be robbery targets was done through computer printout and an extensive analysis of robbery patterns. As the squad increased in proficiency and became more aware of the modus operandi of the active robbery offenders, it became a natural course of action for them to assist in robbery oriented homicides.

In the sixteenth of a series of truck hijackings, the truck driver was the victim of a homicide. Shortly after responding to the scene of the crime, homicide investigators called the robbery officer where the robbery STOP Squad was being briefed before beginning their tour of duty. In previous weeks the truck hijacking pattern had been studied, information developed, and six potential suspects selected. All three teams responded to the scene of the robbery-homicide with information about these six potential suspects, including their pictures. Four of the six were identified as the individuals who had committed the crime.

Squad members also used video cameras and 35mm still cameras, and when they saw groups of suspects known to be active, would stop, point a camera, and take pictures or feign taking pictures. When concentration of this type was instituted in high crime areas, a significant decrease in the number of expected robberies was frequently observed.[6]

Impact. During the four years immediately preceding the instigation of the project, robbery offenses had increased at an average annual rate exceeding 25 percent. During the first 27 months of the project a substantial decrease in the reported robbery offense rate did occur. In 1971, robbery offenses (2,829) declined 1.3 percent compared to previous years. In 1972 and 1973 the rates

5. *Final Report of Robbery Control Project,* City of Miami, Florida Police Department, January 1975.

6. Such blatant harassment of "suspicious characters" without probable cause clearly raises civil liberties issues which the community and courts must carefully consider.

of decline were 9.6 percent and 6.4 percent, respectively.[7] The project was acclaimed a success.

However, by 1974 the robbery offense rate was no longer on the decline. By October the department was reporting a 35 percent increase over the same time period in 1973.[8]

Total departmental clearances and arrests showed a consistent pattern of increase over the life of the project. The clearance rate increased from 17.6 percent in 1971[9] to 26.2 percent in 1973. Robbery arrests increased from 408 in 1971 to 526 in 1973—a 29 percent increase. During 1974 clearances and arrests appeared to keep pace with the growing crime rate.

During the first 15 months of the project, the six-man STOP Unit made 367 felony arrests,[10] of which 168 were for robbery. During 1973 they made 280. This is a felony arrest productivity of approximately 4 arrests per man per month. During their first 15 months, the unit also conducted 809 on-scene investigations, 365 stakeouts, and 741 field interviews.[11]

During the first half of 1974, after the unit was expanded to 12 men, it continued to average approximately 3.9 arrests per man-month. However, during the months of July, August, and September, a new policy was adopted of providing surveillance teams to sit on stakeouts in suspected premises.[12] During August and September more than 1000 man-hours were devoted to this stakeout activity, which resulted in only one intercepted robbery and arrest. The arrest productivity for the squad dipped to an average of 1.75 felony arrests per man-month.

In a sample[13] of 30 robbery arrest cases examined by our staff, the STOP Robbery officers were involved in 11. However, in 9 of these arrests, the STOP officers were executing arrest warrants resulting from regular detectives' investigative activity. In another case, STOP Robbery men were accompanying

---

7. According to the FBI's Annual Reports, substantial decreases in robbery offense rates were being reported in about one-third of the nation's major counties and cities during this same time period. The national rate of change for robbery offenses in the years 1971, 1972, and 1973 were +11, −3, and +2, respectively.

8. The Uniform Crime Reports 1974 Preliminary Annual Release shows that the national robbery offense rate increased by 14 percent in 1974.

9. During the previous eight years, the robbery clearance rate had shown considerable random fluctuation between a high of 30.0 and a low of 14.1. It was 24.5 in 1969.

10. *Miami Police Robbery Control Project, Annual Report 71-DF-1061*, City of Miami, Florida Police Department, Appendix III, p. 26.

11. Ibid.

12. This policy was apparently adopted to sooth the public, primarily the small business community, rather than because the police thought they would make many arrests.

13. The sample consists of a random selection of cases assigned to either of two robbery detectives during 1973 or 1974. Cases were limited to these two detectives so that they could be interviewed to fill in missing data.

the assigned investigator when he made an arrest. Apparently in only 1 case out of 11 were STOP Robbery officers operating on their own initiative (in response to a description of the suspect, an establishment he frequents, and the names of his associates) when they apprehend a suspect.

Interpretation. When Miami began the project, they had both an unusually low arrest rate[14] for robberies (0.17 compared to a national average of 0.33) and a high offense rate (744 compared to a national average of 235 offenses per 100,000 population).[15] These figures would appear to indicate that either Miami has a somewhat unique robbery problem or that they have been less effective than most other cities in dealing with it. We suspect the former is at least partially true. Our review of cases suggested that there were fewer cases in which the victim and suspect were previously acquainted than we have encountered elsewhere. These victim identifications can account for a significant fraction of the arrests.

Whatever the reasons, the STOP Unit was apparently more successful than other units had been in executing arrest warrants, which undoubtedly accounts for their high arrest activity. We are still unsure why other units were unable to complete these arrests or whether the STOP Unit's success was due primarily to the time it had to devote to such arrests, as opposed to other activities it performed to set up the arrest. In 90 percent of our sample robbery cases, the STOP Unit arrest involved execution of a warrant resulting from work of regular investigators. If the STOP men are nothing more than legmen for the detectives, then these arrests alone are no clear measure of their value. Some means must be found to distinguish those arrests which the regular investigator or patrolman would not have been able to make on his own.

The overall impact of the Robbery Control Project on crime rates is difficult to interpret. One could argue that the project initially did have a large impact on robbery offense rates, which diminished over time as either external factors caused an increase in the underlying base rate or offenders became more used to the project and its deterrent effect lessened.

Another explanation could be that the robbery offense rate is determined by factors beyond the reach of the police and that the initial decrease was simply a fortuitous coincidence. Some support for this theory can be found in the fact that the trend in robbery offenses began to decline even before the project was fully operational (1971).

Long Beach—Supression of Burglary (SOB) Unit

After recognizing the rapidly rising rate of burglary in its city, the Long Beach (California) Police Department decided in 1972 to supplement its burglary control efforts by developing a dual facet tactical strike force. Their approach

---

14. Fraction of cases resulting in an arrest.

15. Most big city robbery rates appear consistently higher than the national average.

was to develop a Burglary Crime Prevnetion Unit, consisting of two separate teams. The first team of five police officers concentrates on burglary prevention measures. This team conducts property identification campaigns, inspects security systems, distributes burglary prevention literature, and conducts other activities aimed at securing the cooperation of those elements of the community that are particularly susceptible to burglaries.

The second team in the Crime Prevention Unit consists of 11 police officers who are responsible for suppressing burglary activities. The Suppression of Burglary (SOB) Unit is made up of officers who were carefully recruited from the narcotics, vice, burglary, and juvenile divisions. The men in the unit always work in plainclothes as a flexible tactical unit.

The emphasis of SOB is primarily on eliminating the source of revenue for the burglar by reducing the number of available outlets for stolen property. The unit attempts to do this primarily by receiving information from the relationships they cultivate with informants about burglars, fences, and related activities. The LEAA grant that supports the SOB Unit has appropriated money for paying informants for valid information. Once the unit receives information on such activities, they will often put a tail on the suspected offender, conduct a stakeout at an anticipated target, or raid a location where stolen property is bought, sold, or stored. They also frequently visit pawnshops or secondhand stores, where they try to match articles being sold against reported stolen property.

The unit is closely supervised by a lieutenant. All officers must report into the SOB headquarters every morning, and sign out when they leave to work in the field. When they sign out they must specify where they plan to be—for what purpose, and the specific case they are working on. Each officer carries a police radio with him, and if there are changes in his plans, he is expected to report to the lieutenant. Although the lieutenant monitors the overall activities of the men in his unit, he does not usually become involved in individual cases unless asked to do so by one of his men. In addition to making sure the men are kept busy, the lieutenant is responsible for assigning all incoming leads for follow-up investigation, processing all recovered property, compiling monthly statistics on the unit's activities, and making certain that the officers are prepared to testify in court.

The SOB Unit maintains several offender files, including MO, vehicle descriptions, nicknames of burglars, locations of fences, and the names of suspected burglars and fences. Each evening the SOB officers return to headquarters and dictate daily notes, which recapitulate the officer's work and the information he obtained that day. These notes are subsequently transcribed, and the pertinent information, either regarding a particular case or a suspect, is entered into the appropriate offender file.

The SOB Unit operates as a separate unit within the police department. Although a very tightly knit group among themselves, the unit does not work particularly closely with regular burglary investigators. It does not normally rely on leads provided by the burglary investigators, but uses its own innovative tactics for gathering intelligence—primarily informants and undercover operations.

However, if the burglary unit thinks they have a suspect but don't have the time to follow it up, they may ask the SOB Unit to put a surveillance on the person.

The additional funds available to the strike force often make it possible to experiment with innovative equipment and/or other crime control tactics. Although only a year old, the SOB squad has developed several unique programs. During 1974, the unit operated a secondhand store where members of the Unit knowingly purchased stolen property from burglars. All of the transactions were recorded on a videotape machine hidden in the store. Not only did this experiment enable many burglarized persons to get their property back, but it also exposed many of the burglars in the local community to the police department. Nineteen burglars were arrested as a result of this experiment.

The SOB Unit was also instrumental in putting into action a plan to combat a particularly serious problem in their area, which until this time had been recognized but not dealt with. Many California police departments recognized swap meets as places where many fences were selling stolen merchandise to the public. The SOB Unit formed a Swap Meet Task Force and raided several of these locations, confiscating stolen property. These raids substantiated the belief that swap meets were serving as outlets for stolen property, and the unit has since begun to engage in a serious regional effort designed to limit such activities. Not only has the task force recovered a considerable amount of stolen property (over $100,000 in two swap meet raids), but the unit feels that the widespread publicity surrounding the swap meet raids has served to discourage some fences from selling stolen property in this manner. The SOB Unit has received national attention for their unique efforts to combat this particularly serious local problem.

The overall impact of the SOB Unit during its first three years can be observed from the figures in table 13-1. Total annual arrests increased from 167 in 1972, to 291 in 1974. This apparently increasing trend is due to the fact that the unit operated for only nine months in 1972, and for most of that period with less than eight men. In 1974 the size of the unit was increased to ten.

Overall arrest productivity is better examined by looking at the average individual officer's performance, which in 1972 was 3.2 felony arrests per man-month.[16] In 1973 and 1974 this figure declined to 2.4, which might be due to any of the following explanations: (1) The high arrest rate during the first year was a rare statistical fluke. (2) If the very best men had been initially selected to man the unit, manpower changes over time might dilute the average capability of the unit's officers. (3) Criminals may have adjusted to the unit's novel technique or the first arrests represented the easy cases.

Table 13-1 also shows that the high arrest productivity was maintained without sacrificing the quality of arrests and that the unit's average monthly property recovery rate fluctuated between $10,000 and $23,000 over the three years.

Examination of similar units in the past has shown that their arrest figures are often inflated by allowing them to make many simple arrests which some other police unit could just as easily have made. To test that possibility in the

---

16. Assuming 12 months per man-year.

Table 13–1
SOB Unit Productivity

	1972[a]	1973[b]	1974[c]
Total arrests	167	226	291
Arrests per man-month	3.2	2.4	2.4
Percentage of cases filed as felonies	40	41	30
Percentage of arrests for burglary or receiving stolen property	54	44	52
Average monthly value of recovered stolen property	$20,000	$10,500	$23,000

[a]Nine months.

[b]Eight months.

[c]Ten months.

case of SOB, we examined a sample of 48 cases, two cases selected at random from each month in 1973 and 1974.

The SOB Unit maintains a log containing an entry for every arrest it makes. These entries provided the basis for the summary figures reported earlier.

A case is established and an SOB number assigned only when an arrest involves some investigative effort on the part of SOB or when it might be of interest later. Arrests in support of other units, pickup arrests on observation for non-burglary offenses, or arrests of fugitives are not likely to become SOB cases because they require no unusual efforts on the part of SOB officers.

In our sample of 48 cases, 31 (65 percent) were assigned SOB case numbers. Most of the 17 that were not assigned numbers involved fugitives, narcotics, or juveniles. Of the 31 cases assigned to SOB, four were missing from the files and could not be examined.

Each of the remaining cases was examined to determine how the identification and arrest of the suspect came about. The responsible investigator was interviewed where the records were unclear. We were primarily interested in distinguishing those cases in which the unique characteristics and capabilities of SOB played a significant role in the arrest.

As table 13-2 demonstrates, we identified six categories of cases in which the SOB initiative appeared essential. Patrol observation arrests were made as a result of the SOB officers' presence on the street in casual clothing. Arrests in response to alarms came about because the unit was monitoring patrol frequencies while they cruised the streets. This might possibly be one type of arrest that patrol could have made just as well.

The intensive investigation arrests resulted from the SOB investigators' assembling a group of cases that reflected a distinct pattern. The investigative effort devoted to these cases is greatly in excess of that normally accorded a burglary or robbery.

Table 13–2
Comparison of SOB and Other Arrests

Item	Total	GT	Robbery	Burglary	RSP	Poss. Narc.	Federal Prison Escape
1. SOB initiated arrests							
1.1 Patrol observation	2		1	1			
1.2 Respond to alarm	2			2			
1.3 Intensive investigation (MO pattern)	3		1	2			
1.4 Informant	3		1	1	1		
1.5 Suspect confession	1			1			
1.6 Personal knowledge	2	1		1			
Sub Total	13	1	3	8	1		
2. Other arrests							
2.1 Pickup referral from other unit[a]	8			5	2[b]		1
2.2 Routine investigation	6	1		3	1	1	
Sub Total	14	1		8	3	1	1
Total	27	2	3	16	4	1	1

[a]Often involve problem locating suspect.

[b]One case required the SOB investigator to complete an undercover sale of stolen property to justify the arrest of a previously identified receiver.

Informant arrests are made only because an SOB informant has supplied essential information concerning the identity or location of the suspect, without which the arrest could not have been made. The suspect confession arrest occurred when the suspect, who had been wounded in a gun battle, called an SOB investigator he knew to give himself up.

The personal knowledge cases involved the SOB officers' making some essential connection between the reported offense and a possible suspect. Thirteen of the 27 cases were classified into one of these SOB initiated categories.

The remaining 14 cases can be classified as either of the following two types:

1. Referral arrest from other units in which SOB is used to effectuate the arrest of a previously identified suspect.
2. Routine investigation in which the SOB officers follow the same investigative steps as would any other police officer to make the arrest. Many of these cases came about due to a departmental policy of assigning any case involving a possible receiver to SOB for follow-up. In most of the cases the identity of the possible receiver is provided by a citizen, or a burglar in the custody of some other unit.

Table 13-2 demonstrates that about half of SOB's assigned cases, or 27 percent of their total arrests, really represent payoffs from the unique type of investigative practices that this kind of unit is supposed to employ. Their other arrests come about because they represent a pool of skilled officers, available on short notice to arrest identified suspects, or because departmental policy gives them the opportunity to pursue some specific types of leads (pertaining to receivers) developed by other units.

These findings should not be interpreted in any way as disparaging the efforts of the SOB officers. As our analysis of how cases get solved has shown, regular investigators are seldom able to make arrests in which the identity of the suspect is not readily apparent from the facts available at the time the incident report is completed. Experimental projects intended to allow the investigators more time to investigate cases have not shown any increase in arrests. Therefore, the SOB initiated arrests represent a real gain in the effectiveness of the department, both in suspects apprehended and property recovered. Whether or not this gain is enough to justify the expense of the unit and the unavoidable invasion of privacy resulting from its operation is a judgment each department and community must make for itself.

Concluding Remarks

Although most of the tactical units have proved to be an overall asset to their respective departments, a few common problems have been encountered. The first and possibly most detrimental impediment to the continued expansion of such units is an evaluative problem. Most of these programs are funded by LEAA for a year's duration. In order to receive continued funding, either by LEAA or their respective cities, they usually must provide their sponsor with data showing that their efforts have in fact contributed positively to crime control efforts. As with evaluations of any crime control program, the impact is often difficult to assess. The Berkeley experiment, as an example, was discontinued because of its inability to reduce the incidence of burglary in the experimental period. Officers in the unit felt they could justify their existence on many qualitative terms, but were frustrated by their apparent inability to have an immediate impact on the burglary pattern. If continued funding of these tactical units is going to depend solely on criminal statistics, then it is likely that, as was the Berkeley program, they will be discontinued.

This evaluative problem has a spillover effect on strike team personnel. According to many unit commanders, lowered morale often results when the men recognize that they are being quantitatively evaluated and that in some instances their unit will not be re-funded. Most commanders feel that a single year is not enough time to demonstrate efficiency, that projects of this nature should be at least two years. Some worthwhile programs, which would require longer than a single year to implement, are not undertaken because of the uncertainty of continued funding.

Despite the problems involved, it is likely that many departments will periodically attempt to employ strike forces out of frustration with more traditional apprehension efforts. Tactical strike teams now exist in many large metropolitan police departments, and smaller departments are beginning to establish cooperative intra-agency strike forces.

Part IV

Conclusions and Policy Implications

14 Summary of Findings

In many ways our work has confirmed the findings of previous researchers, either by repeating their results in different cities or by producing information that helps explain why the earlier findings were correct. We have attempted to assure that our results have national applicability by collecting survey data from 153 departments, by conducting interviews in 29 departments located in various regions of the country, and by reviewing our conclusions with the members of our advisory board and working investigators who are named in the acknowledgments. Nonetheless, many of the studies described in Part III were conducted in a single department or a small number of departments, so that undoubtedly exceptions exist.

Certainly no department should take any action based on our findings without assuring itself of the applicability of our work to its own situation. Especially for types of information that could readily be obtained in most departments, we have shown how the data were tabulated, so that others can replicate our analysis. It is our hope that this will be done in the near future, so that firmer conclusions can be drawn about the generality of our findings.

Arrest and Clearance Rates

Department-wide arrest and clearance rates are unreliable measures of the effectiveness of investigative operations. The vast majority of clearances are produced by activities of patrol officers, by the availability of identification of the perpetrator at the scene of the crime, or by routine police procedures.

The fact that clearance rates can be manipulated by administrative practices was previously established by Greenwood (1970), Greenberg et al. (1972), and Skolnick (1966). Our cross-sectional analysis of FBI Uniform Crime Reporting data for 1972 is consistent with this observation, since we showed that the number of clearances claimed for each arrest for a Part I crime ranged from a low of 0.38 to a high of 4.04, a factor of over 10. The ratio from high to low was even larger for each individual crime type, such as robbery or auto theft. Some departments claim a clearance for an auto theft whenever the vehicle is recovered, while others will not claim a clearance unless the perpetrator is arrested and charged for the instant offense. Clearance statistics are also affected by the amount of effort devoted to classifying reported crimes as "unfounded" (i.e., the police find there is no evidence that a crime was actually committed).

225

This practice reduces reported crime rates as well as increasing reported clearance rates.

With administrative discretion playing such a large role in determining a department's clearance rates, any attempt to compare effectiveness among departments using clearance rates is evidently meaningless. Even comparisons over time within a single department are unreliable unless steps are taken to assure that no change occurs in administrative practices concerning clearances and classification of crimes. Arrest rates are also unreliable measures of effectiveness, since arrests can be made without resulting in any clearance.[1] The frequency of such events can be judged from the fact that in half of all departments the number of arrests for Part I crimes exceeds the number of clearances.[2]

Quite apart from the unreliability of arrest and clearance rates is the fact that they reflect activities of patrol officers and members of the public more than they reflect activities of investigators. Isaacs (1967), Conklin (1972), and our analysis of case samples described in Chapter 6 showed that approximately 30 percent of all clearances are produced by pickup arrests by patrol officers who respond to the scene of the crime. After the completion of our study, Bloch and Bell (1976) published findings in Rochester which, although intended for another purpose, permit calculating the fraction of clearances by arrest that were produced by on-scene arrest, most of which are presumably by patrol officers. Their data showed that, for burglary, 31.7 percent of clearances by arrest arose from on-scene arrests, with the analogous figure for robbery being 31.1 percent and for larceny 28.7 percent.

In roughly another 50 percent of cleared crimes (less for homicide and auto theft), the perpetrator is known when the crime report is first taken, and the main jobs for the investigator are to locate the perpetrator, take him or her into custody, and assemble the facts needed to present charges in court. This finding is also consistent with the work of other researchers. Isaacs (1967) studied 1,905 crimes reported to the Los Angeles Police Department and found that of 336 crimes cleared by arrest, 203 (or 60 percent) had a named suspect in the initial crime report, and of 1,556 crimes without a named suspect, 133 (or 8.6 percent) were cleared by arrest. Conklin (1972) studied 259 robberies reported to the Boston Police Department in 1968 and found that in 74 percent of cleared robberies the suspect was known by arrest at the scene or by victim identification. Smith,[3] in a study of 59 cleared robberies in Oakland in 1969, found that a victim or witness was responsible for case solution in 61 percent and that the

---

1. In some jurisdictions, persons may be arrested "for investigation," without a crime being charged. In all jurisdictions persons are occasionally arrested by error and are subsequently released by a prosecutor or magistrate without any clearance being claimed by the police.

2. Instances in which several perpetrators are arrested for a single crime may also explain an arrest/clearance ratio over 1.

3. William Smith, "Robbery: Getting Caught," Chapter 2 in Volume 4 of Feeney (1973).

suspect was known at the time the crime report was filed in 80 percent of cleared robberies. Recent studies by Greenberg et al. (1975) and Bloch and Bell (1976), while not specifically addressing the exact topic of this finding, provide adequate information for the reader to deduce that the same pattern prevails for the times and locations studied.

Hence, with around 30 percent of clearances produced by on-scene arrest and another 50 percent (approximately) by initial identification, around 20 percent of cleared crimes could possibly be attributed to investigative work, but we found in Chapter 9 that most of these were also solved by patrol officers, members of the public who spontaneously provide further information, or routine investigative practices that could also have been followed by clerical personnel.

In fact, for Kansas City we estimated that at most 2.7 percent of all Part I crime clearances could be attributed to special techniques used by investigators. (These are the "special action cases" in table 9-6.) The results for individual crime types in five other departments were not significantly different from those in Kansas City. Therefore, somewhere around 97 percent of cleared crimes will be cleared no matter what the investigators do, as long as the obvious routine follow-up steps are taken. Of course, included in the 2.7 percent are the most interesting and publicly visible crimes reported to the department, especially homicides and commercial burglaries. But the thrust of our analysis is that all the time spent by investigators on difficult cases where the perpetrator is unknown results in only 2.7 percent of the clearances.

This finding has now been established for a sufficiently large number of departments that there can be little doubt of its general correctness, with some variation, in all departments. By establishing a restricted interpretation of what constitutes "routine processing," a department might find that investigative skill or "special action" contributes to as much as 10 percent of all its clearances. Even so, the basic conclusion remains the same. Only in cases of homicide, robbery, and commercial theft did we find that the quality of investigative efforts could affect the clearance rate to any substantial extent. Conversely, the contribution of victims, witnesses, and patrol officers is most important to the identification and apprehension of criminal offenders.

Department-wide arrest and clearance statistics vary primarily according to the size of the department, the region of the country in which it is located, and its crime workload (number of reported crimes per police officer). Variations with investigative training, staffing, procedures, and organization are small and do not provide much guidance for policy decisions.

Once the nature of investigators' contributions to arrest and clearance rates is understood, it must be anticipated that variations in these rates among departments are explained primarily by characteristics that have nothing to do with the organization and deployment of investigators. This is in fact what we found from our national survey data. The three most important determinants of a department's arrest and clearance rates are its size, the region of the country it is located in, and its crime workload.

Large departments (measured by number of employees, budget, or population of the jurisdiction) claim more clearances per arrest in all crime categories than do smaller departments. However, the arrest rates of large departments do not differ from those in small departments.

Departments in the South Central states claim higher clearance rates than those in other regions, which follow in the order North Central, South Atlantic, Northeast, and West. However, arrest rates vary in almost exactly the reverse order. Evidently these differences reflect administrative practices or patterns of crime commission rather than differences in effectiveness.

In regard to crime workload, we found that departments having a large number of reported crimes per police officer have lower arrest rates than other departments. This relationship arises in the following way. The number of arrests per police officer in a year was found to rise nearly (but not quite) in direct proportion to the number of reported crimes per police officer until a certain threshold was reached. Beyond this threshold, increasing workload is associated with very small increases in the number of arrests per police officer. The thresholds are at approximately 35 Part I crimes per police officer per year and 3.5 crimes against persons per police officer per year. These thresholds are fairly high, as only about 20 percent of departments have greater workload levels.

These findings are consistent with the assumption that a city can increase its number of arrests or decrease the number of crimes (or both) by increasing the size of its police force,but the effect of added resources would be greatest for cities above the threshold.

In regard to clearance rates, the data showed that departments with high crime workload tend to claim more clearances per arrest than cities with low crime workload. As a result, clearance rates are less sensitive to workload than arrest rates. Although clearance rates for every crime type were found to decrease with increasing workload, the decreases were not significant for some types of crimes.

These workload relationships apply to all police officers, not just investigators. Although investigators are known to make more arrests per year than patrol officers, and our data confirmed this, the effect was not large enough that we could find a significant variation according to the fraction of the force in investigative units. In other words, if the total number of officers in a department is kept fixed, switching some of them into or out of investigative units is not likely to have a substantial effect on arrest or clearance rates.

Aside from the effects of size, region of the country, and workload on clearance and arrest rates, we did find a few smaller effects of possible interest. Departments that assign a major investigative role to patrolmen have lower clearance rates, but not arrest rates, than other departments. This appears to reflect the fact that patrolmen cannot carry files around with them and therefore do not clear old crimes with new arrests. Departments with specialized units (concentrating on a single crime such as robbery) were found to have lower arrest rates, but not clearance rates, for the types of crimes in which they specialize, as compared with departments having generalist investigators. Departments in which investigators work in pairs had lower numbers of arrests per officer than those in which they work singly. Since we did not collect data permitting a comparison of the quality of arrests produced by solo and paired investigators, this finding must be interpreted with caution. The practice of pairing investigators, which is common only in the Northeast, is nonetheless brought into sufficient question that further research appears warranted.

Most other characteristics of investigators were found to be unrelated to arrest and clearance rates. These include the nature and extent of training for investigators, their civil service rank or rate of pay, and the nature of their interactions with prosecutors. However, this absence of correlations probably indicates more about the inadequacies of arrest and clearance rates as measures of effectiveness than about the inherent value of training and other characteristics.

How Investigators' Time Is Spent

While serious crimes are invariably investigated, many reported felonies receive no more than superficial attention from investigators. Most minor crimes are not investigated.

From an analysis of the computer-readable case assignment file maintained by the Kansas City Police Department, described in Chapter 8, and observations during site visits, it was determined that although a large proportion of reported crimes are assigned to an investigator, many of these receive no more attention than the reading of the initial crime incident report; that is, many cases are suspended at once. The data show that homicide, rape, and suicide invariably resulted in investigative activity; while other serious types of cases received significant attention (i.e., at least a half-hour of a detective's time) in at least 60 percent of the instances. Overall, however, less than half of all reported crimes receive any serious attention by an investigator, and the great majority of cases that are actively investigated receive less than one day's attention. The data in table 8-3 imply that for homicides, rape, other felony sex crimes, kidnapping, aggravated assault, robbery, burglary, auto theft, and larceny *together,* 64.8 percent did not receive as much as a half-hour's attention from an investigator.

The net result is that the average detective does not actually work on a large number of cases each month, even though he may have a backlog of hundreds or thousands of cases that were assigned to him at some time in the past and are still theoretically his responsibility. Table 8-4 showed that in Kansas City the number of worked-on cases per detective was generally under one per day, with the exception of the Missing Persons Unit.

An investigator's time spent on casework is preponderantly consumed in reviewing reports, documenting files, and attempting to locate and interview victims. For cases that are solved (i.e., a suspect has been identified), an investigator's average time in post-clearance processing is longer than the time spent in identifying the perpetrator. A substantial fraction of time is spent on noncasework activities.

In Kansas City, the breakdown of investigators' time was as follows. About 45 percent was spent on activities not attributable to individual cases. This includes administrative assignments, speeches, travel, reading teletypes, general surveillance of junkyards, pawnshops, gathering spots for juveniles, and the like, as well as slack time (for example, in a unit that is on duty at night to respond to robberies and homicides). The remaining 55 percent of the time is spent on casework. Of this, 40 percent (or 22 percent of the total) is spent investigating crimes that are never solved, just over 12 percent (or 7 percent of the total) is spent investigating crimes that are eventually solved, and nearly 48 percent (or 26 percent of the total) is spent on cleared cases after they have been solved. While these figures apply only to Kansas City, we have reviewed them, as well as more detailed tabulations, with investigators from other cities and compared them with our observational notes. We concluded they are approximately correct for other cities, with variations primarily in the areas of slack time (if investigators are not on duty at night) and time spent in conference with prosecutors.

Thus, investigators spend about 93 percent of their time on activities that do not lead directly to solving previously reported crimes. How are they to be judged on the quality of these activities? The time they spend on cases after they have been cleared serves the important purpose of preparing cases for court (this activity will be discussed below). The time they spend on noncasework activities serves a general support function for casework activities and therefore may be useful in ways that are difficult to quantify. The time they spend on crimes that are never solved can only be judged in terms of its public relations value and a possible deterrent value, because most of these crimes can be easily recognized at the start. (They are primarily the ones for which there is no positive identification of the perpetrator available at the scene of the crime.) Police administrators must ask themselves whether the efforts devoted to investigating crimes that are initially unsolved are justified by either the small number of case solutions produced by these activities or the associated public relations benefits.

Collecting and Processing Physical Evidence

Many police departments collect more physical evidence than can be productively processed. Allocating more resources to increasing the processing capabilities of the department is likely to lead to more identifications than some other investigative actions.

The ability of a police agency to collect and process the physical evidence at crime scenes is thought to be an important component of the criminal investigation process. However, in our study we focused on the role of physical evidence in contributing to the *solution* of crimes, as distinguished from its value in proving guilt once the crime is solved.

Earlier studies by Parker and Peterson (1972) and the President's Commission on Crime in the District of Columbia (1966) showed that in only a small number of felony offenses were evidence technicians requested to process the crime scene, and even when the crime scene was processed a significant portion of the available evidence might not be retrieved. Police administrators, aware of these deficiencies, have begun to experiment with a variety of organizational changes designed to increase the number of crime sites processed for physical evidence.

Our analysis of the physical evidence collection and processing activities of six police departments which employ different procedures, described in Chapter 10, confirmed that a department can assure a relatively high recovery rate of latent prints from crime scenes by a sufficient investment in evidence technicians and by routinely dispatching technicians to the scene of felonies. The latent print recovery rate is also increased by processing the crime scene immediately following the report of the incident rather than at a later time.

However, the rate at which fingerprints were used to identify the perpetrator of a burglary was essentially unrelated to the print recovery rate. In fact, as shown in table 10-3, 1 to 2 percent of the burglary cases in each of three departments were cleared by identification from a latent print, despite substantial differences in operating procedures. In Richmond, evidence technicians are dispatched to nearly 90 percent of the reported burglaries and recover prints from 70 percent of the scenes they process, but the fraction of burglaries solved by fingerprints is about the same as in Long Beach or Berkeley, where evidence technicians are dispatched to the scene less frequently and lift prints less often.

The most plausible explanation as to why lifting more prints does not actually result in a higher rate of identifications appears to be that the fingerprint file searching capabilities of police departments are severely limited. If a suspect is known, there is little difficulty in comparing his prints with latent prints that have been collected. Thus, latent prints may help to confirm suspect identifications obtained in other ways. But in the absence of an effective means to perform "cold searches" (where the suspect is unknown), the availability of a latent print cannot help to solve the crime.

From a comparison of the fingerprint identification sections in Washington, D.C., Los Angeles, Miami, and Richmond, we determined that 4 to 9 percent of all retrieved prints are eventually matched with those of a suspect in each of the departments. However, the number of "cold-search" matches produced per man-year differed substantially among departments, according to the size of their inked print files and the attention devoted to this activity. In some departments, technicians performing cold searches produced far more case solutions per man-year than investigators.

The inference we reached was that an improved fingerprint *identification* capability will be more productive of identifications than a more intensive print *collection* effort. Although some techniques and equipment currently available to police departments were found to enhance identification capability, the technology needed to match single latent prints to inked prints is not fully developed and appears to us to be a high-priority item for research.

Preparing the Case for Prosecution

In many large departments, investigators do not consistently and thoroughly document the key evidentiary facts that reasonably assure that the prosecutor can obtain a conviction on the most serious applicable charges.

Police investigation, whether or not it can be regarded as contributing significantly to the *identification* of perpetrators, is a necessary police function because it is the principal means by which all relevant evidence is gathered and presented to the court so that a criminal prosecution can be made. Thus, police investigators can be viewed as serving a support function for prosecutors.

Prosecutors have frequently contended that a high rate of case dismissals, excessive plea bargaining, and overly lenient sentences are common consequences of inadequate police investigations. The police, in response, often claim that even when they conduct thorough investigations, case dispositions are not significantly affected. We undertook the study described in Chapter 11 to illuminate the issues surrounding the controversy between police and prosecutor about responsibilities for prosecutorial failures.

A data form containing 39 questions that a prosecutor might want the police to address in conducting a robbery investigation was developed on the basis of discussions with prosecutors, detectives, and police supervisors. When this form was used to analyze the completeness of robbery investigations in two California prosecutors' offices, chosen to reflect contrasting prosecutorial practices concerning felony case screening, but similar workload and case characteristics, it was found that the department confronted by a stringent prosecutorial filing policy (Jurisdiction A) was significantly more thorough in reporting follow-on investigative work than the department whose cases was more permissively filed (Jurisdiction B). Yet, even the former department fell short of supplying the prosecutor with all of the information he desired; the data show that each of 39 evidentiary questions considered by a prosecutor to be necessary for effective case presentation was, on the average, covered in 45 percent of the cases in Jurisdiction A, while 26 percent were addressed by the department in Jurisdiction B.

We then determined whether the degree of thorough documentation of the police investigation was related to the disposition of cases, specifically to the rate of dismissals, the heaviness of plea bargaining, and the type of sentence imposed. Our analysis showed differences between the two jurisdictions. For example, none of the sampled cases was dismissed in Jurisdiction A; furthermore, 60 percent of the defendants pled guilty to the charges as filed. By comparison, in Jurisdiction B about one-quarter of the sampled cases were dismissed after filing, and only one-third of the defendants pled guilty to the charges as filed.

A comparison between the two offices concerning the heaviness of plea bargaining was shown in table 11-6. Although plea bargaining appears lighter in Jurisdiction A, this may simply reflect that the gravity of criminal conduct in the A cases was less than in the B cases, i.e., special allegations were considerably more frequent to begin with in B. One cannot conclude that only the quality of documentation of the police investigation accounted for the difference.

A similar conclusion was reached with respect to sentence imposed. That is, differences in sentencing were found, but in light of variations in other case characteristics these differences might not necessarily be related to thoroughness of documentation. This analysis leads us to suggest that police failure to document a case investigation thoroughly *may* have contributed to a higher case dismissal rate and a weakening of the prosecutor's plea bargaining position.

Relations Between Victims and Police

Crime victims in general strongly desire to be notified officially as to whether or not the police have solved their case, and what progress has been made toward convicting the suspect after his arrest.

How much information to give the victim and when it is appropriate to convey it were the questions behind a telephone survey taken of robbery and burglary victims, described in Chapter 12. This study must be regarded as exploratory; the survey was conducted simply as an initial attempt to explore how victims feel about receiving information feedback regarding their specific case, and which types of information they feel are most important.

Responses to questions about the victim's desire to know the progress of his or her case showed a large majority in favor of such information. Responses on whether or not the victim desired to be told of a police decision to suspend or drop investigative effort on his or her case, if such a decision were made, suggested a consistent preference for knowledge about this police decision, but with an observable tendency in cleared robbery cases (a relatively small segment of the underlying population) to the contrary.

Responses that the victims made when asked what their reactions would be if they had been told that no further investigation was intended on their cases revealed that approximately one-third of our sample would react negatively to unfavorable feedback (and the proportion would be higher if the data were weighted to reflect the relative numbers of each crime type).

To the extent that our survey results may reach beyond the confines of our small sample, they broadly underscore the belief that there exists a strong market for information feedback to victims from the police. But they also tend to confirm the view that giving unfavorable information to victims creates undesirable reactions in attitude toward the police in some of these victims. Finally, our results suggest that other repercussions from information feedback, of which the police are sometimes apprehensive, are of slight significance. Few victims, no matter how much distressed by information coming to them from the police, indicated they would act inimically to police interests.

Proactive Investigation Methods

Investigative strike forces have a significant potential to increase arrest rates for a few difficult target offenses, provided they remain concentrated on activities for which they are uniquely qualified; in practice, however, they are frequently diverted elsewhere.

In contrast to the typically reactive mode of most investigators assigned to Part I crimes, some police departments have shifted a small number of their investigators to more proactive investigation tactics. These units are usually established to deal with a particular type of offender such as known burglars, robbery teams, or active fences.

The proactive team members often work quite closely with other investigators, but unlike regular investigators they are not assigned a caseload of reported crimes. Instead they are expected to generate other sources of information to identify serious offenders. These other sources may include informants they have developed, intelligence data from surveillance activities, or undercover fencing operations which the police operate themselves.

The primary objective in establishing these units is to reduce the incidence of the target crime. The reduction is supposed to result from the containment effect of successfully arresting and prosecuting offenders and the deterrent effect which the publicity given these programs is expected to have on others. Therefore, the arrest productivity of these units is typically used as a measure of their primary effect. Changes in the incidence rate for the target crime type is also cited for this purpose. The chief problem in using these two measures is the difficulties in isolating the unique effects of the proactive units from either other activities of the police department or external factors affecting crime or arrest rates.

In the course of our study we looked at several such units by either examining evaluation reports or direct observation. In general, they all seemed to result in a much higher number of arrests for the officers assigned than other types of patrol or investigative activities. Consistent effects on targeted crime rates could not be identified.

In order to determine which activities of these units actually resulted in arrests, we examined a sample of cases from two of them in considerable detail. These units were the Miami STOP Robbery Unit and the Long Beach (California) Suppression of Burglary (SOB) Unit.

By examining a sample of robbery cases in Miami, we determined that although the STOP officers averaged 4 arrests per man-month, half of which were for robbery, in 10 out of 11 of these arrests the STOP officer was simply executing a warrant obtained by some other unit or accompanying another officer to make the arrest.

In Long Beach, the Suppression of Burglary officers averaged 2.4 arrests per man-month, half of which were for burglary or receiving stolen property. An analysis of 27 of their arrests disclosed that just half (13) resulted from their own work, with the remainder representing referral arrests or routine investigation which any other unit could have handled.

Our general conclusion from these observations was that proactive techniques can be productive in making arrests, particularly for burglary and fencing. To be effective, such units must be staffed with highly motivated and innovative personnel. Their efforts must also be carefully monitored to ensure that they do not become diverted to making arrests for other units and that their tactics do not become overly aggressive so as to infringe on individual liberties.

15 Policy Implications

We have identified several distinguishable functions performed by investigators: preparing cases for prosecution after the suspects are in custody, apprehending known suspects, performing certain routine tasks that may lead to identifying unknown suspects, engaging in intensive investigations when there are no suspects or it is not clear whether a crime has been committed, and proactive investigations. In addition, investigators engage in varous administrative and paperwork tasks related to these functions.

The information we obtained about the effectiveness of each function is adequate to begin asking whether the function should be performed at all and, if so, who should do it. The notion that all these functions must be performed by a single individual, or by officers having similar ranks or capabilities, does not stand up to scrutiny, and in fact many police departments have begun to assign distinguishable functions to separate units. Our own suggestions, to be presented in this chapter, support this development and extend it in certain ways. If a function now assigned to investigators can be performed as well or better, but at lower cost, by patrol officers, clerical personnel, or information systems, it should be removed from investigators; if it serves the objectives of the prosecutor, then it should be responsive to the needs of the prosecutor; and if especially competent investigators are required, the function should be assigned to a unit composed of such officers.

Preparing Cases for Prosecution

Postarrest investigative activity is not only important for prosecution but is also one of the major activities now performed by investigators. This activity can perhaps be performed in a less costly or more effective manner.

From our observations, the current coordination, or lack thereof, between the police and prosecutorial agencies does not support a healthy working relationship. It allows a situation where each can blame the other for outcomes in court that they view as unfavorable.

Most prosecutors do not have investigators on their staff. If they do, these investigators are usually occupied with "white-collar" offenses rather than street crime. Generally, then, the prosecutor relies on police investigators to provide the evidence needed to prosecute and convict arrestees. But this situation contains an inherent conflict between prosecutor and police. An arrest is justified by *probable cause*—i.e., an articulatable, reasonable belief that a crime was committed and that the arrestee was the offender. Often, the police are satisfied to document the justification for the arrest rather than expending further investigative efforts to strengthen the evidence in the case. The prosecutor, on the other hand, may be reluctant to file the charge preferred by the police, or to file at all, if he believes the evidence would not suffice for a conviction, i.e., *proof beyond a reasonable doubt.* Many cases appear to be affected by the conflicting incentives of police and prosecutor, as reflected in failures to file, lenient filing, early dismissals, or imbalanced bargaining.

One way of ameliorating this problem is to make explicit the types of information the prosecutor and police agree are appropriate to collect and document, given the nature of the crime. The form we designed for robbery cases (summarized in table 11-1) gives an example of how such information can be made explicit. Each jurisdiction should develop appropriate forms for major categories of crimes. Such written documents would assist the police in becoming more knowledgeable about the type and amount of information that a prosecutor requires to establish guilt for each type of offense and in allocating their investigative efforts to provide this information.[1]

We observed that the strictness of the prosecutor with respect to filing decisions can affect the thoroughness of case preparation. In turn, the thoroughness of documentation may affect the percentage of cases subsequently dismissed and the degree of plea bargaining. Given this finding, we suggest that prosecutors be mindful of the level of investigative documentation in their jurisdictions, especially in offices where the officer presenting the case may not have participated in the investigation.

One rationale advanced in some police departments for minimizing the factual content of formal investigative reports is that these reports are subject to discovery by defense counsel and thereby facilitate the impeachment of prosecution witnesses, including policemen. Such departments believe the results of detailed investigations are better communicated orally to the prosecutor's office. The results of our research would tend to refute this argument, although they are not conclusive. In the jurisdiction where detailed documentation is prepared, no such negative consequences were noted, but in the jurisdiction having less information in the documentation, oral communication failed in some instances to reach all the prosecutors involved with the case.

Above and beyond merely improving coordination between police and prosecutors, it is worthy of experimentation to assign the prosecutor responsibility for certain investigative efforts. We feel that a promising approach would be to place nearly all postarrest investigations under the authority of the

---

1. Other alternatives which might accomplish some similar aims include having the prosecutor provide the investigator with periodic evaluations of their case preparation efforts; training for new investigators in case preparation; or on-call attorneys to assist in the preparation of serious cases.

prosecutor, either by assigning police officers to his office or making investigators an integral part of his staff, depending on the local situation. A test of this arrangement would permit determining whether it is an effective way of assuring that the evidentiary needs for a successful prosecution are met.

Apprehending Known Suspects

We have noted that in a substantial fraction of cases ultimately cleared, the perpetrator is known from information available at the scene of the crime. If he or she is already in custody, the case becomes a matter for postarrest processing, as discussed above. If the perpetrator is not in custody, it is important for the responding officer(s), whether from investigative or patrol units, to obtain and make a record of the evidence identifying the suspect. This requires that the responding officers be permitted adequate time to conduct an initial investigation, including interviewing possible witnesses, and that the crime-reporting form be designed in such a way that the presence of information identifying a suspect is unmistakably recorded.

Apprehending a known suspect may or may not be difficult. Assigning all such apprehensions to investigators does not appear to be cost-effective, especially if the investigators are headquartered at some distance from the suspect's location and a patrol officer is nearby. We believe that certain patrol officers, whom we shall call generalist-investigators, could be trained to handle this function in such a way that the arrests are legally proper and a minimum number of innocent persons are brought in for questioning. Only when apprehension proves difficult should investigative units become involved.

Routine Investigative Actions

For crimes without an initial suspect identification, we found that many of those eventually cleared are solved by routine investigative actions. These actions include listing a stolen automobile in the "hot car" file, asking the victim to view a previously assembled collection of mug shots for the crime in question, checking pawnshop slips, awaiting phone calls from the public, tracing ownership of a weapon, etc.

One implication of this finding is that any steps a police department can take to convert investigative tasks into routine actions will increase the number of crimes solved. Technological improvements, especially information systems, produced many of the clearances we identified as "routine." Such clearances might never have occurred in the absence of such systems or might have been difficult to achieve. The ability of patrol officers to check rapidly whether a vehicle is stolen or, more important, whether the owner is wanted for questioning produced numerous case solutions in our samples. Well-organized and maintained mug shot, *modus operandi,* or pawn slip files also lead to clearances.

A second implication is that it may not be necessary for *investigators,* who are usually paid more than patrol officers or clerks, to perform the functions that lead to routine clearances. We believe an experiment should be conducted to determine the cost and effectiveness of lower-paid personnel performing these tasks.

Once clerical processing is complete, some action by a police officer may still be needed (e.g., apprehending the suspect). Such cases should be assigned to the generalist-investigators.

Investigating Crimes Without Suspects

Basically, two different objectives are served by taking more than routine investigative action when the suspect is unknown. One is a genuine desire to solve the crime, and the other is to perform a public service function, demonstrating that the police care about the crime and the victim. The latter function can be performed by generalist-investigators who are responsible to a local commander who is concerned with all aspects of police-community relations. This type of investigative duty does not require specialized skills or centralized coordination. The officers performing it could readily shift between patrol and investigative duties. In departments with team policing, such investigation could be a duty rotated among team members.

If the objective is actually to solve the crime, police departments must realize that the results will rarely be commensurate with the effort involved. An explicit decision must be made that the nature of the crime itself or public concern about the crime warrants a full follow-up investigation. A significant reduction in investigative efforts would be appropriate for all but the most serious offenses. If a thorough preliminary investigation fails to establish a suspect's identity in a less serious offense, then the victim should be notified that active investigation is being suspended until new leads appear, for example, as a result of an arrest in another matter.

Serious crimes (homicide, rape, assault with great bodily injury, robbery, or first-degree burglary) warrant special investigative efforts. These efforts can best be provided by a Major Offenses Unit, manned by investigators who are well-trained and experienced in examining crime scenes, interpreting physical evidence, and interrogating hostile suspects and fearful witnesses, and who are aided by modern information systems. One reason to establish such a unit is to identify the investigative positions that require special skills and training and that demand knowledge of citywide crime patterns and developments. Our observations suggest, by way of contrast, that with current staffing patterns, most investigators rarely see these highly serious cases. Therefore, when they arise, the investigators are frequently ill-equipped to cope with them and unduly distracted by the burden of paperwork on their routine cases.

The Major Offenses Unit would concentrate efforts on a few *unresolved* serious felonies. The team would consist of a relatively small number of experienced investigators who would be closely supervised by a team commander. From our observations, the most serious impediment to high-quality investigative work appears to us to be the traditional method of case assignment and supervision. In nearly every department, cases are normally assigned to an individual investigator and become his sole responsibility whether he is a generalist, specialist, or engaged in team policing. Supervisors do not normally review the decisions he makes on how to pursue the case investigation—decisions that are largely unrecorded in the case file. Consequently, the relative priority an investigator gives to the tasks on one case assigned to him results largely from the number and nature of his other case assignments and from his personal predilections and biases. It may frequently turn out that caseload conflicts and personal predilections lead an investigator to unduly postpone or improperly perform important elements of a particular case assignment.

Assigning cases to investigative teams rather than to individuals could eliminate this impediment. For effective operations, this team should number approximately six men and be led by a senior investigator who is knowledgeable in the local crime situation, in criminal law, and in police management. The leader's primary responsibility would be to keep informed of progress on the cases assigned to his team and make the broad tactical decisions on the team's expenditure of effort. Each day the subordinate investigators would perform individually assigned tasks. A clerk delegated to the team would prepare progress reports to document the daily accomplishment on open cases and assist the leader in making the allocation for the following day. These reports would also help the leader identify which of his men was most effective at which tasks. This approach should assure that significant steps in an investigation are objectively directed by a senior experienced investigator.

Proactive Investigations

Our research into proactive investigations, or strike force operations, leads us to conclude that these units can be relatively productive. In instances where such units did achieve an advantage, the units were manned by motivated and innovative personnel. The gain in employing them becomes illusory when mere quantity of arrests is emphasized, for then the efforts of this force tend to be diverted into making arrests that are not the result of unique capabilities. We feel that departments should employ strike forces selectively and judiciously. The operation of strike forces necessitates careful procedural and legal planning to protect the involved officers and to ensure that the defendants they identify can be successfully prosecuted. They also require close monitoring by senior officers to ensure that they do not become overly aggressive and infringe on individual privacy.

In all likelihood, the relative advantage of strike force operations in a particular department will not persist over a long period of time. The department must accustom itself to creating and then terminating strike forces, as circumstances may dictate.

Processing Physical Evidence

Most police departments collect far more evidence (primarily fingerprints) than they can productively process. Our work shows that cold searches of inked fingerprint files could be far more effective in increasing the apprehension rate than routine follow-up investigations.

We believe that fingerprint-processing capabilities should be strengthened as follows. First, the reference print files should be organized by geographic area, with a fingerprint specialist assigned to each area, of no more than 4,000 to 5,000 sets of inked prints. Second, to assure a large number of "request searches," which imply a cooperative effort between investigator and fingerprint specialist, some communication links should be devised to help motivate and facilitate the reciprocal exchange of information between these two parties. And, third, the persons performing this function should be highly trained, highly motivated, and not overloaded with other tasks which detract from their primary function.

Several existing systems for storing and retrieving inked prints having specified characteristics (of the latent print or the offender) appear useful and were widely praised by departments that have them. However, further research might contribute a major technological improvement in the capability of police departments to match latent prints with inked prints.

Role of the Public

Our research persuaded us that actions by members of the public can strongly influence the outcome of cases. Sometimes private citizens hold the perpetrator at the scene of the crime. Sometimes they recognize the suspect or stolen property at a later time and call the investigator. In other cases, the victim or his relatives conduct a full-scale investigation on their own and eventually present the investigator with a solution. Collectively, these types of citizen involvement constitute a sizable fraction of cleared cases.

Police departments should initiate programs designed to increase the victim's desire to cooperate fully with the police. Resources allocated to such programs may serve to increase apprehension rates as well as improve the quality of prosecutions. Specifically, police departments should announce, when major crimes are solved, the particular contribution of members of the public, although of course their desires for anonymity should be respected. A realistic picture of how crimes are solved will help eliminate the public's distorted image of detectives and will impress on them the importance of their cooperation with police in order to solve crimes.

Reallocation of Investigative Resources

If, after appropriate test and evaluation, the suggestions we have made for improving the investigative function prove to be effective, the ultimate implication of our work would be a substantial shift of police resources from investigative units to other units. First, most initial investigations would be assigned to patrol units under the direction of local commanders. To improve the quality of initial investigations, the patrol force would have to be augmented with a large number of generalist-investigators. These officers would also perform certain follow-up work such as apprehending known suspects and improving communications with victims and witnesses of crimes. The resources needed to field generalist-investigators would be obtained by reducing the number of investigators.

Additional major reallocations of resources away from "traditional" reactive investigative units are implied by our suggestions to have clerical personnel and generalist-investigators perform routine processing of cases, to increase the use of information systems, to enhance capabilities for processing physical evidence, to increase the number of proactive investigative units, and to assign investigative personnel to the prosecutor for postarrest preparation of cases. If all these changes were made, the only remaining investigative units concerned wtih Part I crime would be the Major Offenses Units. The number of investigators assigned to such units would ordinarily be well under half the current number of investigators in most departments.

Our study does not in any way suggest that total police resources should be reduced. On the contrary, our analysis of FBI data suggests that such a reduction might lower arrest and clearance rates. Reallocating resources may lead to somewhat increased arrest and clearance rates, but our suggestions are primarily intended to result in more successful prosecution of arrestees and improved public relations.

Most of our suggestions for change are known to be practical, because we observed them in operation in one or more departments. For example, a number of departments have recently introduced "case screening," which means that each crime report is examined to determine whether or not a follow-up investigation should be conducted. Our findings indicate that the decision rule for case screening can be quite simple. If a suspect is known, the case should be pursued; if no suspect is known after a thorough preliminary investigation, the case should be assigned for routine clerical processing unless it is serious enough to be assigned to the appropriate Major Offenses Unit. The definition of "serious" must be determined individually by each department, since it is essentially a political decision.

Another current innovation is "team policing," in which investigators are assigned to work with patrol officers who cover a specified geographical area. While there are many organizational variations on team policing,[2] most forms would permit the introduction of generalist-investigators having the functions we describe, and some already incude such personnel.

We are not aware of any jurisdiction in which the prosecutor currently administers postarrest investigations, although investigators have been assigned to several prosecutor's offices (for example, in Boston, New Orleans, and San Diego) to facilitate interactions with the police. To determine the feasibility and effectiveness of prosecutor responsibility for postarrest investigations, a careful experiment will be required.

The National Institute of Law Enforcement and Criminal Justice has funded the introduction of revised investigative procedures in six jurisdictions. The experimental changes, which are based partly on the findings of our study, will be carefully evaluated to determine whether, to what extent, and under what circumstances they actually lead to improved effectiveness.

---

2. See, for example, Bloch and Specht (1973).

Appendixes

Appendix A

Police Departments Surveyed

City Police Departments

*Birmingham, Alabama
Huntsville, Alabama
Mobile, Alabama
*Montgomery, Alabama
*Tuscaloosa, Alabama

*Phoenix, Arizona
*Tucson, Arizona
*Little Rock, Arkansas
*Anaheim, California
Bakersfield, California

*Berkeley, California
Burbank, California
Compton, California
*Fremont, California
*Fresno, California

*Fullerton, California
Garden Grove, California
*Glendale, California
Huntington Beach, California
Inglewood, California

*Long Beach, California
*Los Angeles, California
*Oakland, California
*Pasadena, California
Pomona, California

*Richmond, California
*Riverside, California
Sacramento, California
*San Bernardino, California
*San Diego, California

*San Francisco, California
*San Jose, California
* Santa Ana, California
Santa Barbara, California
Santa Monica, California

*Stockton, California
Sunnyvale, California
*Torrance, California
*Colorado Springs, Colorado
*Denver, Colorado

*Lakewood, Colorado
*Pueblo, Colorado
Bridgeport, Connecticut
*Greenwich, Connecticut
*Hartford, Connecticut

New Britain, Connecticut
New Haven, Connecticut
Norwalk, Connecticut
Stamford, Connecticut
Waterbury, Connecticut

*Wilmington, Delaware
*Washington, D.C.
*Clearwater, Florida
Daytona Beach, Florida
*Fort Lauderdale, Florida

*Gainesville, Florida
Hialeah, Florida
*Hollywood, Florida
*Miami, Florida
*Miami Beach, Florida

---

*Responded to survey questionnaire.

247

City Police Departments

Orlando, Florida
*St. Petersburg, Florida
Tallahassee, Florida
Tampa, Florida
*West Palm Beach, Florida

*Atlanta, Georgia
Augusta, Georgia
*Columbus, Georgia
Macon, Georgia
*Savannah, Georgia

*Hilo, Hawaii
Honolulu, Hawaii
Chicago, Illinois
*Evanston, Illinois
Joliet, Illinois

Peoria, Illinois
*Rockford, Illinois
*Springfield, Illinois
East Chicago, Indiana
*Evansville, Indiana

*Fort Wayne, Indiana
*Gary, Indiana
Hammond, Indiana
Indianapolis, Indiana
*South Bend, Indiana

*Cedar Rapids, Iowa
Davenport, Iowa
*Des Moines, Iowa
*Kansas City, Kansas
*Topeka, Kansas

*Wichita, Kansas
*Lexington, Kentucky
Louisville, Kentucky
*Baton Rouge, Louisiana
New Orleans, Louisiana

*Shreveport, Louisiana
*Portland, Maine
Baltimore, Maryland
*Boston, Massachusetts
Brockton, Massachusetts

Brookline, Massachusetts
Cambridge, Massachusetts
Fall River, Massachusetts
Lawrence, Massachusetts
*Lowell, Massachusetts

Lynn, Massachusetts
New Bedford, Massachusetts
Newton, Massachusetts
*Quincy, Massachusetts
Springfield, Massachusetts

*Worcester, Massachusetts
Ann Arbor, Michigan
Dearborn, Michigan
*Detroit, Michigan
*Flint, Michigan

Grand Rapids, Michigan
*Kalamazoo, Michigan
Lansing, Michigan
Livonia, Michigan
*Pontiac, Michigan

*Saginaw, Michigan
Warren, Michigan
Duluth, Minnesota
*Minneapolis, Minnesota
St. Paul, Minnesota

*Jackson, Mississippi
*Independence, Missouri
*Kansas City, Missouri
St. Louis, Missouri
*Springfield, Missouri

City Police Departments

*Lincoln, Nebraska
*Omaha, Nebraska
 Las Vegas, Nevada
*Reno, Nevada
 Manchester, New Hampshire

 Atlantic City, New Jersey
*Bayonne, New Jersey
 Camden, New Jersey
 East Orange, New Jersey
 Elizabeth, New Jersey

 Hoboken, New Jersey
*Jersey City, New Jersey
*Newark, New Jersey
*Passaic, New Jersey
 Patterson, New Jersey

*Trenton, New Jersey
 Woodbridge, New Jersey
*Albuquerque, New Mexico
 Albany, New York
 Binghamton, New York

 Buffalo, New York
*Mount Vernon, New York
 New Rochelle, New York
*New York, New York
 Niagara Falls, New York

*Rochester, New York
 Schenectady, New York
*Syracuse, New York
 Utica, New York
*White Plains, New York

*Yonkers, New York
 Charlotte, North Carolina
*Durham, North Carolina
*Greensboro, North Carolina
*Raleigh, North Carolina

*Winston-Salem, North Carolina
 Akron, Ohio
 Canton, Ohio
*Cincinnati, Ohio
*Cleveland, Ohio

 Columbus, Ohio
 Dayton, Ohio
 Parma, Ohio
 Toledo, Ohio
 Youngstown, Ohio

 Oklahoma City, Oklahoma
 Tulsa, Oklahoma
*Eugene, Oregon
*Portland, Oregon
 Allentown, Pennsylvania

*Bethlehem, Pennsylvania
 Chester, Pennsylvania
 Erie, Pennsylvania
 Harrisburg, Pennsylvania
*Philadelphia, Pennsylvania

*Pittsburgh, Pennsylvania
*Reading, Pennsylvania
 Scranton, Pennsylvania
 Upper Darby, Pennsylvania
*Pawtucket, Rhode Island

 Providence, Rhode Island
 Warwick, Rhode Island
*Charleston, South Carolina
 Columbia, South Carolina
 Greenville, South Carolina

 Chattanooga, Tennessee
 Knoxville, Tennessee
 Memphis, Tennessee
 Nashville, Tennessee
*Amarillo, Texas

City Police Departments

Austin, Texas
*Beaumont, Texas
*Corpus Christi, Texas
*Dallas, Texas
*El Paso, Texas

*Fort Worth, Texas
*Houston, Texas
*Lubbock, Texas
Pasadena, Texas
*San Antonio, Texas

*Waco, Texas
*Salt Lake City, Utah
*Alexandria, Virginia
*Arlington, Virginia
Chesapeake, Virginia

*Hampton, Virginia
Norfolk, Virginia
*Newport News, Virginia
*Portsmouth, Virginia
*Richmond, Virginia

Roanoke, Virginia
Virginia Beach, Virginia
*Seattle, Washington
Spokane, Washington
*Tacoma, Washington

Charleston, West Virginia
Green Bay, Wisconsin
Kenosha, Wisconsin
Madison, Wisconsin
Milwaukee, Wisconsin

Racine, Wisconsin
West Allis, Wisconsin

County Police Departments and Sheriffs

Jefferson County, Alabama
*Mobile County, Alabama
*Pima County, Arizona
Maricopa County, Arizona
*Alameda County, California

*Contra Costa County, California
*Fresno County, California
Kern County, California
Los Angeles County, California
Marin County, California

Monterey County, California
Orange County, California

Appendix B

Survey Instrument

1-3 *Serial Number*

1

4

4-5 *Card* | 0 | 1 |

Date:_____

I. GENERAL INFORMATION ABOUT YOUR POLICE DEPARTMENT OR LAW ENFORCEMENT AGENCY

1 Department's official name:_____

2 Geographical jurisdiction (Name of City, Town, County, or other jurisdiction):_____

3 Police chief or highest ranking career officer:

NAME:_____

TITLE:_____

ADDRESS:_____

_____

4 Person or organization to whom the person named in question 3 reports:

TITLE:_____

NAME:_____

ADDRESS:_____

_____

5 Estimated population of department's jurisdiction:

6-9   a. Total daytime popula-tion (weekday)

10-13   b. Total residential population

c. Check the year for which these estimates apply.

14-0   ☐ 1970

14-1   ☐ 1971

14-2   ☐ 1972

14-3   ☐ 1973

6 Estimated minority group population:

15-17 ☐☐.☐ percent Black or Negro

18-20 ☐☐.☐ percent Hispanic, Chicano, other Spanish-American

21-23 ☐☐.☐ percent other large minority group

24 → Specify: ____________________

7 Area of agency's jurisdiction:

25-31 ☐,☐☐☐,☐☐☐ square miles

8 Department's budget for current fiscal year:

32-37 $ ☐☐☐,☐☐☐,☐☐☐ salaries and wages

38-43 $ ☐☐☐,☐☐☐,☐☐☐ facilities and equipment

44-49 $ ☐☐☐,☐☐☐,☐☐☐ total budget

9 Department's present manpower:

	Authorized	Actual	
50-59	☐☐,☐☐☐	☐☐,☐☐☐	number of sworn officers
60-67	☐,☐☐☐	☐,☐☐☐	number of full-time civilian employees
68-75	☐,☐☐☐	☐,☐☐☐	others (reserve officers, crossing guards, part-time, etc.)

10 Does the department have separate commands for geographical subdivisions (precincts, districts, or divisions)?

76-1 ☐ Yes → How many subdivisions? 77-78 ☐☐

76-2 ☐ No → SKIP TO QUESTION 12

11 Are investigators* organized along the same geographical lines?

79-1 ☐ Yes
79-2 ☐ No

12 Please fill in the following table for the year 1972. If certain information is not available, mark N/A.

Crime Type (FBL Categories)	Number Reported	Number Unfounded	Actual Number	Number of Arrests					Number Cleared*	
				Total	By Patrol	By Investigation	Total	By Arrest	Other	
Card 0 2 Homicide and non-negl. m. sl.										
Card 0 3 Forcible rape										
Card 0 4 Robbery										
Card 0 5 Agg. or felonious assault										
Card 0 6 Burglary										
Card 0 7 Larceny, $ 50 and over										
Card 0 8 Auto theft										
Card 0 9 All other felonies										
Card 1 0 All other crimes										
Card 1 6 Total crimes										

*See GLOSSARY for explanation of items marked with an asterisk.

II. INVESTIGATORS' RANK, QUALIFICATIONS, TRAINING AND SUPERVISION

13 Some departments have a special title for officers assigned to investigative duties (such as "detective" inspector" or "investigator"), whether or not they have a special official rank. Does your department have such a job title?

Card
4 5

| 1 | 1 |

6-1 ☐ Yes

6-2 ☐ No → SKIP TO QUESTION 17

14 What is this title?

_____

15 How many officers in the department have this title?

7-10 ☐ , ☐☐☐

16 Is the job title in question 14 a civil service rank?

11-1 ☐ Yes

11-2 ☐ No → Who is authorized to appoint officers to this title?

_____

17 Do investigators ordinarily work in pairs?

12-1 ☐ Yes

12-2 ☐ No

18 How many hours of formal _investigative_ training are provided to recruits when they enter the department?

13-15 ☐☐☐

19 How many hours of additional formal investigative training are provided to newly appointed investigators?

16-18 ☐☐☐

20 If routine refresher training is provided to investigators, please specify frequency.

19-21 ☐☐☐ number of hours of training

22 _____ how often provided to an investigator

III. ORGANIZATION OF THE INVESTIGATIVE FUNCTION

21 Total number of personnel in the department assigned primarily to investigative duties.

23-26 ☐, ☐☐☐ sworn

27-30 ☐, ☐☐☐ civilian

22 Are the investigators (or most of them) responsible to a centralized commander?

31-1 ☐ Yes ➡️ What is his title?
_____

31-2 ☐ No

23 In some departments investigators can specialize in one or more of the crime types listed below. Add to the list the other specialties in your department.

Code Letter	Specialty
A	Homicide
B	Sex crimes
C	Commercial theft
D	Juvenile crime
E	Auto theft
F	Internal inspection

	Code Letter	Specialty
32-33	G	_____
34-35	H	_____
36-37	I	_____
38-39	J	_____
40-41	K	_____
42-43	L	_____
44-45	M	_____
46-47	N	_____

Card [1] [2]

24 In this table list in detail the investigative units in the department. Include all geographical subdivisions. Do not include personnel primarily assigned to uniformed patrol duty. In last column enter code letters from questions 23 for specialties which investigators in the unit may have. (Mark N/A if no specialties).

Name of unit	Number of Personnel		Check Primary functions			Rank use. 0 = never, 1 rarely 2 = sometimes, 3 = frequently				Special-ties
	With title in quest. 14	Other Investi-gators	Investig. Reported Crimes	Internal Inspec-tion	Intell., Vice, Org. Crime, Narcotics	Arrest * Warrants	Search Warrants	Under-Cover agents	Certified or regis-tered in-formants	

TOTAL _____   Should agree with question 15.

Use additional pages (copies of this page) if more than 14 investigative units.

Card 1 3

4 5

25 How is the quality of investigative units monitored? On each line enter one of the following codes: 0 = Not used   2 = Important
1 = Minor importance   3 = Very important

6 ☐ Supervisory review of investigators' reports, initiative, etc.

7 ☐ Audit (detailed follow-up investigation of randomly selected cases)

8 ☐ Arrest statistics

9 ☐ Clearance statistics

10 ☐ Caseload

11 ☐ Property recovered

12 ☐ Success in a major investigation

13 ☐ Prosecution or indictment statistics

14 ☐ Court conviction statistics

15 ☐ Other
      ↳Specify:_____

26 Do <u>uniformed patrol officers</u> perform investigative functions other than preparing crime reports, securing crime scenes, notifying investigative units, and necessary actions related to pickup arrests?

16-1 ☐ Yes ➡ | Fill in table on next page (Question 27) |

16-2 ☐ No ➡ | SKIP TO QUESTION 28 |

27 List the crime types for which the patrol force has an investigative function (e.g., all crimes, all misdemeanors, burglary, etc.), and check the roles of the patrol force.

Crime Type	Check Crime Scene	Prelim-inary Investi-gation	Full Investi-gation	Stake-out or sur-veillance	Other ►(Specify)	Other ►(Specify)
17-24						
25-32						
33-40						
41-48						
49-56						
57-64						

28 Has there been any significant reorganization of the investigative units during the last two years?

65-1 ☐ Yes

65-2 ☐ No ⟶ | SKIP TO QUESTION 30 |

29 Please describe briefly the change and how it improved operations or management.

_____

_____

_____

_____

_____

30 Is a significant reorganization of the investigative units planned for the next year?

66-1 ☐ Yes.

66-2 ☐ No

66-3 ☐ Can't say

IV. INTERACTION WITH OTHER CRIMINAL JUSTICE AGENCIES

31 Does your department have formal organizational arrangements for sharing investigative or intelligence information with one or more local law enforcement agencies?

67-1 ☐ Yes

67-2 ☐ No

32 Are misdemeanors and felonies both handled by the same prosecuting agency in your jurisdiction?

68-1 ☐ Yes

68-2 ☐ No

33 How soon after an arrest must the arrestee be arraigned or a complaint* sought? (By statute or administrative practice.)

69-70

_____

_____

34 Who in the department generally seeks a complaint from the prosecutor or court?

71-1   ☐   Arresting officer

71-2   ☐   Investigating officer

71-3   ☐   Liaison or escort officer

71-4   ☐   Varies by unit or crime type ▶

Explain

71-5   ☐   Other

    └▶Specify:_____

_____

35 For each of the listed crime types, indicate the extent to which a representative of the local prosecutor's office would be involved in an-investigation <u>prior</u> to an arrest.
Enter the highest applicable code for each crime:

    0 = Prosecutor <u>never</u> involved before an arrest
    1 = Prosecutor <u>sometimes</u> advises on whether to arrest
    2 = Prosecutor <u>always</u> advises on whether to arrest
    3 = Prosecutor <u>sometimes</u> involved in investigation
    4 = Prosecutor <u>always</u> involved in investigation
    5 = Prosecutor <u>has primary responsibility</u> for the entire investigation

72   ☐   Homicide

73   ☐   Robbery

74   ☐   Large theft or burglary

75   ☐   Major drug case

76   ☐   Official misconduct or corruption

77   ☐   White-collar crime

_____
*See Glossary

36 If an investigation of one of the listed crimes was necessary <u>after</u> an arrest, to what extent would the prosecutor supervise the investigation? Enter the appropriate code on each line:

> 0 = Prosecutor <u>never</u> supervises
> 1 = Sometimes
> 2 = Usually
> 3 = Always

4 5
Card 1 4

6 ☐ Homicide

7 ☐ Robbery

8 ☐ Large theft or burglary

9 ☐ Major drug case

10 ☐ Official misconduct or corruption

11 ☐ White-collar crime

37 Do any local prosecutors have their own investigative staff?

12-1 ☐ Yes

12-2 ☐ No → SKIP TO QUESTION 39

38 Are the investigators who are assigned to the prosecutor members of your department?

13-1 ☐ Yes, all of them

13-2 ☐ Yes, some of them

13-3 ☐ No

39 What percentage of felony arrests are screened out or rejected by the prosecutor without drawing of an affidavit or formal complaint?

14 (If data not available please check here ☐ and record estimated percent below.)

15-1 ☐ less than 5%

15-2 ☐ 5 - 20%

15-3 ☐ 20 - 50%

15-4 ☐ 50 - 70%

15-5 ☐ more than 70%

40 Does your department grant or seek leniency for defendants who will provide information to the department on criminal activities?

16-1 ☐ Yes

16-2 ☐ No

41 How many <u>search</u> warrants were obtained by your department in 1972?

17-21 ☐☐,☐☐☐

42 How many arrests in 1972 were made pursuant to an arrest warrant?

22 (If number of <u>arrests</u> is unavailable, but you have data for the number of arrest <u>warrants</u>—including warrants that were not executed—check here ☐ and enter the number of warrants below.)

23-27 ☐☐,☐☐☐ number of arrest warrants obtained as the result of an investigation in your jurisdiction

28-32 ☐☐,☐☐☐ number of other arrest warrants (including out-of-jurisdiction, bail jumping, and so forth)

33-37 ☐☐,☐☐☐ total number of arrest warrants

V. INVESTIGATIVE POLICIES, OPERATIONS, AND PROCEDURES

43 Does your department use evidence technicians who are sent to the crime scene?

38-1 ☐ Yes ➡️ How many are there?

39-41 ☐☐☐ number of civilians

42-44 ☐☐☐ number of sworn officers

38-2 ☐ No

44 Please estimate how frequently the following physical evidence checks
are made at the crime scene.

Enter 0 = never, 1 = rarely, 2 = sometimes,
3 = usually, 4 = always

Physical Evidence Check

CRIME TYPE	Finger prints	Tool marks	Chemical Analysis	Shoeprint and tire casting	Other ►(Specify)
Homicide					
Residential burglaries					
Commercial burglaries					
Robberies					

45

46-50

51-55

56-60

61-65

45 Does your department monitor or regulate pawn shops or other
potential outlets for stolen goods?

66-1 ☐ Yes ➡

┌─────────────────────┐
│ Monitor? ☐ 67-1   │
│ Regulate? ☐ 67-2   │
└─────────────────────┘

66-2 ☐ No

46 Once a case is assigned to a unit, what is the usual method for
assigning cases to investigators?

68-1 ☐ By rotation *

68-2 ☐ By assigned period of time

68-3 ☐ According to specialty of investigator

68-4 ☐ Other
└►Specify:_____

47 Does your department have any innovative investigative programs or
policies showing enough success or promise that other departments
should know about them?

69-1 ☐ Yes

69-2 ☐ No ➡ ┌──────────────────────┐
            │ SKIP TO QUESTION 49 │
            └──────────────────────┘

*See Glossary.

48 Please describe the programs or policies briefly, or attach previously prepared descriptions. Include all LEAA-funded grants or contracts related to investigation and all anti-burglary and anti-robbery programs.

_____

_____

_____

_____

_____

_____

VI. RECORDS AND FILES

49 Do investigators complete any kind of formal activity log* to account for how their time was spent?

70-1 ☐ Yes ➔ Are individual or unit activities periodically summarized?

   71-1 ☐ Yes

   71-2 ☐ No

70-2 ☐ No

50 Are crime, arrest, and disposition records available to the department in computer readable form?

		-1		-2	
72	Crime Reports	☐	Yes	☐	No
73	Arrest Reports	☐	Yes	☐	No
74	Court Dispositions	☐	Yes	☐	No
75	Summary Statistics	☐	Yes	☐	No

51 Does the department have any file (manual or computer readable) in which all of the following information is available in one place for any reported crime?

● crime report
● whether an arrest made

_____

*See Glossary.

Cont.

Cont.

- whether cleared
- whether prosecuted
- court disposition

76-1 ☐ Yes

76-2 ☐ No

Card 1 5

52 Please check the files maintained by the department to support investigations.

FILE	Manual	Computerized
6 M.O. file		
7 fingerprints		
8 known offender		
9 sex offender		
10 hot car		
11 mug shot		
12 organized crime intelligence		
13 14 other►(specify:_____)		
15 16 other		
17 18 other		
19 20 other		
21 22 other		
23 24 other		

53 Does your department have a crime analysis section which analyzes patterns* of past crime?

25-1 ☐ Yes

25-2 ☐ No

54 For each search warrant obtained, do the department's records indicate whether the warrant led to successful recovery of property?

26-1 ☐ Yes

26-2 ☐ No

*See Glossary.

VII. GENERAL

55 After the return of these questionnaires, The Rand Corporation will prepare a report summarizing the responses of all the departments. What information about the responses of other departments would be of particular interest to your department?

_____

_____

_____

_____

_____

_____

_____

56 What information (other than topics covered in this questionnaire) about the organization and effectiveness of investigative units in other departments would be useful to your department?

_____

_____

_____

_____

_____

_____

_____

57 A small number of departments which respond to this questionnaire will be selected for detailed analysis of their investigative function. This will involve interviews with department officials, review of sample case folders, observation of investigative activities, and collection of data for further analysis by Rand. Does your department wish to be considered for selection?

27-1 ☐ Yes

27-2 ☐ No

58 It would be helpful if you could attach documents and forms referred
to in this questionnaire. Please check below all materials you have
attached.

√	Document	Question Number
	Department's annual report	
	Current organization chart	
	List of ranks and pay ranges	
	Description of evidence technician unit	43
	Description of innovative programs or policies	48
	Blank copy of investigator's activity log	49
	Example of summarized activities	49
	Coding form or data format for computer readable records: Crime report	50
	Arrest report	
	Court disposition	
	Recent computer summary of crime & arrests	
	Coding form for computerized files: M.O. file	52
	fingerprints	
	known offender	
	sex offender	
	hot car	
	mug shot	
	organized crime intelligence	
	other	

59 Who completed this questionnaire?

Title & Name _____

Unit _____

Telephone
Number   Area Code _____

GLOSSARY

ACTIVITY LOG: In Question 49, this refers to a written breakdown of the duty hours of an officer. The categories in the breakdown may be activities such as investigation, crime lab, court time, and special detail, or they may indicate how much time the officer spent on individual cases.

ARREST WARRANTS: In Question 24, this refers to warrants obtained from a magistrate or judge prior to apprehension of a suspect, as a result of an investigation or grand jury proceeding. It does *not* refer to service of bench warrants by the police, or to warrants obtained after the suspect is in custody.

CLEARED CRIMES: Does not include unfounded crime reports.

COMPLAINT: A sworn written statement made to a magistrate or court charging the accused with responsibility for a specified offense.

INVESTIGATOR: A sworn officer who devotes most of his time to criminal investigations. Included are those officers specially designated as "detective," "inspector," "investigator," "agent," or whatever title is used in your department, *and also* plainclothes or uniformed officers assigned to investigative duties and the commanding officers of investigative units. *Not included* are civilians having investigative duties, such as laboratory technicians, legal staff, and intelligence or information specialists, who are counted separately in Question 21.

PATTERNS OF CRIME: This refers to aggregated information showing variations by time of day, location, M.O., or other crime characteristics. It does not refer to daily, monthly, or annual crime and arrest statistics.

ROTATION: In Question 46, assignment of cases by rotation refers to the practice of dividing cases more or less equally among the investigators in a unit without regard to the characteristics of the crime, the specialty of the investigator, or whether the investigator was on duty at the time the crime was reported.

Appendix C

Sample Cover Letter Used in Survey

March 27, 1974

We are writing to ask your cooperation in a nationwide study of criminal investigation procedures and policies in municipal and county police agencies. This study is being conducted by The Rand Corporation under a grant from the National Institute of Law Enforcement and Criminal Justice, the research and demonstration arm of LEAA.

One of the objectives of the study is to develop a comprehensive picture of investigative units, their organization, their procedures, and the special resources they use--such as computerized information files or mobile laboratory equipment. Your department can help us complete this important task by filling out and returning the enclosed questionnaire.

After the questionnaires are returned, we will select a few interested departments, varying in size, type of community, and organization, for special observation and collection of data. (Question 57 asks whether your department would be interested.) Through a combination of analysis of the questionnaire responses and the detailed studies of selected departments, we expect to produce new insights into the investigative function. We think these insights will provide guidance to you and other law enforcement officials on possible ways to improve your investigative effectiveness through organizational changes, additional training, and adoption of methods that have proved their worth elsewhere.

We have made careful preparation, described in an attachment, to assure that all responses will be analyzed in strict confidence by a team having broad experience in the criminal justice system. We hope you will agree to participate by returning the enclosed postcard and indicating a completion date prior to April 15, 1974.

Sincerely,

Peter W. Greenwood and Sorrel Wildhorn
Project Co-Directors

Encls.

271

Sample Cover Letter Attachment

Confidentiality Conditions

By agreement with the National Institute of Law Enforcement and Criminal Justice, your response to our questionnaire will be held in confidence by Rand, according to the following provisions:

1. Any publication concerning the results of this survey will provide only limited descriptive information about identified departments, such as would always be publicly available—for example, size of department, population of jurisdiction, and total number of investigators.
2. All other published tabulations of data, statistical findings, and illustrative examples will be presented in such a way that individual departments cannot be identified, except in cases where Rand obtains *explicit written consent in advance* from the department in question.
3. The department will not be identified on computer-readable records generated from the returned questionnaires, except by the serial number shown on the first page of the questionnaire.
4. No copies of the completed questionnaires or the computer-readable files will be provided to anyone outside Rand, and the data will not be used by Rand for any purposes other than statistical analysis of the characteristics of investigative units.

The Rand Corporation

Rand is a nonprofit corporation with staff located in Santa Monica, California, Washington, D.C., and at The New York City-Rand Institute. It conducts research on issues of public concern for various federal, state, and local governmental agencies. Rand's criminal justice studies published since 1968, which are available on request, include:

- *Methods for Allocating Urban Emergency Units*, Jan Chaiken and Richard Larson

- *An Analysis of the Apprehension Activities of the New York City Police Department*, Peter Greenwood

- *Aids to Decisionmaking in Police Patrol*, James Kakalik and Sorrel Wildhorn

- *The Impact of Police Activities on Crime: Robberies on the New York City Subway System*, Jan Chaiken, Michael Lawless, and Keith Stevenson

- *Police Background Characteristics and Performance*, Bernard Cohen and Jan Chaiken

- *Evaluation of the Manhattan Criminal Court's Master Calendar Project*, John Jennings

- *Private Police in the United States* (5 volumes), Sorrel Wildhorn and James Kakalik

- *Prosecution of Adult Felony Defendants in Los Angeles County*, Peter Greenwood, Sorrel Wildhorn, *et al.*

- *Dismissal of Narcotics Arrest Cases in the New York City Criminal Court*, Sydney Cooper (Asst. Chief Inspector, ret., New York City Police Department)

Rand's team for the NILECJ project "Analysis of the Investigative Function" includes many of the authors of the studies listed above and also other retired high-ranking law enforcement officers from municipal and federal investigative units.

Appendix D

Sample Postcard Used in Survey

_____
(name of law enforcement agency)

☐ will
☐ will not   respond to your questionnaire.

You may expect a response by _____ / _____ /74.

Signed _____

Appendix E

Sample Follow-up Letter Used in Survey

April 26, 1974

Several weeks ago we sent you a questionnaire entitled "Survey of the Criminal Investigation Process in Municipal and County Police Departments," together with a postcard on which you could indicate whether or not your department planned to return a completed questionnaire.

To date, over 75 of the selected departments have indicated they will respond, and we have received many of their questionnaires. The variation in their answers to questions about the organization of investigative units, their procedures, and special equipment such as computerized files and laboratory equipment indicates that a complete response is needed for us to obtain a truly comprehensive picture.

However, we have not yet received your postcard, and we would appreciate it if you could indicate your plans by filling in the attached card. If your copy of the questionnaire has been misplaced, please call one of us collect, and we will be glad to mail you another one.

Sincerely,

Peter W. Greenwood
Sorrel Wildhorn
Project Co-Directors

Encl.

Appendix F

Sample Coding Sheet Used in Survey

Department

Card No. | 1 | 2 | 5 |

CRIMES AGAINST PERSONS	7					
Homicide	11					
Sex Crimes	15					
Robbery	19					
Banks	23					
CRIMES AGAINST PROPERTY	27					
Burglary (General)	31					
Commercial	35					
Residential	39					
Commercial Theft	43					
Checks and forgery/fraud	49					
Business machines	51					
Safes	55					
Hijacking	59					
Pawn shop detail	63					
Credit cards	67					
Fence detail	71					
Hotel/motel	75					

CARD 126

| 1 | 2 | 6 |

Auto Theft	7					
License detail	11					
Hit and run	15					
Internal Inspection	19					
Missing Persons	23					
Fugitives	27					
Juvenile Crime	31					
Arson	35					
Narcotics and Vice	39					
Vice (only)	43					
Narcotics or drugs (only)	47					
Organized Crime	51					
OTHER SERVICES	55					
Victim Report Check	59					
Warrants	63					
Security Investigation	67					

279

Appendix G

Illustrative Examples of Investigation

To illustrate the daily routine of investigators, this appendix reviews some typical and not so typical cases and other instances of investigative work that demonstrate investigative policies in practice. They are collected together here for ease of reference in the text.

Playing a Hunch

The classic detective story begins with a crime and a population of suspects, quickly narrowed down through insightful deduction—

Of the few cases on his desk this Monday morning, one case struck Detective Smith's interest—a technical burglary. In a single night in the same area, a suspect had entered seven different apartments of women and molested them to varying degrees, except for the last whom he raped. In one case, $10 had been taken from the victim's purse.

Although there was no direct evidence that these entries were the work of one man, Detective Smith immediately thought about G. His kinky sexual behavior, which had once made an interesting office story, came to mind.

Acting on this hunch, Smith put together six mug shots and set up appointments to interview four of the victims. The mug shots were carefully chosen; the picture of G was grouped with that of five other blacks. The interviews with victims were scheduled as a matter of Smith's convenience. Some he telephoned were not home; others worked in areas of town that would be an inconvenient drive that day.

During the remainder of the work day, four victims were interviewed, three at their homes and one at work. Certain patterns could be seen in Smith's handling of the investigation:

- Smith was quite solicitous to each of the victims, giving advice on how to secure the apartment.

- During the day spent with Smith, no notes were taken about the victim's responses to the mug shots. And there was a wide variety of responses—with no positive identification. One girl indicated two individuals—one of whom was G—who "might have been the intruder." However, these persons had Afros and the man she saw was "athletic,

281

with a short haircut."[1] This statement tended to confirm Smith's suspicion that G was the offender because he had an athletic build and had been recently released from prison, which might account for the short haircut. The second interviewee was unable to identify the intruder from the mug shots; the third immediately pointed to the picture of G, stating, "This is not the man." The last person interviewed identified K, a man who could not have committed the offense because he was currently doing time at San Quentin. (Smith discovered this information by calling K's probation officer.)

Physical evidence at the crime scene was not collected. The suspect had apparently entered one second floor apartment by a rear staircase. Fingerprints were visible in the dust on the banister, but Smith found them "not good enough." (In this apartment, the girl had tentatively identified either G or another man as the possible intruder.) In yet another apartment, the intruder left through the same rear kitchen window through which he gained entry. As he was leaving, the tenants heard him knock over a can of cleaning fluid and then place it in an upright position again on the window sill. Again, Smith dismissed the idea of taking fingerprints because "there would be too many other fingerprints" (e.g., the homeowners', the drugstore clerk's).

After the interviews, Smith decided to talk to G. Although G had been checking in regularly, at this particular time his probation officer did not know where he was. G was also not at home. As it was the end of the day, Smith decided to resume work on the case another time. Another time could be any time, depending on the cases on his desk tomorrow and his hunches.

Some Further Observations. The art of investigation as practiced today is in many ways solely and completely a one-man operation. Even with the science and technology that make high-speed data processing a reality, information about criminal activities appears to be noted and disseminated much as it was before the computer—by curiosity and word of mouth. With "modus operandi" only in the mind of each individual investigator, solving a crime perpetrated by an unidentified person becomes a random process. Either a mental bell is rung or it is not. Did the assigned investigator once have contact with a suspect with this type of behavior? And does he remember it? Did he happen to overhear another investigator talking about a similar type of case?

The haphazardness applies to more than hunches. The reliance on memory rather than notes during and about interviews has serious and far-reaching

---

1. Certainly one difficulty with mug shot identification is the time lag between the time the picture was taken and the time of the crime. Hairstyles, for examples, are easily subject to change.

implications. Memory blurs over time, and information becomes garbled or lost. There is no written record of the conduct of a case—either for an eventual prosecutor or for use of another detective on this or other cases.

Working a Tough Case

Within his assigned caseload (typically 30 crimes a month), the investigator can choose what crimes he wants to work on, when, and how. Some decisions, however, are implicitly mandated by state statute. In California, for example, a prisoner must be released at the end of 48 hours if no complaint has been filed. Thus, cases with suspects in custody get first priority.

All detective stories begin with a crime, and this one was not only serious, but also quite frightening. Without apparent motive, a man had been pulled from his parked car outside a restaurant and brutally slashed around his face and chest with a broken beer bottle. Although two suspects made a getaway, witnesses recorded the license plate of the car, which turned out to be registered to X, currently on parole; his last conviction had been for assault with a deadly weapon (ADW).

This ADW was assigned to Detective Jones, who ran the check on the license plate, and then went to the suspect's home to question and perhaps arrest him. The suspect was not at home. Jones did not put out an alert for the car, but instead left his card, with a request that X call him. In the meantime, X was being arrested for a robbery in Oaktown.

Through X's probation officer, Jones learned of X's arrest in Oaktown. Since the robbery charge could not be made to stick, the suspect was released to Jones on the ADW charge. The interrogation of the suspect, who was obviously undergoing withdrawal symptoms, began in the car, and continued in the station during arrest processing.

It was a long, slow, and exceedingly frustrating process. Both men were working against time. X had already spent 24 hours in custody in Oaktown. In another 24 hours he would have to be released unless charged.

Questions were asked and reasked and answers were sidestepped and completely avoided.

At first the suspect would admit only that he was present during the assault:
"Who was your companion?"
"Don't know."
"You admitted being there. Who were you with?"
"I don't know?—I can't remember—Some guy"—etc., etc.

Each applied pressure to the other. The detective promised to drop the robbery charge, trying to sell the suspect what he already had, in the hope that he did not know this.

X, on the other hand, had information Jones wanted. By withholding this information as long as possible and by promising much needed information, yet eventually delivering only bits, X exercised the only power he had.

At the same time, during the banter, leads were mentioned that Jones did not catch. For example, hours later, after telling a half-dozen obvious and easily refuted lies, X stated that he had not participated in the actual assault, but had in fact tried to stop it by wresting the bottle from the now "identified" companion, Joe Mendez. "Mendez" was someone X served time with—but this means of identifying him was not pursued.

The suspect then related that after meeting Mendez downtown, and prior to the fight, they had gone to some house for a party. Again, this clue went unnoticed. If the house had been located, it could then have been determined if there had been a burglary there (and perhaps more clues), or if anyone at the house could identify X. Only after the interview, which lasted most of the day, did Jones contact the Bureau of Criminal Identification and Investigation for a rapsheet on X and some information on his friend. Had Jones requested it earlier, this background information on X, which arrived the next day, could have proved a useful psychological ploy during the interrogation.

The last action of the day, and as it turned out, the last action taken on this case, was showing mug shots to the victim, who picked X tentatively as the man who had been there, but had not participated in the action.

Lack of a chargeable offense meant X was released the next morning. No effort was made to put him under surveillance to find out the identity of "Mendez." The case remains unsolved.

Wheeling and Dealing

Interrogation and informants are two key weapons in the investigator's bag of tricks—These attributes are supposed to distinguish him from the patrolman— the ability to use one and to rely on the other.

When Danny the Burglar was brought to the Beachtown stationhouse, he was recognized and greeted by all at the investigators' table. A career burglar since graduating from high school five years ago, Danny had been arrested many times, received a variety of convictions—including several terms in facilities for drug addicts—but had never been sent to the state prison.

Two partially masked men had robbed a liquor store; although they had managed to escape, the getaway car, registered to Danny, had been found and impounded. Since the burglary had been committed in Oaktown, Danny was to be returned there for arrest processing. But before this, Beachtown's investigators wanted to question him; he lived in Beachtown and, besides, they thought of him as a good informer.

From the outside looking in, the efforts to solve this crime resembled an elaborate con game. But it was hard to tell who was conning whom.

From a distance we observed a seemingly friendly and animated discussion between Danny and two Beachtown detectives.[2] During the course of this, Danny's girl had been brought in so that Danny could see her—and was being questioned separately. We were told that the police had gone to her house on the chance of finding something connected with the robbery, and had arrested her for possession of marijuana. It became apparent later that she was to be used as a counter in negotiations with Danny.

That afternoon, Danny was booked in Oaktown. So far, the upshot of the interrogation was Danny's denial of participation in the robbery, and no information about the men who allegedly borrowed his car. But as if this were a routine gone through many times before, the detectives seemed pleased and quite sure that they would get what they wanted.

The Beachtown detectives drove to Oaktown the following afternoon to continue the interrogation. This time, after a half-hour interview, they were apparently quite successful. In return for his release and that of his girl, Danny promised to identify the two men and find out where the robbery goods had been sold.

In the meantime, having done some investigation of their own, the Oaktown detectives were beginning to suspect Danny as one of the actual robbers. Danny, for example, had some distinguishing marks on his upper teeth that resembled those observed by the victim. When shown the mug shots, the victim did not think Danny was the robber because his skin tone was not as dark as that in the picture—not very conclusive evidence since pictures can have any kind of shading.

The Oaktown police were quite ready to pursue the case against Danny, and it was with great effort that the Beachtown investigators convinced them to release him, so that they would get the men Danny identified, the goods, and perhaps the fence. Danny was released, and it was hard to tell who had really out-manipulated whom.

On Patrol

Not all investigators get to pick and choose what cases they want to work on and when. Some departments have patrolmen/investigators who work from patrol cars rather than desks. Beats are assigned and when a felony is reported, the appropriate investigator is dispatched—

---

2. This followed a detective modus operandi of "protecting" informants by keeping their conversation confidential.

At 9 a.m. Detective Morefield began his day of cruising the streets in his district, an inner-city mostly black area. Today seemed much like other days, and as he looked around he felt the old bitterness rising. On street corners and in front of shops he saw small clusters of males and females whom he felt sure were dealing drugs, pimping, and soliciting.

Many he knew by name, some by reputation, and others because he had tried to arrest them before for dealing and crimes of violence of every conceivable kind. Although they saw each other, they did not exchange greetings. Some stared aggressively at the police car, and others turned abruptly away or went into the nearest building.

The futility of the day already weighed heavily on him. Suspecting that a person is dealing drugs does not constitute the "reasonable grounds for suspicion" that allow a search. So, he went on, "the dealers aren't easy to bust and even if you do, prosecutors only take sure wins to keep their noses clean. And besides, the judges let 'em all go anyway."

"You see that man." Morefield said, pointing out a very muscular black in a T-shirt. "He's crazy." He went on to say that with the exception of murder, there was no crime he had not been arrested for, including battery of a police officer. And in that case, he went free because when the judge heard that the arresting officer had been pushed so hard down a flight of stairs that he had to be hospitalized, he determined that it was "poor police work" on the part of the officer.

During the course of the day, "crazy" was the epithet most frequently used by Morefield, and he always applied it to people, not to the situation he or they found themselves in.

A call sent him to the scene of a battery. Another investigator had already arrived and was talking to an old black couple and their daughter, a girl with lemon-colored hair, in shiny slacks, holding a baby; a young boy with a smooth face and a sailor's cap; a tall, zombie-like fellow of about 25 with a blue hat; and a tall, thin, but muscular man of 18 who looked more like 25, who had started the commotion. Apparently, he had a fight with the lemon-haired girl, during the course of which he had beaten the fellow with the blue hat over the head with a brick, slashing open the man's scalp but, surprisingly, not breaking his skull. He had then thrown the brick and another one at the man, but missed him. The old couple and the girl were terrified. The boy in the cap whispered some information about the perpetrator, glancing uneasily in his direction to see whether he noticed the action. He reported that the night before the perpetrator had had a gun and a switchblade knife, but Morefield's search of the man's car produced nothing.

Morefield returned to his car, leaving the case to the other investigator. He had arrested this suspect and "lots like him" before—and found conviction was almost impossible. Not only were there problems with the D.A. and judges, but finding effective witnesses was impossible. Either the witnesses were afraid, or they had records "a mile long," so that they would not be believed in court. Besides, they were all "crazy."

After several hours of driving, Morefield was called to a doctor's office that had been burglarized that morning—only one of several typewriters had been stolen, and nothing else had been disturbed. The questions that followed were routine, and the investigation perfunctory. On the basis of the information gathered, Morefield was able to explain to the victims apparently how and when the crime was committed. The burglar probably was on foot (because only one item had been taken) and most likely exited through the backdoor (there were marks on the recently painted doorframe). He recorded the names of janitors who had access to the building and the serial number of the typewriter, and walked around the building to determine access points. Before leaving he told the doctor that the typewriter could probably be recovered in some pawnshop, and he admonished all in the office not to touch the typewriter stand until an evidence technician dusted for prints. Privately, Morefield stated that there was no hope of finding the burglar and that he had done all he could. He regarded the case closed.

The "investigation" at the doctor's office had once been interrupted by a call over Morefield's walkie-talkie that an armed robbery was in progress. Fortunately, on this case the interruption did not prove too disruptive to the investigation. Rushing from one crime scene to another, Morefield unlocked his shotgun as he was advised over the radio that the suspects were fleeing by foot down Paloma. The chase was short and ended abruptly after about 10 minutes when no fugitives were sighted, and Morefield guessed that they had gone into a house. This meant "it is practically impossible to find them." Having arrived at this decision without contacting other personnel involved in the search, he returned to the doctor's office for a few closing remarks, and continued cruising while tape-recording his notes on the case.

Administrative Details

In many departments, the organization chart denotes a hierarchy of investigation skills. The patrolman visits the scene of each crime and files a preliminary report. A senior investigator may make decisions about follow-up and assign cases to the less senior investigators—

Senior Investigator Johnson always finds Monday mornings the busiest time of the week. Over the weekend, a fairly large volume of reported crime and in-custody reports have accumulated for him to process. As one of the most experienced investigators on his team, his job as investigation administrator is to process these reports, which involves reviewing each case, assigning it to the appropriate investigator, and entering each case into his "control log," which records all active cases assigned to the team.

Among the other cases, he found more than 20 reported burglaries, all of the same ilk: the victims left their homes locked in the morning. When they returned in the evening, they found their homes had been broken into. Losses varied from hundreds to thousands of dollars. "The same familiar story," Johnson muttered as he designated *none* of these cases for follow-up.

Skimming through the pile, we noted that not one of the reports contained serial numbers for property identification. Either the victims did not have this information or the patrolman did not inquire.

Various administrative tasks stretch out the remainder of the day. As the division receives descriptions of reported crimes and arrested suspects from other law enforcement agencies, the teletypes are sorted by crime type. Johnson, as robbery coordinator for the division, goes through all robbery related alarms, identifying material relevant to his district, e.g., crimes by white suspects are quite uncommon in his district and therefore ignored. Pertinent automobile and gun identifications are underlined and distributed to robbery specialists, who are to use their memory to make connections between these items and past crimes. Although much information is passed to the individual detective, he is given no help in processing it.

Even though a clerk could easily handle the sorting task, Johnson insts that as the most experienced man on the team only he can perform this screening or key pieces of evidence may be lost. But it seems even more true that these tasks must have inflated importance to give his job meaning. There must be some justification for having the most experienced men in the department daily tied to their desks while the rookie detectives are doing the more sensitive work in the field.

Occasionally, a citizen may call to complain about the conduct of officers in the division. One call concerned rough treatment: as two officers approached a car that they had stopped for a moving violation, they noticed a revolver above the car's visor. As the citizen reached for the weapon (when he heard one officer warn, "Watch out—he's got a gun"), the officers pulled him out of the car and handcuffed him.

Johnson spent close to a half hour on the phone, trying to appease the citizen and promising to reprimand the officers, even though the citizen was somewhat in the wrong.

When asked about his behavior, Johnson explained that he was trying to avoid a written complaint, which would count as a black mark against the division, and to which he would have to make a response that would involve more work than a regular investigation.

For the most part, the day of the senior investigator is filled with administrative trivia of the sort that a clerk could perform. The atmosphere of the team room, where the investigators work, is one of boredom; the slightest distraction in the office grabs their attention—whether it is a good-looking clerk walking to a file cabinet, a stranger entering the room, or a confiscated weapon being passed around and admired.

Once in a while, one of the team members will consult with the senior investigator about a particular case—but it is not clear whether he really needs help or just wants to be friendly and maintain contact. Essentially, however, the teams are organized to run without administrators. Yet day in and day out here sit the most experienced men in the department—monitoring paperwork.

Appendix H

Detailed Tabulations from the Kansas City Case Assignment File

This appendix contains tables supporting the analysis of the Kansas City Case Assignment File in Chapters 8 and 9. Table H-1 shows how the crime types appearing in Chapter 8 were defined in terms of the codes used by detectives in Kansas City on their case assignment cards.

Table H-2 is an expanded version of table 8-4 in Chapter 8 showing the average number of cases worked on per detective per month. The table not only breaks down the total workload into its components by crime type, but also indicates how the calculations were performed. We classified detectives into groups according to the unit they worked in during the study period and the mix of cases they worked on. Some officers changed units, and others began work as detectives during this period. In addition, two officers in the Crimes Against Property Unit were borrowed to work on homicide cases for a substantial portion of their time. We counted the number of man-months of work performed in each unit and converted this to an average number of detectives in the unit. As a result, the number of detectives in a unit is not always an integer and may not correspond to a count of the names on a roster of the unit.

The final column of table H-2 shows the percentage of cases of the specified crime type that were handled partly or entirely by the unit. For example, 82 percent of aggravated assaults were handled partly or entirely by the Crimes Against Persons Unit. The remaining 18 percent were handled by some other unit, almost always Youth and Women's.

Table H-3, an expanded version of table 8-5, shows the percentage of crimes in the Case Assignment File that were cleared, as compared to the percentage of *all* reported crimes that were cleared. Some categories of crimes as coded in the Case Assignment File are not directly comparable with categories for the department's tabulations of reported crimes; for these categories it was not possible to calculate the percentage of all reported crimes that were cleared.

Table H-4 supplements information in Chapter 8 by showing the fraction of casework time spent on various types of activities. The breakdown is shown separately for cases in which an arrest was made and cases for which no arrest was made. Although the table is organized by detective unit, the figures refer to all time spent by all detectives on crimes of the indicated type. These statistics were calculated only for selected crime types. As mentioned in the text, time spent in court may be underestimated in the Case Assignment File, and this should be kept in mind when interpreting the table.

Table H-5 shows the relationship between categories of crimes used in the analysis of how cases are solved (Chapter 9) and the crime types defined in table H-1.

291

Table H-1
Crime Categories Used for Analysis of the Kansas City Case Assignment File

Crime Type	KCPD Code	Includes	Crime Type	KCPD Code	Includes
Auto accessories	AC		Other crimes against persons	HL	Shooting
Auto theft	AA	Auto theft		HW	Abduction
	AB	Attempt auto theft	Larceny	LB	
Other auto	AD	Auto theft by deceit	Bicycle larceny	LD	
	AE	ATL auto	Larceny from auto	LE	
Safe burglary	BL		Shoplift	LI	
Residential burglary	BR	Apartment	Arson	LM	
	BU	Residence garage	Checks	LP	
	BW	Residence	Destruction of property	LQ	
Commercial burglary	BA	Appliance	Counterfeit/forgery	LR	
	BB	Barber	Fraud/embezzlement	LS	
	BC	Church	Larceny by deceit	LT	
	BD	Laundry	Extortion	LV	
	BE	Drugstore/liquor	Bomb or threat	LO	Bomb threat
	BG	Grocery store		LZ	Bomb
	BH	Professional office	Bunco	LA	Con game
	BJ	Recreation parlor		LW	Credit cards
	BK	Restaurant/cafe	Larceny other	LC	Larceny interstate
	BM	Service station		LH	Pickpocket
	BN	School		LL	Larceny miscellaneous
	BO	Tavern		LU	Lost property
	BV	Hotel/motel	Larceny commercial	LF	Hotel/motel
Miscellaneous burglary	BI	Miscellaneous		LJ	Till taps
	BT	Possess burglary tools		LK	Vending machines
Homicide	HA		Runaway	MA	
Rape	HB		Escaped juvenile	MB	
Aggravated assault	HC		Attempt to locate	MH	
Common assault	HD		Lost	ME	Lost child
Suicide	HJ			MF	Lost senile
Dead body	HK			MG	Lost mentally retarded
Kidnapping	HS		Mental	MC	Juvenile mental
Felony sex crimes	HE	Molestation		MD	Adult mental
	HF	Exhibitionism	Bank robbery	RA	
	HG	Incest	Residential robbery	RH	
	HH	Sodomy			
	HI	Other sex			

Crime Type	KCPD Code	Includes	Crime Type	KCPD Code	Includes
Taxicab robbery	RL		Incorrigible	YD	
Miscellaneous robbery	RM		Trespassing	YG	
Robbery concealed weapon	RW		Disorderly conduct	YJ	
Robbery commercial	RB	Delivery boy	Youth/women's miscellaneous	Y	Unknown type
	RC	Drugstore		YL	Prostitution
	RD	Grocery store		YS	Procuring
	RE	Hotel/motel		YW	Resist officer
	RG	Laundry		YZ	Miscellaneous Y/W
	RI	Restaurant/cafe	Youth other	YA	Child abuse
	RJ	Service station		YB	Child neglect
	RK	Tavern/liquor store		YE	Contributing to delinquency
Pursesnatch	RU	Pursesnatch by white		YF	Accidental shooting
	RV	Pursesnatch by black		YH	Loiter at school
Strongarm	RR	Strongarm by white		YK	Minor with alcoholic beverage
	RS	Strongarm by black		YN	Drunk in public
Robbery outside-street	RO	Robbery outside		YO	Gambling
	RP	Robbery street by white		YT	Firearms
	RQ	Robbery street by black		YU	Fireworks
Protective custody	YC		Possession of drugs	YP	Possess marijuana
				YQ	Possess stimulants
				YR	Possess narcotics

Table H-2
Caseload of Detectives in Kansas City

Crime Type	Handled Entirely by Unit		Total Handled by Unit		Percentage of Cases of Type in File
	N[a]	Per Month Per Detective	N[a]	Per Month Per Detective	
Crimes Against Persons Unit					
Homicide (15)[b]	*1106*	*10.53*	*1176*	*11.20*	*88*
Homicide	42	0.40	55	0.52	100
Aggravated assault	619	5.90	662	6.30	82
Common assault	217	2.07	229	2.18	76
Dead body	192	1.83	192	1.83	100
Suicide	22	0.21	22	0.21	88
Shootings	14	0.13	16	0.15	89
Robbery (14)	*629*	*6.41*	*755*	*7.70*	*86*
Bank	8	0.08	17	0.17	90
Commercial	191	1.95	221	2.26	99
Residence	74	0.76	83	0.85	100
Taxicab	23	0.23	29	0.30	97
Outside-street	165	1.68	194	1.97	81
Strong arm	49	0.50	73	0.74	57
Pursesnatch	16	0.16	24	0.24	65
Concealed weapon	35	0.36	37	0.38	93
Miscellaneous	68	0.69	77	0.79	95
Sex Crimes (8)	*309*	*5.52*	*345*	*6.16*	*93*
Rape	209	3.73	238	4.25	96
Felony sex crimes	88	1.57	94	1.68	84
Kidnapping	12	0.16	13	0.17	100
Total [c] (37)	*2077*	*8.02*	*2373*	*9.16*	*88*
Crimes Against Property Unit					
Auto (12)	*1447*	*17.23*	*1639*	*19.51*	*91*
Theft	1252	14.91	1428	17.00	95
Accessories	89	1.06	101	1.20	78
Other auto	106	1.26	110	1.31	100
Nonresidential burglary (13)	*657*	*7.22*	*853*	*9.37*	*93*
Safes	32	0.35	36	0.40	97
Other commercial	162	1.78	192	2.11	87
Miscellaneous	463	5.09	625	6.87	94
Residential burglary and larceny (11)	*1466*	*19.04*	*1763*	*22.90*	*71*
Residential burglary	1022	13.27	1234	16.03	89
Larceny	345	4.48	386	5.01	83
Larceny bicycle	31	0.40	63	0.82	44
Theft from auto	68	0.88	80	1.04	67
Total (36)	*3570*	*14.17*	*4255*	*16.88*	*83*

[a] Number of cases worked on during May-November 1973.

[b] Numbers in parentheses are number of detectives in unit.

[c] Includes some miscellaneous crimes not listed in the above categories.

Crime Type	Handled Entirely by Unit		Total Handled by Unit		Percentage of Cases of Type in File
	N[a]	Per Month Per Detective	N[a]	Per Month Per Detective	
General Assignment Unit					
Incendiary (1.5)[b]	69	*6.57*	82	*7.81*	*83*
Arson	60	5.71	73	6.95	96
Bomb or threat	9	0.86	9	0.86	69
Forgery, fraud, bunco (9.5)	658	*9.89*	691	*10.39*	*93*
Fraud/embezzlement	368	5.53	384	5.77	97
Forgery/counterfeit	237	3.56	251	3.77	99
Extortion	14	0.21	14	0.21	93
Larceny by deceit	2	0.03	2	0.03	100
Bunco	37	0.56	40	0.60	75
Shoplifting and pickpocket (3)	390	*18.57*	438	*20.86*	*54*
Shoplifting	222	10.57	258	12.29	54
Larceny other	168	8.00	180	8.57	53
Execute warrants (14)	267	*2.72*	267	*2.72*	*100*
Total[c] (14)	*1509*	*15.40*	*1818*	*18.55*	*92*
Youth and Women's Unit/Other Units					
Youth and Women (18)					
Protective custody	84	0.67	86	0.68	99
Incorrigible	115	0.91	120	0.95	100
Trespassing	54	0.43	54	0.43	100
Disorderly conduct	125	0.99	127	1.01	100
Possession of drugs	92	0.73	95	0.75	99
Y-W miscellaneous	190	1.51	193	1.53	98
Youth-other	70	0.56	72	0.57	99
Pursesnatch	12	0.10	20	0.16	54
Strongarm	53	0.42	76	0.60	59
Destruction of property	107	0.85	121	0.96	63
Larceny commercial	17	0.13	20	0.16	67
Larceny bicycle	78	0.62	111	0.88	77
Crime types usually assigned other units					
Aggravated assault	135	1.07	176	1.40	22
Burglary residential	153	1.21	339	2.69	24
Auto theft	69	0.55	220	1.75	15
Theft from auto	39	0.31	51	0.40	43
Larceny	74	0.59	111	0.88	24
Shoplifting	213	1.69	244	1.94	51
Juvenile escape	67	0.53	155	1.23	39
Runaway	133	1.06	330	2.62	24
All other	312	2.48	551	4.37	
Total (all cases)	*2192*	*17.40*	*3272*	*25.97*	
Missing Persons Unit					
Missing Persons (4.5)					
Runaway	1044	33.14	1244	39.49	90
Escaped juvenile	243	7.71	329	10.44	83
Attempt to locate	597	18.95	6.04	19.17	98
Lost	219	6.95	221	7.02	93
Escaped mental	322	10.22	331	10.51	97
All other	9	0.29	55	1.75	
Total	*2434*	*77.27*	*2784*	*88.38*	

Table H-3
Clearance Rates from Kansas City Case Assignment File

Crime Type	Percentage Cleared[a]	Percentage in File Cleared[a]
Homicide	*78.1*	*78.1*
Robbery	*29.7*	47.4
Bank		81.8
Commercial		33.5
Residence		41.0
Taxicab		40.0
Outside-street		59.6
Strongarm		65.9
Pursesnatch		73.0
Concealed weapon		25.0
Miscellaneous		32.1
Sex crimes	*51.2*	*55.8*
Rape	64.0	52.4
Felony sex crimes	37.4	63.4
Other crimes against persons	*27.7*	*53.4*
Aggravated assault	40.5	63.4
Common assault	26.5	66.3
Kidnapping	33.3	38.5
Shootings		27.8
Auto	*22.4*	*29.5*
Theft		29.0
Accessories		56.6
Other auto		4.6
Nonresidential burglary	*21.8*	*60.1*
Safes		24.3
Other commercial		59.3
Miscellaneous		63.7

Crime Type	Percentage Cleared[a]	Percentage in File Cleared[a]
Residential burglary and larceny	6.8	48.0
Residential burglary	15.1	50.2
Larceny	2.3	41.5
Other property crimes		62.0
Larceny bicycle		59.0
Theft from auto		65.6
Destructive acts		57.8
Arson	35.2	50.0
Destruction of property	4.2	62.7
Bomb or threat		30.8
Fraud and larceny		55.4
Fraud/embezzlement	27.9	46.9
Forgery/counterfeit	41.6	46.1
Extortion		13.3
Larceny by deceit		100.0
Larceny other		37.1
Bunco		69.8
Shoplifting		80.0
Execute warrants		*34.1*
Youth and women's total		*73.7*
Protective custody		80.5
Incorrigible		81.7
Trespassing		90.7
Disorderly conduct		81.1
Possession of drugs		76.0
Y-W miscellaneous		56.4
Youth-other		71.2
Larceny commercial		73.3

[a] Cleared by arrest.

Table H-4
Breakdown of Activities on Cases
(Percentage of time on each activity)[a]

Crime Type	Interrogation	Interview	Arrest	Arraignment	Reports	Surveillance	ATL	Crime Scene	Prosecutor	Court	Administration
Homicide unit	*7.5*	*36.0*	*1.3*	*1.4*	*26.5*	*4.7*	*11.5*	*5.9*	*0.0*	*1.7*	*3.3*
Homicide											
No arrest	2.6	35.3	–	–	16.0	5.7	23.0	4.1	–	–	13.2
Arrest	8.5	34.0	0.0	1.4	21.9	7.6	13.1	6.5	0.0	2.9	3.0
Aggravated assault											
No arrest	2.5	47.2	–	–	30.5	2.8	11.6	5.1	–	–	0.0
Arrest	11.9	33.1	3.2	3.5	35.2	1.6	4.6	3.7	0.0	2.4	0.0
Common assault											
No arrest	4.6	46.3	–	–	37.8	5.1	5.1	0.0	–	–	–
Arrest	15.5	29.1	6.0	2.1	37.1	1.1	6.6	1.0	–	1.1	0.0
Dead body	0.0	44.1	–	–	31.5	0.0	3.3	19.4	–	–	0.0
Suicide	–	39.6	–	–	35.5	–	–	24.9	–	–	–
Sex crimes unit	*6.7*	*34.1*	*1.5*	*2.2*	*19.2*	*0.0*	*28.1*	*2.2*	*1.5*	*2.1*	*0.0*
Rape											
No arrest	3.1	35.7	–	–	15.6	0.0	41.5	1.9	0.0	–	1.0
Arrest	7.5	31.0	2.2	3.8	20.7	0.0	24.5	2.8	1.8	3.1	1.0
Felony sex crimes											
No arrest	6.8	48.8	–	–	23.3	–	16.7	–	2.1	–	2.1
Arrest	14.9	39.3	3.7	2.0	21.3	2.5	8.9	–	1.2	5.3	0.0
Kidnapping											
No arrest	4.5	42.7	–	–	23.6	–	16.9	12.4	–	–	–
Arrest	4.4	38.5	–	2.2	20.0	–	23.7	2.2	5.2	–	–
Robbery	*12.3*	*31.3*	*0.0*	*3.8*	*27.9*	*7.2*	*6.0*	*4.8*	*0.0*	*1.8*	*0.4*
Bank											
No arrest	–	35.7	–	–	14.3	–	14.3	35.7	–	–	–
Arrest	19.0	26.7	–	5.7	35.2	–	1.9	11.4	–	–	–
Residence											
No arrest	4.8	41.6	–	–	26.2	7.1	5.0	14.0	–	–	–
Arrest	11.4	30.1	1.3	7.5	29.0	6.9	6.0	7.5	–	–	–
Taxicab											
No arrest	11.6	22.3	–	–	28.6	7.1	30.4	1.8	–	–	–
Arrest	23.8	31.6	–	6.2	30.1	–	8.3	–	–	–	–
Miscellaneous											
No arrest	2.6	33.8	–	–	22.6	25.2	2.6	12.2	–	–	–
Arrest	17.7	34.9	–	9.0	30.8	–	1.0	3.3	1.3	–	0.0
Concealed weapon											
No arrest	36.4	12.1	–	–	46.4	1.4	–	1.4	–	–	–
Arrest	25.9	15.5	3.4	12.1	43.1	–	–	–	–	–	–
Commercial											
No arrest	3.9	33.3	–	–	23.5	12.8	9.6	16.1	–	–	0.0
Arrest	12.4	26.9	1.6	6.8	26.0	6.0	4.9	8.0	0.0	6.2	0.0

[a] May not add to 100% due to categories not shown: warrants, subpoenas, extradition.

Table H-4 — Cont.

Crime Type	Interrogation	Interview	Arrest	Arraignment	Reports	Surveillance	ATL	Crime Scene	Prosecutor	Court	Administration
Robbery (cont'd.)											
Pursesnatch											
No arrest	29.2	33.3	—	—	29.2	—	8.3	—	—	—	—
Arrest	25.5	34.9	—	3.0	35.3	—	—	—	—	0.0	—
Strongarm											
No arrest	9.2	50.4	—	—	31.8	5.6	7.7	0.0	—	—	—
Arrest	21.6	26.8	2.0	1.9	31.2	2.4	2.6	3.8	—	0.0	2.4
Strongarm-outside											
No arrest	5.7	40.8	—	—	28.3	7.2	12.4	7.1	—	—	—
Arrest	18.9	27.1	1.4	6.4	31.0	4.1	4.3	2.4	0.2	2.8	—
Crimes against property	16.7	28.4	2.0	4.3	24.1	2.5	9.7	7.3	0.6	4.5	0.5
Auto											
Auto theft											
No arrest	4.2	33.9	—	—	26.6	2.3	20.7	9.4	—	—	1.7
Arrest	19.7	15.0	3.1	8.1	27.7	3.0	4.6	3.0	0.9	11.5	0.0
Accessories											
No arrest	7.5	33.7	—	1.6	31.3	—	11.5	6.7	—	4.8	1.2
Arrest	24.2	17.8	2.6	6.0	35.6	0.7	2.4	2.2	—	8.2	—
Other auto											
No arrest	1.3	48.3	—	—	37.8	1.3	3.3	5.0	1.7	—	—
Arrest	7.8	23.5	7.8	11.8	41.2	—	—	7.8	—	—	—
Nonresidential burglary											
Safes											
No arrest	3.8	33.5	—	—	11.1	0.3	32.5	17.6	—	—	1.2
Arrest	15.7	29.3	2.2	5.0	16.3	0.6	20.4	7.2	—	2.5	—
Other commercial											
No arrest	7.8	40.6	—	—	—	1.5	21.8	8.7	0.7	—	0.8
Arrest	21.7	21.5	2.0	9.0	—	0.2	8.7	1.8	0.3	6.4	—
Miscellaneous											
No arrest	10.1	32.7	—	—	18.6	2.7	25.1	9.1	0.4	—	0.3
Arrest	20.3	20.4	2.8	7.5	21.8	3.3	8.2	3.5	0.5	8.8	0.3
Residential burglary and larceny											
Residential burglary											
No arrest	10.6	48.1	—	—	24.0	4.6	7.9	2.9	0.6	—	0.4
Arrest	24.0	25.8	3.7	6.4	27.8	1.1	3.1	1.3	0.8	4.9	0.1
Larceny											
No arrest	6.9	40.4	—	—	23.3	1.0	25.8	0.9	—	—	1.1
Arrest	18.7	24.7	2.0	3.2	26.7	7.2	9.3	0.8	1.5	3.4	0.7
Larceny bicycle											
No arrest	8.7	49.2	—	—	36.8	—	3.7	—	—	—	—
Arrest	27.1	25.9	0.9	1.5	43.6	—	0.5	—	0.5	—	—
Theft from auto											
No arrest	6.3	47.2	—	—	32.7	—	11.3	2.5	—	—	—
Arrest	29.2	21.5	0.9	1.4	40.8	0.9	2.8	—	1.4	—	—

aMay not add to 100% due to categories not shown: warrants, subpoenas, extradition.

Table H-5
Definition of Crime Categories Used in Chapter 9

Crime Category	Crime Types Defined in Table H-1
Forgery/fraud	Fraud/embezzlement Larceny by deceit Extortion Bunco Counterfeit/forgery Checks
Auto theft	Auto theft Other auto
Theft	Shoplift Larceny from auto Bicycle larceny Larceny Larceny other Larceny commercial
Commercial burglary	Safe burglary Commercial burglary Miscellaneous burglary
Residential burglary	Residential burglary
Robbery	Bank robbery Residential robbery Taxicab robbery Miscellaneous robbery Robbery commercial Pursesnatch Strongarm Robbery outside—street
Felony morals	Rape Felony sex crimes
Aggravated assault	Aggravated assault Common assault Bomb or threat Arson Other crimes against persons
Homicide	Homicide Suicide Dead body

Appendix I

Examples of Model Investigation Reports

This appendix contains examples of three reports that are typically found in the cleared robbery case files of Jurisdiction A, described in Chapter 11. This jurisdiction was found to be unusually thorough in documenting all facets of a case, and as such these reports can be viewed as model police reports.

The Incident Report completed by the responding patrol unit is shown, as well as the Arrest Report which describes the evidence that led to the arrest and the circumstances under which it was made. Finally, there is an Investigation Report which attempts to sort out the accounts reported by the different participants.

In our estimation, the collection and evaluation of this information is extremely useful in making an accurate filing decision. The information will also be valuable if the participants begin to change their accounts at some later date.

Type of Report ARMED ROBBERY (211 CPC)	Report No. 7605581	POLICE DEPARTMENT

		INCIDENT REPORT

Victim's Name (Firm Name if Business) HARRIS, Keith	Amount of Loss $ .80	

Residence or Firm Address 102 SANDSTONE BLVD.	Res. Phone (or Firm) N/P	CRIMES AGAINST ☐ PROPERTY ☒ PERSON

Sex	Desc.	D.O.B. 05-28-35	Social Security No. 224-79-0624	Occupation NONE	Name of Premises PUBLIC STREET
M	N				

Victim's Employer UNEMPLOYED	Days Off/ Work Hrs.	Location (Off., Res., St., etc.) E/W ALLEY S/O CALIF. E/O L.A.	Code DD RL

Business Address	Bus. Phone	How Attacked GRABBING & STABBING	Code D

Location of Occurrence E/W ALLEY S/O SEPULVEDA E/O ARIZONA	Report Dist.	Means of Attack 4" SWITCHBLADE KNIFE	Code

Occ.on or Bet.	Mo. 02	Date 23	Yr. 74	Time 0130	Day SAT	&	Mo.	Date	Yr.	Time	Day	Object of Attack	Code

Rptd.	Mo. 02	Date 23	Yr. 74	Time 0200	Invest.Unit L	Investigator Asgd:	Type Prop. Taken or Obtained	Code

Trademark of Susp. (Actions or Conversation) VICTIM WALKS IN ALLEY, SUSPECT #2 GRABS VICTIM FROM BEHIND, SUSPECT #1 ASKS FOR MONEY, STABS VICTIM FLEES UNK DIRECTION.	Codes					

Connecting Report Nos. ONE	Vict. Injured ☒ Yes ☐ No	Vict. Removed to ST. JOAN'S

☐ In Custody   See Narrative   S U S P E C T   I N F O R M A T I O N

Suspect's Name	Address	Phone	Sex M	Desc. N	DOB/Age 34-37	Hgt. 5-4/5	Wgt. 145-50	Hair	Eyes

Clothing BRN ARMY JACK	Identifying Characteristics (Build, Facial Hair, Comp., etc.)

VEH	License No. NONE	State	Make and Model	Year	Type	Color(s)	Ident. Features

CODE:	R - REPORTING PERSON X - RELATIVE W - WITNESS				ADDRESS	CITY	ZIP	PHONE/EXT.
V	HARRIS, Keith	Sex	Desc.	D.O.B.	RES. BUS.			
		Sex	Desc.	D.O.B.	RES. BUS.			

Reporting Officer(s) JACKSON, T. L. FRYE, R. A.	Photo Number 2885 2828	Div./Watch ONE ONE	Approved 2006	TECH.REQ'D.	Yes ☐	No ☒

Date/Time Dict. 02-23-74, 0610	Dictated by JACKSON, T. L.	Date & Time Typed 02-23-74, 0610	Typed by STRICKER, A.	Recorder No.	SPEC.REQ'D.	Yes ☐	No ☒

ADDITIONAL OFFENSE: ADW (245 CPC)   SUSPECT #2: "SONNY," M/N, 6-3, 195, 18-20

Offs. dispatched to 905 Sepulveda, regarding ADW stabbing 901Y. Upon arrival Offs. observed Paramedics RESCUE #4 to be rendering emergency first aid to a M/N subj. lying on the ground at that location. At that location Officer JACKSON contacted a F/W, 32 yrs., TOKES, Rose M., 905 Long #3, who related the following. Mrs. TOKES told filing off. she was watching TV when she heard a knock on the front door of her apt. Mrs. TOKES further stated she asked who it was and the subject I.D. himself as Mr. HARRIS, who stated, "I want to talk to your husband." At this time Mrs. TOKES awakened her husband who proceeded to the front door and at this time was asked by the subj. Mr. HARRIS if he (Mr. TOKES) would transport the above VICTIM to the hospital because he had been stabbed. Mr. TOKES advised the VICTIM Mr. HARRIS that he could not because he did not have enough gas. At this time Mr. TOKES contacted BYERS AMBULANCE, who arrived at the scene a short time later.

PAGE 1 OF 2

ADDITIONAL INFORMATION TO BE ADDED TO REPORT MADE AND
FILED COVERING CASE MENTIONED ON FILING MARGIN

Victim   HARRIS, KEITH (NMI)   DATE: 02-23-74, SAT., 0130

Accused M/N's   No.   730-0621

Page 2 -- INCIDENT REPORT--ARMED ROBBERY (211 CPC) ADW (245 CPC)

Officer Adison further contacted RESCUE 4 (paramedics), who stated that
the above VICTIM had a puncture wound to the lower abdomen, that he was
in good condition but had lost a large amount of blood. Officer ADISON
did not attempt to converse with VICTIM at this time due to the state
of his semiconsciousness. VICTIM was then transported to ST. JOAN's
EMERGENCY HOSPITAL by BOWER #2.

At the hospital Officer ADISON talked to VICTIM HARRIS, who made the
following statement to filing officer. VICTIM stated that he had just
left the MEJI CAFE, 112 Arizona, and was walking in an Easterly direction
in the E/W alley S/O Sepulveda E/O Arizona, when he was grabbed from
behind by a suspect #2 known to him as "SONNY." VICTIM stated that
SUSPECT #2 held his arms while SUSPECT #1 asked him for his money which
the VICTIM stated, "All I have is $.80." SUSPECT #1 then stated to
VICTIM, "You're lying. I saw you cash a $10.00 bill at the cafe."
VICTIM then stated that he told SUSPECT #1 that he gave the money to
a F/companion prior to his leaving the cafe. VICTIM stated at this time
for no apparent reason SUSPECT #1 stabbed him in the lower abdomen area
after taking the $.80 in change and fled in an UNK direction. VICTIM
stated that he walked from the location from which he was attacked to
the address of the CP.

VICTIM HARRIS stated he has seen both SUSPECT(S) on numerous occasions
and they are known to frequent the area of 17th and Alamitos, and
Anaheim and Lewis.

Officers talked with the Emergency Dr. PAGE, who stated to officers that
the VICTIM had a deep puncture wound on the lower abdomen and would
require surgery to close the wound. Dr. PAGE further stated that the
VICTIM would be admitted and a specialist would be called to perform
the operation.

LOSS: $.80

Report by ADISON, T. L. Unit 3.

POLICE DEPARTMENT

| Report of Arrest |

Case Rep. No. 730-0621
Booking No. 621-000
Opr. Lic. No. None
Soc. Sec. No. 224-79-0624

ADA: SONNY

Defendant Smith, James nmn   Date of Arrest March 5, 1974 Time 1030
Address 10 Long Avenue, #10
 M Race Negro Age 19 DOB 4/20/54 Hgt. 6-4 Wht. 190 Hair blk Eyes brn
Description of Clothing brn tee shirt, brn trousers
Occupation maintenance engineer   Place of Employment Los Angeles Hospital
Address Studio City, Calif.   Date of Offense   prior

Offense ARMED ROBBERY 211 cpc
Where Arrested 1025 Long Avenue LA   Where Committed prior
Victim HARRIS, Keith   Address 102 Sandstone Blvd. PH none
Address   Address   PH

CIRCUMSTANCES OF ARREST

ARRESTED IN COMPANY OF: White, Ken   #666-999

Defendant arrested after officers investigation indicated he took part in
and assisted in a robbery (armed) with the above listed Incident
Report 730-0621 and victim Harris.

Officer Brown was dispatched 2/1/74 to St. Joan's Hospital and subsequently
took an additional information report at that location from victim Harris,
who was a patient at the hospital in Room #343. The victim informed officer
that he was the victim of a robbery within the past week during which he was
stabbed with a knife. He informed officer further that due to his severe
condition and only semi-consciousness, he was unaware whether a report was
filed at that time or not. He stated, however, he believed he remembered
some police officers asking him questions at the hospital.

Officer later checked and ascertained that a report was filed shortly after
the armed robbery incident was taken by Los Angeles Police Officers at
St. Joan's Hospital. Officer did find out, however, that at that particular
time the victim was not conscious enough to relate any suspect information
which at the time was supplied to investigating officer. The victim described
the two suspects as follows:
... 1 ... MNe 26-28 years, 5-6/7, 150 lbs. blk hair, brn eyes, moustache,
          and goatee, dark grn or blk floppy hat, fatigue army jkt, jeans

... 2 ... Smith, James M Ne 22 yrs, aka: Sonny, blk short hair, brn eyes,
          6-0 to 6-2, 175 lbs, blue shirt and jeans NFD, possible living
          on Long between Anaheim and 9th Streets, LA.

ADDITIONAL INFORMATION TO BE ADDED TO REPORT MADE AND
FILED COVERING CASE MENTIONED ON FILING MARGIN

Victim   Harris, Keith   Date   March 5, 1974

Accused Smith, James #621-000   No.   730-0621

PAGE # TWO ARREST REPORT   ARMED ROBBERY 211 cpc

Officer ascertained that the defendant was residing with his grandmother at
10 Long Avenue and proceeded to that location. Officer Brown in company with
officers Albright and Jackson located the suspect Smith at the Long Apartment
and placed him under arrest for the above crime. Defendant was advised of
his rights from PD Form 300 by officer Brown in the presence of officer
Jackson and Albright to which he responded yes to both waiver questions.

Officer advised the defendant of the allegations made against him by the victim,
and asked him if he would explain to officers in his own words what happened on
the night in question. Defendant stated that he knew the victim, and that he was
in a cafe with the victim on Arizona south of Sepulveda on that night. Defendant
stated he was in company of co-defendant White, that the victim, whom he knew,
was in possession of a large amount of money, around $400.00. Defendant said he
and the co-defendant White discussed robbing the victim, and subsequently did so
a short time later in the alley next to the cafe between Arizona and Lewis Avenue
south of Sepulveda Street.

Defendant stated he approached the victim from behind, placed his arms under
the victim's arms, and interlaced his fingers behind the victim's neck, rendering
the victim immobile. Stated at this time the co-defendant White removed the money
that the victim had, from the victim's pocket. This was found out by them to be less
than ten dollars. Defendant stated prior to their accosting the victim, co-deft.
White asked the defendant for his pocket knife, which he gave him. Defendant
stated he had no idea the co-defendant White was going to use the knife. Stated
he thought he was only going to scare the victim with it. The defendant stated,
however, after co-defendant White took the money, co-defendant White stabbed the
victim in the side. Stated at this time he was scared and fled with the co-deft.

Defendant stated he got the knife back from the co-defendant after the incident.
The defendant further stated that he knew of co-defendant White's location and
would take officers there. The defendant did so and co-deft White was subsequently arrested. Officer returned to the defendant's residence where the defendant
turned over to Officer Albright the weapon used in the crime, who subsequently
placed it into evidence. Defendant booked as charged.

Report by J. J. BROWN 3/5/74 1367

ADDITIONAL INFORMATION TO BE ADDED TO REPORT MADE AND
FILED COVERING CASE MENTIONED ON FILING MARGIN

Victim   Harris, Keith (x) - MN, DOB 5/29/39   Date 3/5/74
          102 Sandstone Blvd., no phone
Accused   SSN: 669-40-5041   No. CR #730-0621
          Occupation: Disabled

RE: ARMED ROBBERY (211) - OCCURRED 2/23/74, 0130 - E/W ALLEY S/OF
                SEPULVEDA, W/OF LEWIS

PAGE # THREE ARREST REPORT ARMED ROBBERY 211 cpc

Officer contacted this date 2/28/74 at approximately 1400 hours by the above
victim at St. Joan's Hospital. The victim stated he was robbed and believed
that a police report had been taken. He stated however he was only semi-
conscious when he arrived at the hospital; and therefore, was unable to give
Officers a full description and account of what occurred regarding the robbery
incident.

The victim stated he knew suspect #2 personally by name as he once dated his
aunt. He stated that suspect #1 was also familiar to him, however, he did not
know this suspect's name. He described the two suspects as follows: SUSPECT
#1) M/N, 26-28 yrs, 5'6/7, 150, blk hair, brown eyes, wearing dark green or
black floppy hat, fatigue Army jacket and jeans, moustache, goatee. SUSPECT
#2) SMITH, James, AKA "Sonny", M/N 22 yrs, blk short hair, brown eyes, 6'0/6'2,
175, wearing blue shirt and jeans. The victim stated he was entertaining a
young lady at the pool hall or bar south of Sepulveda on Arizona and noted
that the suspects were present at this location.

Victim stated he was taking this young lady home through the above mentioned
alley when suspect #2 grabbed him from behind as suspect #1 went through his
pockets and subsequently stabbed him with the weapon. He stated both suspects
fled in unknown direction.

Victim stated he walked southbound on Lewis Avenue to the vicinity of his
house where he was finally taken to St. Joan's Hospital, and officers
were summoned.

                              Report by___ J. J. BROWN PW#2 #1367_____

ADDITIONAL INFORMATION TO BE ADDED TO REPORT MADE AND
FILED COVERING CASE MENTIONED ON FILING MARGIN

Victim   HARRIS, Keith   Date   March 5, 1974

Accused   SMITH, James, BN 621-000   No.   CR 730-0621
          WHITE, Ken, BN 666-999

| INVESTIGATION REPORT |

RE: ARMED ROBBERY, E/W ALLEY S/O SEPULVEDA, E/O ARIZONA, 2/23/74 AT 0130 HRS

On 3/4/74 Sgt. Kampbell contacted victim Harris in Room 347 of St. Joan's Hospital.
Victim is in the hospital as a result of abdominal wounds suffered during the
robbery. Victim states that he will be hospitalized for at least another week.
He stated that the wounds suffered included some intestines being severed plus
other wounds in the stomach and chest area. Harris was asked to view two groups
of Los Angeles photos and at this time was advised that a picture of the suspect
might or might not be included in the group of photographs and that he was under
no obligation to pick anyone. Harris viewed Group I consisting of the following
photographs:

Group I

        1.   Photo #286437 dated 10/10/73
        2.   "   #289081   "   2/1/74
        3.   "   #282659   "   3/2/74 Smith
        4.   "   #180113   "   12/16/72
        5.   "   #289770   "   8/25/72
        6.   "   #284895   "   6/10/72

Harris thumbed through this group of photographs and almost immediately picked
the photograph of SMITH, stating that this was "Sonny" and that he had known him
ever since he had been in California. He stated that Sonny was the one who had
held his arms while he was being robbed. Victim then viewed Group II consisting
of the following Los Angeles photographs:

Group II

        1.   Photo #299002 dated 1/28/74
        2.   "   #290785   "   2/18/73
        3.   "   #299778   "   9/2/73 WHITE
        4.   "   #299531   "   4/5/72
        5.   "   #292945   "   4/2/72
        6.   "   #294797   "   3/17/71

After viewing this group, the victim was unable to identify anyone included in
that group. He stated that he would be able to identify the assailant should he
see him in person. He further stated that all Sonny did was to hold him, that he
did not go through his clothing, nor did he cut him. Harris, at this time, was
asked if he had been drinking that night, and he stated that he had consumed three

                              Report by Sgt. Kampbell, Robbery Dtl.
                               Trans. by Trinkle, 0835 hrs. 3/5/74

ADDITIONAL INFORMATION TO BE ADDED TO REPORT MADE AND
FILED COVERING CASE MENTIONED ON FILING MARGIN

Victim   HARRIS, Keith   Date   March 5, 1974

Accused SMITH, James, BN 621-000   No.   CR 730-0621
         WHITE, Ken, BN 666-999

RE: ARMED ROBBERY, E/W ALLEY S/O SEPULVEDA, E/O ARIZONA, 2/23/74 at 0130 HRS

PAGE TWO OF FOLLOWUP

large cans of beer plus a standard bar glass of beer but that he was not drunk.

The Inv. Off. checked the victim's Police record and found that the victim had
been arrested for Intox. twelve times since 1969 and that in each case he either
received a sentence or forfeited bail. The victim was asked if he had had $400
at the time of the robbery, and he stated he had not, that he had $10, consisting
of bills and some change. He stated that the bills were in the watch pocket of
his trousers and that the man who had cut and robbed him missed those while he was
searching through his clothing and took only the change from his pocket.

Victim stated he could think of no reason why the robber cut him, that he offered
no resistance. Harris stated that he was also in the company of a female negro
at the time of the robbery, that he did not know her name or where she went to
during or after the robbery. He stated he had met her in the cafe and that she
had asked him to buy her a drink and that they were en route to a bar when he was
robbed.

Sgt. Kampbell contacted deft. WHITE in the fifth floor men's jail at approx. 1315
hours. WHITE was asked if he remembered being advised by the Offs. in the jail
as far as his rights, and he stated that he recalled being advised and was still
willing to talk with the Off. WHITE stated that he and his co-deft. were at a
cafe, he did not remember the name, only that it was near Sepulveda and Arizona,
when he heard a pimp who had a couple of girls in there say that Harris told him
he had $400. Deft. stated that he knows Harris fairly well and that Harris had
bought a couple of beers for him earlier on the day of the robbery. After hearing
this, White and his co-deft. began talking about robbing Harris and decided to do so.

He stated at this time Harris was very drunk and could barely walk without falling.
He stated that Harris left the cafe and went out into the alley and that Sonny came
up behind him and held his arms and that he was holding the knife in his right hand
and going through victim's clothing with his left. He stated that he did not find
any money, only an empty cigarette package. The deft. stated that he is not sure

Report by Sgt. Kampbell, Robbery Dtl.
Trans. by Trinkle 3/5/74 0848 hrs.

ADDITIONAL INFORMATION TO BE ADDED TO REPORT MADE AND
FILED COVERING CASE MENTIONED ON FILING MARGIN

Victim   HARRIS, Keith   Date   March 5, 1974

Accused SMITH, James, BN 621-000   No.   CR 730-0621
         WHITE, Ken, VN 666-999

RE: ARMED ROBBERY, E/W ALLEY S/O SEPULVEDA, E/O ARIZONA, 2/23/74 AT 0130 HRS

                    PAGE THREE OF FOLLOWUP

whether or not he did, in fact, cut the victim. He stated he did attempt to
rob him but that the victim had nothing for him to take.

He stated that the pimp and the girls also planned on robbing Harris of his $400
and that they may have made some attempt to do so after he and the co-deft. had
robbed him. Deft. stated he and the co-deft. returned to the cafe after attempting
to rob Harris and that he became involved in an argument with the pimp because he
would not give him the money taken from Harris. He stated at this time the pimp
hit him alongside the head, causing a bump on the left cheek bone (still slightly
visible). The deft. stated that the knife belonged to his co-deft. and was returned
to him after the robbery.

At 1400 hours deft. Smith was interviewed by Sgt. Kampbell and advised of his
rights per PD 300, responding "Yes" to waiver questions 1 and 2. Deft. at this
time stated he remembered being the deft. in the case handled by Sgt. Kampbell in
May of 1973. Sgt. Kampbell then recalled the case and the deft. The deft. also
informed the Sgt. as they were going through the Interview Room that he guessed
he was sure in big trouble this time, that he had sure done wrong. Deft. stated
that they were in the cafe and had heard that Keith was carrying a large amount
of money.

He stated that he first heard it from a guy he thought was a pimp but he didn't
know for sure because he didn't know the man. He stated that Keith was very drunk
and wasn't able to walk very well. He and his co-deft. then agreed to rob Keith
and get the $400 if the opportunity presented itself. About this time, Keith left
the cafe and started to walk down the alley. His co-deft, White, waited a little
bit and then followed Smith out and then the deft., in turn, followed White. He
stated as they started down the alley, they observed Keith talking with two female
negroes. He stated he couldn't hear for sure, but it sounded like the women were
trying to talk Keith out of his money.

Deft. stated at this time, he got behind Keith and pinned his arms and head in
an armlock and held him while Ken went through his clothing. He stated that he

                          Report by Sgt. Kampbell, Robbery Dtl.
                          Trans. by Trinkle 3/5/74

ADDITIONAL INFORMATION TO BE ADDED TO REPORT MADE AND
FILED COVERING CASE MENTIONED ON FILING MARGIN

Victim   HARRIS, Keith   Date   March 5, 1974

Accused SMITH, James, BN 621-000   No.   CR 730-0621
         WHITE, Ken, BN 666-999

RE: ARMED ROBBERY, E/W ALLEY S/O SEPULVEDA, E/O ARIZONA, 2/23/74 AT 0130 HRS

PAGE FOUR OF FOLLOWUP

doesn't know if Keith was really cut during this time or not, that he did not
learn of the injury until a day or so later. Deft. stated that the two women
wanted part of the money taken from Keith but that neither he nor his co-deft.
talked to them. He stated as soon as Keith was released that he ran away from
them, down the alley, and that they returned to the cafe. About this time, Ken
returned the knife to him. The deft. stated that he knew Keith and liked him
and that had he known he was hurt, he would have stayed and helped him.

Deft. stated that when the Police came to his house for him, his grandmother told
them that he was not home and that they left but returned later and that he
surrendered himself at this time. He stated that he met the victim's brother
sometime later and told him about the robbery and his part in it and that was when
he learned that Keith was in the hospital. Both defts. stated that they would like
to pay for the victim's doctor and hospital bill. Deft. was asked if he and his
co-deft had been drinking, and he stated that he had. He stated that he was
pretty drunk and that he thought his friend Ken was also fairly drunk.

                                   Report by Sgt. Kampbell, Robbery Dtl.
                                     Trans. by Trinkle 3/5/74 0910 hrs.

Bibliography

American Bar Association Project on Standards for Criminal Justice. *Standards Relating to the Administration of Criminal Justice*. American Bar Association, Washington, D.C., June 1974.

Arco Publishing Company. *Police Administration and Criminal Investigation,* 2d ed., Arco Press, New York, 1967.

Arther, Richard O. *The Scientific Investigator*. Charles C. Thomas, Springfield, Illinois, 1965.

_____, and Rudolph R. Caputo. *Interrogation for Investigators*. William C. Copp and Associates, New York, 1959.

Asch, Sidney. *Police Authority and the Rights of the Individual*. Arco Books, New York, 1968.

Aubry, Arthur. *Criminal Interrogation.* Charles C. Thomas, Springfield, Illinois, 1965.

Bailey, F. Lee, and Rothblatt, Henry B. *Investigation and Preparation of Criminal Cases; Federal and State*. Lawyers Cooperative Publishing Company, Rochester, New York, 1970.

Battle, Brendon P., and Paul B. Weston. *Arson*. Arco Publishing Company, New York, 1967.

Bittner, E. "A Theory of Police." In *The Potential for Reform of Criminal Justice*. Sage Publications, Los Angeles, 1974.

Bloch, Peter, and James Bell. *Managing Investigations: The Rochester System*. The Urban Institute, Police Foundation, 1976.

_____, and David Specht. *Neighborhood Team Policing*. Law Enforcement Assistance Administration, U.S. Department of Justice, Washington, D.C., 1973.

_____, and Cyrus Ulberg. *Auditing Clearance Rates*. Police Foundation, Washington, D.C., 1975.

_____, and Donald Weidman. *Managing Criminal Investigations*. The Urban Institute, Washington, D.C., 1975.

Bopp, William J. *Principles of American Law Enforcement and Criminal Justice*. Charles C. Thomas, Springfield, Illinois, 1972.

Brandstatter, Arthur F. *Fundamentals of Law Enforcement*. Glencoe Press, Beverly Hills, California, 1971.

Bristow, Allen P. *A Handbook in Criminal Procedure and the Administration of Justice*. Glencoe Press, Beverly Hills, California, 1966.

_____. *Field Interrogation*. Charles C. Thomas, Springfield, Illinois, 1964.

Bugliosi, Vincent. *Helter Skelter*. W.W. Norton & Company, Inc., New York, 1974.

311

Camps, Francis E. *The Investigation of Murder.* Michael Joseph, Ltd., London, 1966.

Chaffee, Zechariah, et al. *The Third Degree.* Arno Press, New York, 1969.

Chaiken, Jan M. *The Criminal Investigation Process, Volume II: Survey of Municipal and County Police Departments.* The Rand Corporation, R-1777-DOJ, October 1975.

Chamelin, Neil C. *Criminal Law for Policemen.* Prentice-Hall, Englewood Cliffs, New Jersey, 1971.

Chilimidos, Robert S. *Auto Theft Investigation.* Legal Book Corporation, Los Angeles, 1971.

Conklin, John. *Robbery and the Criminal Justice System.* J. B. Lippincott Co., Philadelphia, 1972.

———, and Egon Bittner. "Burglary in a Suburb." *Criminology,* Vol. II, No. 2, August 1973, pp. 206–231.

Diamond, Harry (ed.). *Arrest, Search and Seizure.* Department of Police Science and Administration, Los Angeles State College, Los Angeles, 1963.

Dieckmann, Edward A. *Practical Homicide Investigation.* Charles C. Thomas, Springfield, Illinois, 1961.

Dienstein, William. *Techniques for the Crime Investigator,* 2d ed. Charles C. Thomas, Springfield, Illinois, 1974.

Earhart, Robert S. *A Critical Analysis of Investigator-Criminal Informant Relationship in Law Enforcement.* International Association of Chiefs of Police, Washington, D.C., 1964.

Edelfonso, Edward. *Principles of Law Enforcement.* John Wiley & Sons, Inc., New York, 1968.

Feeney, Floyd, et al. *The Prevention and Control of Robbery, Volume I: The Robbery Setting, The Actors and Some Issues; Volume II: The Handling of Robbery Arrestees: Some Issues of Fact and Policy; Volume III: The Geography of Robbery; Volume IV: The Response of the Police and Other Agencies to Robbery; Volume V: The History and Concept of Robbery.* The Center on Administration of Criminal Justice, University of California at Davis, 1973.

Folk, Joseph F. *Municipal Detective Systems: A Quantitative Approach.* Operations Research Center, Massachusetts Institute of Technology, Technical Report No. 55, Cambridge, 1971.

Fosdick, Raymond. *American Police Systems.* The Century Company, New York, 1921.

Franklin, Charles (Frank Hugh Usher). *The Third Degree.* Robert Hale, London, 1970.

Freedman, Warren. *Societal Behavior: New and Unique Rights of the Person.* Charles C. Thomas, Springfield, Illinois, 1965.

Fricke, Charles W. *Criminal Investigation.* 6th ed. as revised by LeRoy M. Kolbrek, Legal Book Store, Los Angeles, 1962.

George, B. James, Jr. *Constitutional Limitations on Evidence in Criminal Cases.* Institute of Continuing Legal Education, Ann Arbor, Michigan, 1969.

Gerber, Samuel R. (ed.). *Criminal Investigation and Interrogation.* W. H. Anderson, Cincinnati, 1962.

Greenberg, Bernard, et al. *Enhancement of the Investigative Function, Volume I: Analysis and Conclusions; Volume III: Investigative Procedures–Selected Task Evaluation; Volume IV: Burglary Investigative Checklist and Handbook.* Stanford Research Institute, Menlo Park, California, 1972. (Volume II not available.)

_____, et al. *Felony Investigation Decision Model–An Analysis of Investigative Elements of Information.* Stanford Research Institute, Menlo Park, California, December, 1975.

Greenwood, Peter W. *An Analysis of the Apprehension Activities of the New York City Police Department.* The New York City–Rand Institute, R-529-NYC, September 1970.

_____, et al. *Prosecution of Adult Felony Defendants in Los Angeles County: A Policy Perspective.* Lexington Books, D.C. Heath and Company, Lexington, Mass., 1976.

_____, and Joan R. Petersilia. *The Criminal Investigation Process, Volume I: Summary and Policy Implications.* The Rand Corporation, R-1776-DOJ, October 1975.

Gross, H., and R. L. Jackson. *Criminal Investigation.* 5th ed., Sweet and Maxwell, Ltd., London, 1962.

_____, *Criminal Investigation: A Practical Textbook for Magistrates, Police Officers and Lawyers.* Sweet and Maxwell, Ltd., London, var. eds.

Harney, Malachi L. *The Informer in Law Enforcement.* Charles C. Thomas, Springfield, Illinois, 1962.

Harris, Raymond I. *Outline of Death Investigation.* Charles C. Thomas, Springfield, Illinois, 1962.

Hecht, Henry H., and E. W. Zidenis. *A Police Handbook on Confession.* American Legal Publications, New York, 1958.

Hopkins, E. J. *Our Lawless Police, A Study of the Unlawful Enforcement of the Law.* DaCapo Press, New York, 1972.

Inbau, Fred, and John E. Reid. *Criminal Interrogation and Confessions.* Williams and Wilkins Co., Baltimore, Maryland, 1962–1967.

_____, and John E. Reid. *Lie Detection and Criminal Interrogation.* Williams and Wilkins Co., Baltimore, Maryland, 1966.

_____, and John E. Reid. *Truth and Deception.* Williams and Wilkins Co., Baltimore, Maryland, 1966.

——— , Andre A. Moenssens, and Louis R. Vitullo. *Scientific Police Investigation.* Chilton Book Company, Philadelphia, 1972.

Institute for Defense Analyses. *Task Force Report: Science and Technology, A Report to the President's Commission on Law Enforcement and Administration of Justice.* U.S. Government Printing Office, Washington, D.C., 1967.

International Association of Chiefs of Police. *Criminal Investigation.* 2d ed., I.A.C.P., Washington, D.C., 1971.

Isaacs, Herbert H. "A Study of Communications, Crimes, and Arrests in a Metropolitan Police Department," Appendix B of Institute for Defense Analyses, *Task Force Report: Science and Technology, A Report to the President's Commission on Law Enforcement and Administration of Justice.* U.S. Government Printing Office, Washington, D.C., 1967.

Isaacson, Irving. *Manual for the Arresting Officer.* 5th ed., Legal Publications, Inc., Lewiston, Maine, 1968.

Jackson, Richard L. *Criminal Investigation.* Carswell Company, Toronto, Canada, 1962.

Jones, Leland. *Scientific Investigation and Physical Evidence.* Charles C. Thomas, Springfield, Illinois, 1959.

Kansas University Governmental Research Center. *School of Criminal Investigation: A Report.* Governmental Research Center, Lawrence, Kansas, 1968.

Kelling, George L., Tony Pate, Duane Dieckman, and Charles Brown. *The Kansas City Preventive Patrol Experiment.* Police Foundation, Washington, D.C., 1975.

Kessler, William F., and Paul B. Weston. *The Detection of Murder.* Arco Publishing Co., Inc., New York, 1971.

Kingston, C. R., and F. G. Madrazo. *Latent Value Study.* New York State Identification and Intelligence System, New York, 1970.

Kirk, Paul L. *Crime Investigation.* Interscience Publishers, Inc., New York, 1953.

——— *The Crime Laboratory.* Charles C. Thomas, Springfield, Illinois, 1965.

LaFave, Wayne R. *Arrest—The Decision to Take a Suspect into Custody.* Little, Brown and Co., Boston, 1965.

Langford, Beryl. *Stopping Vehicles and Occupant Control.* Charles C. Thomas, Springfield, Illinois, 1960.

Leibers, Arthur. *The Investigator's Handbook.* 3rd ed., Arco Publishing Co., New York, 1972.

Leonard, V. A. *Academy Lectures on Lie Detection.* Charles C. Thomas, Springfield, Illinois, 1957.

——— *Criminal Investigation and Identification.* Charles C. Thomas, Springfield, Illinois, 1971.

_____ *The Police Detective Function.* Charles C. Thomas, Springfield, Illinois, 1970.

Maguire, John M. *Evidence of Guilt.* Little, Brown and Co., Boston, 1959.

Mann, Geoffrey T. *Violent Deaths and Their Differential Diagnosis: (F.B.I.).* U.S. Government Printing Office, Washington, D.C., 1964.

McCann, Michael G. *Police and the Confidential Informant.* Indiana University Press, Bloomington, Indiana, 1957.

McDonald, Hugh C. *The Practical Psychology of Police Interrogation.* Fashion Press, Los Angeles, 1963.

McIntyre, Donald M., et al. *Detection of Crime.* Little, Brown and Co., Boston, 1967.

Morrish, Reginald. *Criminal Law and Police Investigation.* 6th ed., Police Review and Publishing Co., London, 1961.

Motto, Carmine J. *Undercover.* Charles C. Thomas, Springfield, Illinois, 1971.

National Advisory Group on Productivity in Law Enforcement. "Opportunities for Improving Productivity in Police Services." National Commision on Productivity, 1750 K Street, N.W., Washington, D.C., 1973.

Nedrud, Duane R. *The Supreme Court and the Law of Criminal Investigation.* Law Enforcement Publishers, Chicago, 1969.

Nelson, John G. *Preliminary Investigation and Police Reporting: A Complete Guide to Police Written Communication, California.* Glencoe Press, Beverly Hills, California, 1970.

O'Hara, Charles E. *Fundamentals of Criminal Investigation.* 2d ed., Charles C. Thomas, Springfield, Illinois, 1970.

Osterburg, James. *The Crime Laboratory: Case Studies of Scientific Criminal Investigation.* Indiana University Press, Bloomington, Indiana, 1968.

Oughton, Frederick. *Murder Investigation.* Elek Books, Ltd., London, 1971.

Parker, Brian, and Joseph Peterson. *Physical Evidence Utilization in the Administration of Criminal Justice.* School of Criminology, University of California at Berkeley, 1972 (available from the National Criminal Justice Reference Service, U.S. Department of Justice, Washington, D.C.).

Penofsky, Daniel J. *Guidelines for Interrogation.* Aqueduct Books, New York, 1967.

Peper, John P. *Basic Criminal Investigation.* California State Department of Education, Sacramento, California, 1956.

_____ *Elements of Police Investigation.* California Peace Officers' Training Series No. 25, California State Department of Education, Sacramento, California, 1964.

Perkins, Rollin M. *Cases and Materials on Criminal Law and Procedures.* 3rd ed., Foundation Press, Mineola, New York, 1966.

——— *Perkins on Criminal Law.* Foundation Press, Mineola, New York, 1969.

Peterson, Joseph L. "Utilization of Criminalistics Services by the Police: An Analysis of the Physical Evidence Recovery Process." U. S. Department of Justice, Law Enforcement Assistance Administration, National Institute of Law Enforcement and Criminal Justice, Washington, D.C., 1974.

President's Commission on Crime in the District of Columbia. *Report of the President's Commission on Crime in the District of Columbia.* U.S. Government Printing Office, Washington, D.C., 1966.

President's Commission on Law Enforcement and Administration of Justice. *The Challenge of Crime in a Free Society.* U.S. Government Printing Office, Washington, D.C., February 1967.

Rhodes, Henry T. F. *Clues and Crimes: The Science of Criminal Investigation.* John Murray, London, 1963.

Richardson, James R. *Scientific Evidence for Police Officers.* W. H. Anderson Co., Cincinnati, Ohio, 1963.

Ringel, William E. *Arrests, Searches, and Confessions.* Gould Publications, Jamaica, New York, 1966.

——— *Searches and Seizures, Arrests and Confessions.* Clark Boardman Co., Ltd., New York, 1972.

Samen, Charles C. "Major Crime Scene Investigation—Basic Photography, Part II." *Law & Order,* September 1971, p. 16.

——— "Major Crime Scene Investigation—Bloodstain Evidence (Field Testing and Handling), Part VIII." *Law & Order,* April 1972, p. 84.

——— "Major Crime Scene Investigation—Casting (Shoe and Tire Impressions), Part VII." *Law & Order,* March 1972, p. 52.

——— "Major Crime Scene Investigation—Corroborating Evidence, Part VI." *Law & Order,* February 1972, p. 68.

——— "Major Crime Scene Investigation—Developing Invisible Evidence, Part V." *Law & Order,* December 1971, p. 50.

——— "Major Crime Scene Investigation—Search Patterns, Part IV." *Law & Order,* November 1971, p. 76.

——— "Major Crime Scene Investigation—Securing the Scene, Part I." *Law & Order,* August 1971, p. 94.

——— "Major Crime Scene Investigation—Sketching the Scene, Part III." *Law & Order,* October 1971, p. 72.

Schafer, William J. *Confessions and Statements.* Charles C. Thomas, Springfield, Illinois, 1968.

Schultz, Donald O. *Police Operational Intelligence.* Charles C. Thomas, Springfield, Illinois, 1968.

Schwartz, Louis B. *Law Enforcement Handbook for Police.* West Publishing Co., St. Paul, Minnesota, 1970.

Seedman, Albert, and Peter Hellman. *Chief.* Arthur Fields Books, Inc., New York, 1974.

Skolnick, Jerome. *Justice Without Trial: Law Enforcement in a Democratic Society.* John Wiley and Sons, Inc., New York, 1966.

Smith, Bruce. *Police Systems in the United States.* Harper and Row, New York, 1960.

Snyder, LeMoyne, *Homicide Investigation.* Charles C. Thomas, Springfield, Illinois, 1967.

Soderman, Harry. *Modern Criminal Investigation.* 5th ed. rev., Funk & Wagnalls, New York, 1962.

Southwestern Law Enforcement Institute. *Criminal Investigation.* Charles C. Thomas, Springfield, Illinois, 1962.

_____ *Institute on Homicide Investigation Techniques.* Charles C. Thomas, Springfield, Illinois, 1961.

Specter, A., and M. Katz. *Police Guide to Search and Seizure, Interrogation and Confession.* Chilton Book Publications, Philadelphia, 1967.

Svensson, Arne. *Technique of Crime Scene Investigation.* 2d rev. and expanded American ed., American Elsevier Publishing Co., New York, 1965.

Stucky, Gilbert G. *Evidence for the Law Enforcement Officer.* McGraw-Hill Book Co., New York, 1968.

Thorwald, Jurgen. *The Century of the Detective.* Harcourt, Brace and World, New York, 1965.

Tiffany, Lawrence P. *Detection of Crime: Stopping and Questioning, Search and Seizure, Encouragement and Entrapment.* Little, Brown & Co., Boston, 1967.

Turner, William W. *Case Investigation.* 2 vols. (Police Evidence Library), Lawyers Cooperative Publications, Rochester, New York, 1965.

Vanderbosch, Charles G. *Criminal Investigation.* I.A.C.P. Training Keys, Washington, D.C., 1968.

Van Meter, C. H. *Principles of Police Interrogation.* Charles C. Thomas, Springfield, Illinois, 1973.

Ward, Richard H. "The Investigative Function: Criminal Investigation in the United States." unpublished thesis, Doctor of Criminology, University of California, Berkeley, California, 1971.

Washington, D.C. Manual for Crime Scene Search. District of Columbia Police Department, Washington, D.C., 1973.

Weihs, Frederick J. *Science Against Crime.* Collier Books, New York, 1964.

Weston, Paul B., and Kenneth Wells. *Criminal Investigation: Basic Perspectives.* Prentice-Hall, Englewood Cliffs, New Jersey, 1970.

_____ *Elements of Criminal Investigation.* Prentice-Hall, Englewood Cliffs, New Jersey, 1971.

Williams, E. W. *Modern Law Enforcement and Police Science.* Charles C. Thomas, Springfield, Illinois, 1967.

Woods, Arthur. *Crime Prevention.* Arno Publications, New York, 1918 (reprinted 1971).

Index

Accidents, 67
Acquittals, 35
Administrative functions and administrators, 26, 37, 57, 101–106, 118, 143–144, 205, 226, 230–231
Affirmative action programs, 62
Alcoholic beverages and alcoholism, 23, 171, 180
ALERT system, 74n
Alameda County, California, 41
American Bar Association, 35
Anonymity, desire for, 76, 98, 138–139
Antiburglary activities, 207
Apprehension rates, 31–34
Arraignments, 99
Arrestees Section, classification of, 157, 161
Arrests, 3, 41, 47, 51, 83, 99, 210–211; clearance by, 36, 58–59, 103; false, 36, 83; felony, 215–218; on-scene, 40, 130, 135, 226–227; patrol, 16, 40, 56–57, 130, 135, 141, 180, 219–220; pickup, 226; quality, 34–35; rate of, 32–33, 84–87, 91–93, 225–229, 234; referral, 220; reports on, 70–73, 172–175; self-initiated, 206; statistics on, 1, 65, 79–82, 88–89, 181–182; warrants for, 75, 101
Arson, 105, 108–111, 115, 119, 152
Assault, 21, 40, 63, 67, 85, 110, 114, 118, 122–135, 147–148, 240; aggravated, 107, 137–138, 229; critical injury, 152; felonious, 80–81
Assignment to cases, 3, 13, 20–21, 99–105, 108, 123, 230
Attorneys, 38, 60
Auto thefts, 17, 21–22, 63–64, 67, 76, 80, 82, 85, 88, 92, 101, 105, 107, 110–114, 122–127, 132–137, 147–150, 225–226, 229

Autonomy, 97
Autopsies, 116

Bail schedules, 16
Ballistic experts, 116
Bank robberies, 17, 112–114, 119, 138–139
Behan, Cornelius (Neil) J., 3n
Bell, James, 44, 226–227
Berkeley, California Police Department, 5, 18, 21–22, 41, 43, 76–77, 122–127, 148–150, 153–154, 208, 221, 231
Bittner, E., 41–42
Bloch, Peter, 44, 60n, 76n, 226–227, 244n
Bodily injury, 172, 182, 186
Bombings, 152
Boston, Massachusetts Police Department, 41, 43, 226, 244
Budgets, 51, 58, 82, 85–86, 146, 228
Bunco, 63–64, 105, 108, 111–112, 115, 119, 136
Burglaries, 2, 5–6, 17, 19, 32–33, 40–43, 63–64, 67–71, 74, 77, 80, 82, 85–88, 101, 107, 111–112, 118, 122–127, 132–138, 141, 143, 147–152, 159, 165, 191–202, 205, 208–212, 217–221, 231, 233, 240
Business leaders, 10, 24

California, 193, 232; computer system (CLETS), 44; prosecutor's office, 168; University of, 21
Career files and progression, 62, 165–166
Cars: hot, 239; unmarked, 213
Caseloads, 18, 27, 42–43, 65, 74, 88, 208, 210, 212
Cases: assignment of, 3, 13, 20–21, 99–105, 108, 119, 123, 230; disposition of, 35, 171, 182–189; duration of, 117–118; enrichment, 71; files on, 4, 241;

About the Authors

Peter W. Greenwood is Director of the Criminal Justice Research Program at The Rand Corporation. He has directed a number of research projects in education and criminal justice including the implementation of innovative projects and the prosecution of felony defendants. His current research concerns the behavior and treatment of habitual criminals. Dr. Greenwood's principal professional interests focus on the operations of the criminal justice system and its proper role in society.

Jan M. Chaiken graduated from the Massachusetts Institute of Technology with a Ph.D. in mathematics. In 1968 he joined the staff of The Rand Corporation, where his research has focused primarily on analysis of emergency service systems (police, fire, and medical). His work in the criminal justice field has included a study of police officers' background characteristics and performance, design of a patrol car allocation model, a review of criminal justice models, and parts of an evaluation of residential patrols. Dr. Chaiken is coeditor of a forthcoming book on fire department deployment analysis.

Joan Petersilia is a criminologist who has worked on a variety of criminal justice projects since joining the Criminal Justice Program at The Rand Corporation. She received a B.A. in sociology from Loyola University and an M.A. in criminology and sociology from The Ohio State University. Ms. Petersilia has recently begun a major piece of research focusing on the criminal career of the repetitively violent offender. She has published several research reports on the effectiveness of community correctional programs and authored a number of articles relating to the criminal investigation function. Her principal professional interests focus on utilizing research to guide the policy maker in reforming the criminal justice system so that it can deal more effectively with the habitual offender.

Selected List of Rand Books

Bagdikian, Ben H. *The Information Machines: Their Impact on Men and the Media*. New York: Harper and Row, 1971.

Bretz, Rudy. *Handbook for Producing Education and Public-Access Programs for Cable Television*. Englewood Cliffs, New Jersey, 1976.

Bretz, Rudy. *A Taxonomy of Communication Media*. Englewood Cliffs, New Jersey: Educational Technology Publications, 1971.

Cohen, Bernard and Jan M. Chaiken, *Police Background Characteristics and Performance*. Lexington, Massachusetts: D.C. Heath and Company, 1973.

Dalkey, Norman (ed.) *Studies in the Quality of Life: Delphi and Decision-Making*. Lexington, Massachusetts: D.C. Heath and Company, 1972.

DeSalvo, Joseph S. (ed.) *Perspectives on Regional Transportation Planning*. Lexington, Massachusetts: D.C. Heath and Company, 1973.

Downs, Anthony. *Inside Bureaucracy*. Boston, Massachusetts: Little Brown and Company, 1967.

Fisher, Gene H. *Cost Considerations in Systems Analysis*. New York: American Elsevier Publishing Company, 1971.

Greenwood, Peter W., Sorrel Wildhorn, Eugene C. Poggio, Michael J. Strumwasser, Peter De Leon, *Prosecution of Adult Felony Defendants*. Lexington, Massachusetts, D.C. Heath and Company, 1976.

Jackson, Larry R. and William A. Johnson. *Protest by the Poor*. Lexington, Massachusetts: D.C. Heath and Company, 1974.

Leites, Nathan and Charles Wolf, Jr. *Rebellion and Authority*. Illinois: Markham Publishing Company, 1970.

McKean, Roland N. *Efficiency in Government Through Systems Analysis: With Emphasis on Water Resource Development*. New York: John Wiley & Sons, 1958.

Novick, David (ed.) *Current Practice in Program Budgeting (PPBS): Analysis and Case Studies Covering Government and Business*. New York: Crane, Russak and Company, Inc., 1973.

Novick, David (ed.) *Program Budgeting: Program Analysis and the Federal Budget*. Cambridge, Massachusetts: Harvard University Press, 1965.

Pascal, Anthony, *Thinking About Cities: New Perspectives on Urban Problems*. Belmont, California: Dickenson Publishing Company, 1970.

Quade, E.S. *Analysis for Public Decisions*. New York: American Elsevier Publishing Company, 1975.

Quandt, William B. (ed.) *The Politics of Palestinian Nationalism.* Berkeley, California: University of California Press, 1973.

The RAND Corporation. *A Million Random Digits with 100,000 Normal Deviates.* Glencoe, Illinois: The Free Press, 1955.

Sharpe, William F. *The Economics of Computers.* New York: Columbia University Press, 1969.

Sackman, Harold. *Delphi Critique: Expert Opinion, Forecasting, and Group Process.* Lexington, Massachusetts: D.C. Heath and Company, 1975.

Turn, Rein. *Computers in the 1980's.* New York: Columbia University Press, 1974.

Wildhorn, Sorrel, Burke K. Burright, John H. Enns, and Thomas F. Kirkwood. *How to Save Gasoline: Public Policy Alternatives for Automobile.* Cambridge, Massachusetts: Ballinger Publishing Company, 1976.

Williams, J.D. *The Compleat Strategyst: Being a Primer on the Theory of Games of Strategy.* New York: McGraw-Hill Book Company, Inc., 1954.

Wirt, John G., Arnold J. Lieberman and Roger E. Levien. *R&D Management: Methods Used by Federal Agencies.* Lexington, Massachusetts: D.C. Heath and Company, 1975.

Yin, Robert K. and Douglas Yates. *Street-Level Governments: Assessing Decentralization and Urban Services.* Lexington, Massachusetts: D.C. Heath and Company, 1975.